Buried Treasure

Buried Treasure

Unearthing the Riches of the Gospel of Mark

Hunter R. Hill

RESOURCE *Publications* · Eugene, Oregon

BURIED TREASURE
Unearthing the Riches of the Gospel of Mark

Copyright © 2021 Hunter R. Hill. All rights reserved. Except for brief quotations in critical publications or reviews, no part of this book may be reproduced in any manner without prior written permission from the publisher. Write: Permissions, Wipf and Stock Publishers, 199 W. 8th Ave., Suite 3, Eugene, OR 97401.

Resource Publications
An Imprint of Wipf and Stock Publishers
199 W. 8th Ave., Suite 3
Eugene, OR 97401

www.wipfandstock.com

PAPERBACK ISBN: 978-1-6667-1213-1
HARDCOVER ISBN: 978-1-6667-1214-8
EBOOK ISBN: 978-1-6667-1215-5

09/15/21

Scripture quotations are from the New Revised Standard Version Bible, copyright © 1989 National Council of the Churches of Christ in the United States of America. Used by permission. All rights reserved worldwide.

Dedicated to the memory of
Balmer H. Kelly, Master teacher of biblical studies
James L. Mays, who engaged my passion for Mark's Gospel
and Anna Lewis Morton, Grandmother.
She was a good person to be raised by.

Contents

Acknowledgments | ix
Introduction | xi

1. Don't Blink or You'll Miss It | 1
2. "Come off it, Jesus!" A Jesus Who Grows Up | 14
3. The Kingdom of God Is for the Birds | 36
4. Of Parents, Pigs, and Prohibited Powers | 58
5. Splendiferous Failures | 86
6. Choosing Not to Choose | 118
7. The Way of Discipleship | 159
8. Resurrections Begin in the Now | 199
9. The Terrifying Good News Promise | 229

Appendix 1: Human Lack, Divine Love, and Kingdom Inclusivity in Mark 10:17–31 | 249
Appendix 2: Resources for Readers | 253
Bibliography | 259

Acknowledgments

"It takes a village"—true when raising children, true when writing this book. Here are the villagers I want to thank for their support, assistance, and thoughtful "raising" of Buried Treasure. Their efforts make this volume much better than it would have been had I worked in isolation.

Thanks to my many readers, early and late: Larry Barnett, Kristin Long Francisco, Sandra Hamilton, Mary Fran Hughes-McIntyre, Don McKim, David Mucha, Dennett Slemp, Malcolm Turnbull and Eleanor Anders Workman. Their expenditure of time and incisive suggestions encouraged and motivated me to continue on. Special appreciation is due Vic Maloy whose gift of careful reading, honest and supportive comments remained persistently present in my mind as I wrote.

Thanks to members of the Gayton Kirk congregation in Richmond, Virginia, who engaged Mark's Gospel with me face to face. Their participation in a lengthy study of Mark helped me refine and strengthen material appearing in these pages: Robert Chesnut, Betty and Michael Doll, Cecilia Fitzgerald, Ellen Hasty, Kasci Lawrence, Deborah Mueller, and Rebecca Weaver.

Several authors provided valuable knowledge about the adventure of writing and the realities of the publishing experience: Brian K. Blount, President of Union Presbyterian Seminary, Robert Dale, and Michael E. Gunter. I single out for special thanks John T. Carroll, Professor of New Testament at Union Presbyterian Seminary. John inspired a retired minister with limited biblical training and expertise to believe that he could write a work of sound scholarship and the capacity to engage the heart, soul, and intellect of biblically inquisitive readers. And, of course, not the least of John's help came as he provided guidance in several of Mark's texts that were literally "Greek to me."

As for my local editorial team, I owe much to Marylynda Nease for her early struggles to decipher my handwriting and render it readable for others and to Marilyn Johns who in a moment of crisis became my first official editor, moving me toward a more professional stance than I had previously practiced. And it must be said that without the multiple, on-target edits of Kathleen DuVall this work likely would not have passed muster with any publishers worthy of that name. Time and again Kathy's deft editing turned muddle into clarity, wordiness into brevity, and mediocre sentences into words that shine. Thank you, Kathy.

Eternal appreciation goes to my wife, Lyn, who had no idea I would spend much of my retirement closeted in my study, less available for greater participation in our life together. Thank you for the emotional and physical space of a study to pursue a dream.

Any errors discovered by readers rest not with these splendid villagers. Please lay them where they belong—at my doorstep.

And lastly, I wish to thank Betty Greer, a student of mine who long ago planted a seed when she asked, "So, when are you going to write your book on Mark?" Betty, thanks for asking.

Introduction

Harriet

I BEGIN WITH A story. As a member of a class of graduating seminary students in the early 1970s, I remember a baccalaureate sermon delivered by the Reverend James A. Forbes, Jr. In the years to come, Dr. Forbes would be recognized as one of the great pulpiteers of the late twentieth century and for a number of years was the senior minister of the Riverside Church in Manhattan. On the day I am recalling, however, Dr. Forbes was a younger man pastoring a congregation in Richmond, Virginia, where I had attended Union Theological Seminary in Virginia, now Union Presbyterian Seminary. So it was quite by happenstance that our paths crossed—he the guest preacher and I a graduate-to-be.

A sermon delivered to new graduates might have been expected to speak of celebration, with expressions of gratitude, encouragement, and hope. But Dr. Forbes took another direction in his sermon. He chose instead to focus on the existential need of the people we would encounter in our journeys as ministers. He drew on the haunting imagery of the valley of dry bones found in Ezekiel 37, as well as the central question raised there for the prophet in verse 3, "Can these bones live?"[1] Dr. Forbes predicted that many dry bones awaited us as we walked among our people—bones in the form of crushing despair, lives touched by losses beyond counting, bitterness or rage over the all-too-frequent lack of justice in our society, and the economic inequalities prevalent between races and genders. Many bones. He went on to say that in many ways, as representatives of the larger church and a supposed loving God, we would be challenged by heartfelt queries of our congregants similar to the one that

---

1. Unless otherwise noted, all quotations of biblical texts are from the New Revised Standard Version (NRSV).

confronted Ezekiel, "Can these bones live?" Questions like: "Is there any meaningful life to be had by the children of God who are caught up in dire poverty, subsistence living, or other severe circumstances and suffering? Is the end toward which much of humankind moves a dark one filled with spiritual and emotional numbness or consuming rage?" Or perhaps even more personally, "Tell me, preacher, why do I feel so empty inside?"

Having spoken, then, of a painful side of the human condition awaiting us eager would-be shepherds, Dr. Forbes recounted a specific incident drawn from his pastorate. As a young minister he had been called by family members to the home of one of his church members—a man who had died at home unexpectedly of a heart attack. The man's wife, Harriet (not her real name), who was out of town for the day at a conference—had not yet been informed of her husband's death. Since she was driving back to Richmond alone, the family decided for safety's sake to wait to tell her when she was no longer behind the wheel. (Needless to say, this incident occurred prior to the advent of the many means of electronic communication we now use.) As Harriet's pastor, Dr. Forbes had been asked to be present when she arrived home. Soon after Dr. Forbes arrived Harriet walked through the door and immediately knew something was not right. While Dr. Forbes stood a few feet to one side, one of Harriet's sisters—as compassionately as possible—told her of her husband's death.

As a pastor, Dr. Forbes had, of course, been present with other families in similar circumstances; he had, he told us, seen various expressions of a family's grief, from screams and wailing to mute shock and fainting. But never, he said, had he encountered what he did that day with Harriet. Upon hearing of the death of her beloved husband, in the blink of an eye Harriet pivoted to face Dr. Forbes. She stared at him, her trusted pastor, with a ferocity in her eyes that threatened to burn through him. No crushing sadness registered in her demeanor, only the incredulous, angry hurt which comes when an insufferable insult has been rendered upon a person. Moreover, there was in her glare, he said, the nearly palpable expectation that he make this thing right, correct this unspeakable wrong. There was no mistaking, he said, that her eyes demanded that as "God's man" he do something. Now! Dr. Forbes stood immobilized, pinned by the intensity of the moment.

As I recall, Dr. Forbes never told us how he in fact responded to Harriet that day, and this was probably intentional. He wanted in his example to focus not on what he said or did, but on the abyss of Harriet's need as the world she had known began to change forever, collapsing into dust. What Dr. Forbes did speak about to us was his further reflections on Harriet's reaction. Initially, he said, he saw her response as yet another understandable though somewhat unusual expression of overwhelming grief. As he continued thinking about the intense moment, however, he came to believe that her response spoke not only of grief, with all its initial shock and disbelief, but also as giving evidence to the radicalism of a faithful expectation that lies at the center of religious belief. That is, that God somehow do something when there is absolutely nothing humanly to be done. For Dr. Forbes, Harriet's glare came to represent the spiritual reality lived out by so many, the reality of desperate hope that God chart a course to bring dry bones alive, to wrest life from death, and resurrection from crucifixion. Dr. Forbes came to believe, he said, that in the most tumultuous, shaking moment of her life, Harriet held fast to her core expectation about God—that despite all appearances and beyond our paralyzing experiences to the contrary, God can and will act.

I have not forgotten Harriet over the intervening years or what I believe Dr. Forbes wished for us to learn from her. In my mind it has crystallized as follows: that as those who are—at one and the same moment—pilgrims on this earth and connected to a life-giving God, we may well find ourselves, as did Harriet, trusting as we anguish, hoping as we despair, and glimpsing a distant flickering light as we dwell in darkness.

Dry bones there are. But so, too, is God, the great I AM who has promised to make all things new, and we are well within the bounds of faith to expect God to act and accomplish the humanly impossible.

Questions

What does Harriet's story have to do with the Gospel according to Mark?[2] Harriet strikes me as a woman capable of expecting with all her heart, soul, mind, and strength. What she expects is the grand surprise of God's presence and activity among God's children. She is adamant in that conviction. The reality of her life circumstances in the terrible moment when she learns of her husband's death would seem to give the lie to all she holds true, but there she stands, staring her faithful—some would say

---

2. Hereafter I use shortened forms of the title for Mark's work, either the Gospel of Mark or Mark.

delusional—glare.³ If you, as a potential reader of Mark, are at all curious how such a stance of expectancy is possible in life's most bludgeoning times, you may well be ready for a journey with Harriet serving as guide, teacher, and inspiration.

Let me spell this out slightly differently. My fondest hope for you, reader, is that you will be inspired by Harriet's insistent expectancy as you examine Mark's story again or even perhaps for the first time. Out of that expectancy, I urge you to ask questions of the text as you read. As an example of the sorts of questions that you might raise, I am including a list that has proved helpful to me over the years:

- What does a careful and measured reading of Mark's narrative reveal that is easily overlooked in a "quick read" of Mark's Gospel?

- Where are the many unexpected surprises Mark inserts into his work? Think of these as the buried treasures of Mark's Gospel you are trying to unearth.

- What is going on beneath Mark's main plotline? Upon close examination, are there seemingly unconnected scenes that do in fact connect, revealing significant subplots that invite us to a deeper understanding of his Gospel?

- What did Mark hope his readers might discover by taking note of how he shaped his story?

- If Mark sets out to present a good news, what strikes us as good in his sometimes dark account?

- And perhaps most importantly, how might Mark answer the personal and age-old question, "What does this Jesus you write about, Mark, have to do with me in the life I am living in the present moment?"

My experience with Mark leads me to trust that these and similar questions you raise and seek to answer will be worth your effort. In a way, these are risky, even confounding questions. But in a religious analysis, that is, a thoughtful, heartfelt pondering of the joys and griefs of the human experience, they are indeed appropriate queries to put to the Gospel of Mark. Furthermore, it is my hope that as you follow Harriet's lead by

---

3. See Mark 5:21–43, especially 5:38–40, for a story raising issues similar to Harriet's. The crowd's laughter at Jesus's words seems to question at least his perception of the situation and at most, his sanity.

Introduction   xv

adopting her stance of expectancy you may well unearth the author's compelling and intriguing answers to your questions. You may find that these answers evoke a richly complex mix of curiosity, pause, confusion, and courage. It is my conviction that such a mixture lays the foundation for an eventual deepening of one's own religious understanding in life's ongoing pilgrimage. And as Jesus's original followers were impacted by a similar "stew" of thoughts, feelings, and experiences as they began "hanging out" with a strangely different sort of wandering teacher, you, too, may be guided toward the riches in Mark's narrative by the surprising drama of Mark's gospel tale.

Where I Fit In

What is my place in this work? Where do I fit in? Here is what I hope to offer those who use this volume as they move through Mark's narrative. Within the larger context of the grand surprise in Mark—God's enlivening presence and activity in people's lives—I have singled out nine additional treasures found in Mark's story. I believe that Mark is a wonderful craftsman attempting always to interest his readers, thereby beckoning them toward good news. At times Mark is urgently straightforward in laying out his account. However, at other times he is profoundly veiled as he weaves his tapestry about Jesus and his followers. This two-fold approach on Mark's part leads to two challenges for his readers. The first is not to overlook the seemingly ordinary, simple descriptions and vocabulary Mark uses, or the minor plot development he mentions in an off-hand manner. Things can be easily missed in Mark; he is a master at hiding things in plain sight. The second challenge is that Mark constructs deliberately confounding scenes from time to time, seeming to avoid an issue or question that leaps from his pages and demands attention for the readers' sake.[4]

In my selection of nine Markan surprises I try to address both of these challenges. At times I hope to help readers pause, lingering over a seemingly inconsequential moment in Mark's account, to see more deeply into Mark's method and message. At other times, I do my best to assist the reader as we together peer into the fog of a particular passage,

---

4. An example would be in Mark 14:51–52, where the young man who is grabbed by those arresting Jesus slips out of the linen cloth he is wearing and runs away naked. Whatever happens to him and why does Mark mention him in the first place?

hoping for a slowly emerging outline to appear through the mist in at least a preliminary and suggestive way.

My Assumptions and Key Beliefs

It seems only fair to readers that I outline several assumptions and beliefs that undergird my work.

1. Mark employs narrative to advance his central message. While he drew on various materials to shape his work—parables, healing stories, accounts of "miracles," teachings and sayings of Jesus, and especially traditions and accounts of Jesus's passion and death—above all else Mark tells a story. It is the story of a journey taken by Jesus and his disciples. Their travels eventually take them toward Jerusalem, the seat of political, religious, economic, and societal power in Jesus's world. In that world imperial Rome was the supremely dominant military and governing force over all of Israel.

2. Initially, Mark's story was likely delivered out loud in the form of dramatic readings or performances. If this was the case, the original written Markan narrative "functioned as a script for storytelling."[5]

3. Mark used the inherent power of story to engage his hearers and readers. He wanted them to become intrigued by his account and he set out to activate people's imaginations, catching them up in the drama of his narrative. I believe he hoped that they would become curious and wonder, "How is this going to turn out? What will happen to our heroes and heroines? What about the villains? And, what will happen to the ordinary folks, who are at one point brave and at another cowardly; at one point clear and decisive and at another confused and stumbling; at one point emboldened to act and at another paralyzed by fear? What will happen, in other words, to those like us?"

4. I assume that Mark's literary efforts arose out of an animation of his own life. I believe his core being was enlivened and transformed as he encountered One whom he experienced as present and active, that is, risen, in his time on earth. As such, Mark's work is that of both head and heart, thought and driving energy. Jesus's story mattered in an ultimate way to Mark and he hoped it would matter in a similar way to his readers.

5. Rhoads et al., *Mark as Story*, xii.

Introduction xvii

5. Mark is not a "white bread" Gospel. It is full of rich flavor and texture, providing readers much to chew on. Its implications for how humans can choose to live—even into today's times—are radically stunning, surprising, and replete with both ongoing challenge and necessary reassurance in the face of our inevitable moments of failure.

6. There are three main characters in Mark's story. The two obvious ones are Jesus and, collectively, his followers, especially the twelve closest to him, plus an important grouping of women. Perhaps less obvious is the third main character: the body of readers for whom Mark wrote. I believe this includes us in the present age. Additionally, there are numerous minor characters often drawn from the ranks of marginal outsiders who nonetheless serve to reinforce Mark's themes as they are developed throughout the Gospel.

7. I do not assume that Christian faith and experience promotes a single approach to interpreting the Scriptures. While my intent is to offer interpretive remarks from within a Christian perspective, I am aware that my belief system and particular tenets of faith at times vary from others within the larger faithful Christian community and the broad spectrum of biblical interpreters. This means that the reader may at times be persuaded by my efforts and at other moments find my approach lacking. This is as I would expect and as any decent humility on my part would demand.

8. I assume that Mark's narrative offers its readers profound truth. This truth is not presented in the form of literal history or precise biography though this does not subtract from Mark's value. On the contrary, I am persuaded that the surest realities and truths which most satisfactorily anchor our lives and fill them with meaning eventually become shaped into stories of one form or another. Mark is such a story.

9. Mark does not construe Jesus's suffering and death as an elimination of some dark stain on humankind as much as the issuing of an invitation to a life transformed. Mark's portrayal of what Jesus accomplished in dying is not primarily one that emphasizes a taking away of sin, guilt, and shame as much as it sees Jesus's passion and death as the culminating act of one who trusts God with this life and beyond. In doing so, Jesus aims his followers toward a path which offers them a more enlivened, courageous, and meaningful human sojourn here and now and into an unknown future.

10. There is no consensus as to the identity of the Gospel's author. Tradition, however, has attributed authorship to "the John Mark known to us from Acts 15:22–40, assumed to be the same person as the Mark of the Epistles (Phlm 24; Col 4:10; 2 Tim 4:11; 1 Pet 5:13)."[6] At the same time, "Mark" was a name in "common use in the Greco-Roman world."[7] The geographical location for Mark's composition is also uncertain. Various suggestions for the place Mark wrote include Rome, Galilee, or Syria.[8] As for the date of Mark's composition, current Markan scholarship posits a time frame of "shortly before or just after the fall of Jerusalem and the destruction of the temple in 70 CE."[9]

11. The Gospel of Mark ends with 16:1–8.[10]

The Basic Shape of Each Chapter

In an effort to arrive at a clear presentation of Mark's serendipitous themes I have adopted the same basic form for each of the nine chapters.

Each chapter begins with a statement about the Markan treasure that is unearthed in the chapter.

Exploring Mark's Story

This section of each chapter includes a close examination of portions of Mark's account. In most exploratory sections I consider several *focal texts*, selected for their relevance to the particular theme under study. I believe Mark to be a genius who in subtle ways indicates how the thoughts or actions of his characters are evolving or building as his story proceeds. This section of the chapter, then, focuses on how Mark is moving his account along.

---

6. Carroll, *Jesus and the Gospels*, 49.
7. Carroll, *Jesus and the Gospels*, 49.
8. Carroll, *Jesus and the Gospels*, 49.
9. Carroll, *Jesus and the Gospels*, 49.
10. See Chapter 1 for a fuller discussion of this assumption.

Introduction

Personal Reflection

In these sections I write about how my journey has been impacted in both small and significant ways by Mark. Mark challenges and comforts me still, always bringing me home to the sobering choice which is mine alone to make: "Dare I attempt to follow this compelling and beckoning Risen One, or will my courage fail me yet again? And if so, then what?"

Two Encouragements as You Begin

I began this introduction with a story. I end it with a recollection. When I was a seminary student, Dr. Balmer Kelly was one of my professors. Dr. Kelly was a master teacher. Once when speaking of how he perceived his calling as a teacher of the New Testament, he offered that one of his primary tasks was "to strange it up a bit."[11] That is, when teaching New Testament materials that stood a high likelihood of being minimally and sleepily encountered by some students, or on the other hand known by rote by others (who were therefore somewhat smug in their familiarity with Mark), Dr. Kelly believed that part of his role was to make foreign or unfamiliar that which had become incompletely grasped in one instance or too well "learned" in the other. His hope was that as he applied enough judicious jarring, students would get curious and be drawn either to engage or to reengage the Scriptures, becoming careful and precise readers of them. He trusted that if that began to happen for his charges, the life-giving nature of the biblical materials would be rediscovered and vigorously reclaimed by a new generation of pastors as the surprising, radical, and grace-filled living documents that they have continued to be across the centuries.

In the spirit of Dr. Kelly, I offer these two encouragements as you begin. First of all, take time to read through the entirety of Mark. Get a feel for the whole, the sweep of the full story. As you read, do all that you can to see Mark with fresh eyes. For example, use your God-given imagination to pretend you live around 80 or 90 CE (soon after Mark's composition, many scholars believe). Imagine that yesterday, when a friend gave you her copy of a manuscript, which turns out to be Mark, you had heard neither of one Jesus of Nazareth or of a writer calling himself Mark. Your friend said that she would be interested to hear what you think of it.

11. I am indebted to the Reverend Richard H. Lindsey, a colleague in ministry over the years and in our youth a whitewater rafting buddy, for this recollection of Dr. Kelly.

The second encouragement I have is this. As you make use of this volume, you and I will spend time noting numerous Markan passages. (For clarity and the convenience of readers I reproduce as many of these passages as possible in the body of the manuscript.) Whenever I mention particular texts, I urge you to read them as you go along. Read them before you consider whatever I or anyone else might say about them. Based on what you are reading of Mark's narrative, begin to formulate your own impressions and frame your own questions out of your experienced curiosity and reflection. My encouragement to you comes out of the particular religious orientation into which I was born—namely, the conviction that biblical texts are in some way "alive" and capable of speaking for themselves. If this is so, it is worth taking time to dialogue with Mark's story itself, not merely (or even primarily) with what I or what any other persons or commentators may say about Mark. Read the various passages; sit with them; attend to your thoughts, feelings, and impressions as you go along. Be attuned to what impact Mark itself is having on you.

If you begin to sense yourself stirred in some way, I invite you to imagine seeing Dr. Kelly looking your way, his eyes flashing his delight. From his perspective, you may well be experiencing that not only can you engage Mark's story but that Mark's story is engaging you, leading you onward into a good news beyond your fondest and most hopeful imaginings.

Grace for the journey.

1

Don't Blink or You'll Miss It

Mark employs the word "for" (*gar* in Greek) as a red flag to readers, alerting us to frequently overlooked but extraordinarily interesting emphases in his narrative.

Exploring Mark's Story

FOR. WHAT A PECULIAR place to begin. It is such a common word, serving the ordinary function of a conjunction. It is in the same category as "and" or "but." Indeed, as one reads along in Mark's account, it would be easy to overlook his "for" clauses. Either that or one could just as easily chalk up Mark's use of "for" clauses as statements of the obvious, akin to redundancy. However, years ago I was lucky enough to have sensitivity to Mark's "for" clauses instilled in me by Dr. Kelly, the same Dr. Kelly mentioned in the introduction. Dr. Kelly glanced up from his lectern in class one day to make a seemingly off-hand remark—"Ladies and gentlemen, whenever you see 'for' in Mark's story, pay attention. Something very interesting or unexpected is getting ready to happen." While originally skeptical, I have found that Dr. Kelly's comment has become central to my understanding of Mark's literary and theological purposes at key junctures in his story.

Focal Text: Mark 1:16–20
Jesus Calls Four Followers

¹⁶As Jesus passed along the Sea of Galilee, he saw Simon and his brother Andrew casting a net into the sea—for they were fishermen. ¹⁷And Jesus said to them, "Follow me and I will make you fish for people." ¹⁸And immediately they left their nets and followed him. ¹⁹As he went a little farther, he saw James son of Zebedee and his brother John, who were in their boat mending the nets. ²⁰Immediately he called them; and they left their father Zebedee in the boat with the hired men, and followed him.

In 1:16, the author first uses a "for" clause. Jesus is walking near the Sea of Galilee and sees the brothers Simon and Andrew fishing. They are using a method of shore fishing where a weighted net is cast from the shore into the water. The net settles through the water and fish are captured as the net is pulled back toward shore by the fishermen. In Jesus's time, net casting was used by poorer fishermen who could not afford a boat.[1] Mark comments on the casting activity of the brothers, adding "for they were fishermen" (1:16). At first glance this clause hardly seems necessary, given that the fishing description, casting the nets, had already been provided about Simon and Andrew. But suppose for a moment that rather than being needlessly repetitive here, Mark is signaling to his readers with his "for" clause, saying in effect, "Hey, don't miss that these two soon-to-be followers start out in their encounter with Jesus as fishers. Fishing is not only what they do; fishing is who they are! Please note, reader, that their identities are firmly established as fishers when Jesus first notices these two."

This line of interpretation is bolstered by noting how Mark presents James and John, whom Jesus next encounters. They, too, are involved in the business of fishing, attending to the repair of their nets. They appear to be better off economically than Simon and Andrew, since Mark references both boats and hired workers who assist them. But note how Mark emphasizes what is more important about James and John than their fishing or even their economic standing: James and John are identified by Mark as first and foremost members of a family. Mark writes: "[Jesus] saw James, son of Zebedee, and his brother John" (1:19). Zebedee's status as

---

1. Schweizer, *Good News*, 47–48.

father is repeated in 1:20. So, just as Mark highlights Simon and Andrew as fishers, he identifies James and John (and Zebedee) as members of a family. As the Markan Jesus begins to encounter these four men, the locus of identity is firmly in place for each. Simon and Andrew are fishers, and James and John are brothers and sons—family members above all else.

However, two additional observations are necessary to complete our focus on this story and how Mark uses the "for" clause of 1:16 to invite our more focused attention. First, as noted, Mark has pointed us toward the established identities of Simon and Andrew as fishers and James and John as family members. In speaking to or calling each of these sets of brothers in turn, Jesus employs language asking them to follow him. In the case of Simon and Andrew, the call to follow is explicit; for James and John, it is implied. In Markan vocabulary, "to follow" Jesus is the author's shorthand for moving toward discipleship. In short, to follow is to pursue becoming a disciple. And following is what both sets of brothers do in the story: Simon and Andrew "immediately left their nets and followed him" and James and John "left their father Zebedee in the boat with the hired men and followed him" (1:20). All four men follow and so commence their discipleship.

Second, it is no coincidence, I believe, that Mark writes that just as they follow, they also leave (1:18 and 1:20). Note precisely what they leave behind. According to Mark, they leave behind the very things that have been markers of their identities up to this point in their adult lives. In the case of the fishers, nets are left behind. In the case of family members, father is left behind. Is Mark hoping that his readers will see that it is not merely a treasured possession of a net that is left behind, nor the patriarchal and honored head of a family, as central as these may be? And as the four men follow—leaving behind nets and father—is Mark hinting that they leave behind their old identities, their former selves? I believe the most likely answer to these questions is that in this scene Mark is shifting the locus of identity for the four; who they have been is transforming into "someone" new. A new path is opening to them in Jesus's call, as each man takes action to leave and follow. Granted, there remains fogginess about the road ahead and what it will mean to be a disciple. Nonetheless, Mark 1:16–20 makes this point: fishers and family members are becoming followers. Formerly well-established identities have begun to dim as new ones emerge.

In summary, then, beginning with an undistinguished "for" clause in 1:16, Mark alerts us that those who decide to follow a call from this stranger, Jesus, may never quite be the same again. Whoever folks have been up to the moment of following—butcher, baker, or candlestick maker[2]—they commence a journey toward a new and different identity, that of follower. In using "for" in 1:16, Mark has begun to spell out what it means to follow Jesus, becoming his disciple. We as readers are invited to stay alert to the advancing narrative to explore the nature of this transformation, and to determine further whether leaving and following will lead these four men, and perhaps also us, toward Mark's predicted good news.

Focal Text: Mark 8:34—9:1
Jesus Speaks of a New Direction for Followers

³⁴He called the crowd with his disciples, and said to them, "If any want to become my followers, let them deny themselves and take up their cross and follow me. ³⁵For those who want to save their life will lose it, and those who lose their life for my sake, and for the sake of the gospel, will save it. ³⁶For what will it profit them to gain the whole world and forfeit their life? ³⁷Indeed, what can they give in return for their life? ³⁸Those who are ashamed of me and of my words in this adulterous and sinful generation, of them the Son of Man will also be ashamed when he comes in the glory of his Father with the holy angels." ⁹:¹And he said to them, "Truly I tell you, there are some standing here who will not taste death until they see that the kingdom of God has come with power."

The next examples of the importance of "for" clauses appear in Mark 8:34—9:1. Within these six verses Mark has embedded four consecutive "for" clauses. Not one, not two, but four "for" clauses, one after another. This number of "for" clauses grouped together is unusual even for Mark.[3] Moreover, because of the inherent challenges of translating Mark's Greek into English, his placement of the four clauses is not obvious to the readers of some translations. The NRSV does not reflect all four of the "fors,"

---

2. Of course, I am alluding to the traditional English nursery rhyme, "Rub-A-Dub-Dub."

3. The only other passages of Mark I have located that group as many as four "for" clauses in close proximity (although not in consecutive order) are found in the story of the beheading of John the Baptist in 6:14–29 (see 6:14, 6:17, 6:18, and 6:20) and in Mark's first feeding story (see 6:31, 6:50, and 6:52 in the NRSV; the fourth "for"—found in Greek in 6:48—is not evident in the NRSV).

so in this instance, I refer the reader to its predecessor, the RSV. In it, the four clauses can be visually identified more easily:

- For whoever would save his life . . .
- For what does it profit a man . . .
- For what can a man give . . .
- For whoever is ashamed of me . . . (8:35–38 RSV)

This series of "for" clauses again alerts readers that something unexpected and worthy of our close attention stands before us in the text. What is so important here that Mark's very design and use of these multiple clauses should catch our eye?

An answer arises from the following observation. With the six verses of Mark 8:34—9:1 and its preceding context of Mark 8:27–33, Mark positions his readers at the very point in the story where his entire narrative shifts. Prior to 8:27, Mark is telling one sort of story. Commencing with 8:27, a different story begins to unfold, one that will initiate significant changes for both Jesus and his followers, especially for the Twelve closest to him.

Before mentioning some of the changes Mark introduces beginning with 8:27, a clarifying word is needed about the nature of the turning point. It is not the sort of turning point where the whitest white becomes blackest black or where all things are turned to their polar opposite. Instead, Mark's turning point is more in the nature of a plot thickening, where themes introduced earlier in the story become more fully developed and implications of earlier sections of Mark's narrative begin to come into view. Mark's story becomes more tightly focused as the stakes for Mark's central characters become immeasurably higher. From this point on Jesus grows more intentional in his direction and more outspoken in his message. As for his followers, however, confusion waxes and composure wanes. As the full ramifications of Jesus's words and actions dawn on them, these more complete understandings give birth not to joy or satisfaction but to quite understandable fear.

The following is a partial list of the changes introduced by Mark in 8:27—9:1, trusting they may illustrate that with this section of material, Mark is engaging in the most significant turning point in his story. In these verses,

- **Jesus predicts his death.** Jesus declares openly and for the first time that he, as the Son of Man, will be killed and rise. (He repeats this claim in alternative forms in 9:30–32 and 10:33–34.) Mark alerts us that Jesus is now aware that his fate includes passion, being killed, and a hoped-for rising of some as of yet undefined sort.

- **The journey shifts from Galilee toward Jerusalem.** With apparent intentionality, Jesus heads toward the seat of religious, political, military, and societal power in his world.

- **Jesus's focus turns to the disciples.** With 8:27, Jesus begins to focus more intensely on his followers, especially the Twelve. Much of this focus plays out in Jesus's teachings about the nature of discipleship and what the implications of following are. (See especially these three teachings: 8:34—9:1, 9:33–37 and 10:41–45.)

- **A pattern begins: stories of discipleship.** Many have observed that beginning with 8:31—9:1, Mark uses a series of three similarly structured encounters between Jesus and his followers. In addition to 8:31—9:1, there is 9:30–37 and 10:32–45. Each of these contains a three-fold plot structure:

    1. Jesus announces his fate as the Son of Man.
    2. His followers show they have misunderstood him.
    3. Jesus corrects the misunderstanding with a teaching about discipleship and reissues his call.

- **Jesus presents a paradox.** "For those who want to save their life will lose it, and those who lose their life for my sake, and for the sake of the gospel, will save it" (8:35). The heart of Jesus's expanded and truth-bearing teaching about discipleship is indeed paradoxical.[4] Paradox, by its contradictory nature, leaves its audience pondering how what is heard can be true, and thereby calls for thought and deliberation. Mark uses paradox here for two purposes. First, in the narrative itself, Jesus provides those who are drawn to him—members of the crowd and his more active followers—the chance to ponder and reflect before they make an impulsive commitment to

---

4. Myers, *Binding the Strong Man*. In this illuminating work, Myers refers to Mark 8:35 as "introducing the central paradox of the Gospel" (247). Myers also notes that Jesus's two additional teachings regarding discipleship (9:30–37; 10:32–45) include paradox (237).

follow. Second, Mark presents an opportunity for us—his readers—to slow down and puzzle our way toward the deeper and sobering side of Jesus's good news and the choices that are ours to make.

With the numerous shifts outlined above, it is certainly believable that Mark's four "for" clauses serve, as did our initial example of 1:16–20, to alert us to pay special attention at this point in Mark's narrative. In this case the four "for" clauses sensitize us to a major turning point in Mark's Gospel. The plot thickens. The four "for" clauses serve as a signal that both slows us down and awakens us. Yet again, Mark is up to something, and we had better pay attention.

Focal Text: Mark 16:1–8
Human Failure and God's Promise

¹When the sabbath was over, Mary Magdalene, and Mary the mother of James, and Salome bought spices, so that they might go and anoint him. ²And very early on the first day of the week, when the sun had risen, they went to the tomb. ³They had been saying to one another, "Who will roll away the stone for us from the entrance to the tomb?" ⁴When they looked up, they saw that the stone, which was very large, had already been rolled back. ⁵As they entered the tomb, they saw a young man, dressed in a white robe, sitting on the right side; and they were alarmed. ⁶But he said to them, "Do not be alarmed; you are looking for Jesus of Nazareth, who was crucified. He has been raised; he is not here. Look, there is the place they laid him. ⁷But go, tell his disciples and Peter that he is going ahead of you to Galilee; there you will see him, just as he told you." ⁸So they went out and fled from the tomb, for terror and amazement had seized them; and they said nothing to anyone, for they were afraid.

There is perhaps no better place to go in Mark's story to understand the importance of "for" clauses as Mark's hint to stay alert than the final verse of his good news, Mark 16:8. I offer it as our third example of how Mark employs "for" to take hold of his readers and invite them to see more deeply.

Mark 16:8 contains two "for" clauses, each of which elaborates on one of the two behaviors of the three women disciples. In 16:1–2, Mark describes how the women made their way to the tomb hoping to anoint the lifeless body of their friend and teacher. It is a nobly intended effort. However, after their encounter in the tomb with a young man, and in light of what he says to them, the three women react in two distinct and disturbing ways. They bolt from the tomb and they remain absolutely silent about what they have seen and heard, thereby completely disregarding the young man's directive to speak to the other disciples regarding future contact with Jesus. To call additional attention to both the fleeing from the tomb and the complete silence of the women, Mark adds his two "for" clauses: "for terror and amazement [befuddlement, confusion] had seized them" and "for they were afraid." Each of the "for" clauses serves to accentuate the women's fear and panic; they are seized in terror's grip and left literally shaking in reaction to the young man's words. Their collapse is all-encompassing and devastating.

In 16:8 Mark spares none of the three from a withering description of their failure. Parenthetically, neither does he spare us, his readers. Ever since the first verse of his story, Mark has implied, for all his readers, that we will encounter a good news. Instead, we too see the disturbing vision of the three women laid out on the page before us. We too collide with the darkness of 16:8. We too may sense a confusion and slight trembling as we ponder, "Where is the good news we were promised?" It seems nowhere to be found.

A brief historical note at this point may provide some relief to those who need it after reading the previous paragraph. For centuries, Mark 16:8 has been unsettling the faithful, beginning only a few years after Mark's ink dried upon the page. The clearest evidence of this can be seen in the several extant versions of Mark 16 that are outlined in most translations. As attentive readers discover these various "endings" to Mark and digest the study notes often provided by the translators, they learn that these endings may have been added to the earlier known and more authentic copies of Markan manuscripts that conclude with 16:8. For example, the study notes for the HarperCollins Study Bible that accompany the NRSV include the following about Mark 16:8: "Some of the most ancient authorities bring the book to a close at the end of verse 8."[5] Differing theories have been put forward to explain the various endings of Mark and to argue for the validity of one or more of them. Many scholars agree that it is likely that the various endings were added by later writers or copyists to soften or neutralize the starkness of Mark's abrupt

---

5. Black, "The Gospel of Mark," note t.

and disquieting ending. I am persuaded that Mark's account does come to an intentional ending with 16:8 despite its disturbing character. What follows will outline why I am so persuaded, and—more important—why such an ending is necessitated by Mark's understanding of "the good news of Jesus Christ" (1:1).

To begin to examine Mark's view of the nature of Jesus's good news, we return to the three women disciples to further delineate the bleak picture Mark paints of them and why he does so. The key to understanding Mark's portrayal of the women's collapse in 16:8 is to realize how overwhelmingly positive Mark has been in his general presentation of women followers of Jesus prior to 16:8 and in his specific presentation of the three who go to the tomb. Women disciples, and most particularly the three who make their way toward Jesus's body, are presented by Mark as the best of the disciples: they are the most loyal and courageous of all of Jesus's followers. Mark's overall picture of disciples suggests that while the twelve male disciples closest to Jesus repeatedly fall into bickering over which of them is most prominent or privileged (the "first" and the "greatest") even as Jesus is trying to talk to them about his own approaching death (9:30–37 and 10:32–45), the women disciples are portrayed as following him quite close to the dangerous, soldier-surrounded site of his execution. They stick with him as long as they dare. Mark calls the reader's attention to the women's compassionate and practical providing for (or ministering to, or serving) Jesus before the crucifixion (15:41).[6] And finally, it is only the three women who have the daring and determination to do the one thing left for them to do for their dead leader: anoint his body for burial. Meanwhile, the male disciples are nowhere to be seen. Their courage has failed them again.

If this is so, why does Mark seem to change gears in 16:8, ending his story with the portrayal of three of Jesus's most faithful followers in full, frantic, and fear-filled retreat? (See chapter 9 for a fuller exploration of this question.) As best as I have come to understand Mark, an integral part of what makes for human well-being—that is, for one's *life* (psyche, core, soul) being saved—is the recognition that all human initiatives and systems of security, power, and standing fail. Even the most noble, most courageous, and most well-intentioned of humankind cannot secure for themselves a sense of safety, meaning, aliveness, and soulful peace for which they (and we) long. Given this, of course the three women

---

6. Black, "The Gospel of Mark," note on Mark 15:41.

must fail in their best efforts, as graciously intended as they are. They fail nobly, but fail they do. They fail in no way because they are women, but they fail *because* they represent the best and most faithful of human intention and initiative.

Mark's narrative ending leads readers to encounter the theological truth that what is humanly our best is insufficient to find life and wholeness. Humans are incapable of providing for our own salvation. Rather, in Mark's understanding of the things that make for a resurrected and transformed life, the only thing that matters in the long run is following Jesus. This is a difficult and truly shocking realization, but I believe it is Mark's conviction that such a vivid realization and acceptance of our profound human limitation is woven into the warp and woof of the good news. It is not the whole of it, as we shall see, but it is at the very least a requisite and ongoing aspect of discipleship life. The failure of the women, then, leads us to uncover or remember this great treasure—that it is God who saves. That reality cannot be undone by human failure of courage, heart, or deed.

For. What a peculiar place to begin. And yet with Mark, it is the only place for us to come to in the end. It urges us to stay awake, keep alert and not grow despondent in the face of inevitable human failure.

Personal Reflection: Grandma Laughs

One of the most enlivening memories from my childhood is of my Grandma Anna laughing. The context for her laughter could be considered unusual, in that it occurred as she read from a collection of Bible stories.[7] Except for Sundays, each evening after dinner it was our family's custom to finish the meal with a story. On this particular evening I was about eight years old and my brother Morton was about thirteen. Granddaddy Morton rounded out the familial tableau as we sat around the kitchen table.

In addition to seeing to it that the family went to the local Presbyterian Church on Sundays, Grandma was an elementary school teacher who knew how to read so as to make stories interesting for squirmy kids. She often made a game of our story time by offering a dime or, on grand occasions, a quarter if, for example, my brother or I could name eight of Joseph's eleven brothers—the rascals who threw Joseph into a deep pit, sold him into slavery, and convinced their father that Joseph had

---

7. Bowie, *The Story of the Bible*.

ended up being lunch for some wild beast. What an evocative story of sibling revenge was presented to me as a lad of eight, one from which I could take some unspoken comfort when I felt picked on or teased by my older, bigger, and stronger brother Morton. Although he was bigger and stronger, Morton was good to me most of the time, so I normally kept my imagined revenges to myself. Luckily, no pit ever magically appeared during our more difficult times, offering itself for use by my darker angels. Though there would be no revenge, there at least remained the chance, through Grandma's impromptu quizzes, of monetary gain in the form of dimes and quarters. Financial incentive has its place, I suppose, even in one's moral and religious development.

On the evening when Grandma laughed, she was reading as usual. She was recounting the story of Balaam's ass. My impression is that this story, found in the Hebrew Scriptures in the book of Numbers, is about the only thing in Numbers with even a trace of comedy about it. The story involves an encounter between Balaam and Balaam's ass, that is, his donkey. Balaam is traveling by ass to put a curse on the Israelite army. The story goes that the ass is able to see an angel blocking his master's path, while Balaam cannot. Understandably, the animal veers and balks. Balaam becomes so infuriated with the ass that he violently beats it, to the point that the poor creature breaks into conversation with Balaam about the whole situation.

I don't know for sure what got her started. Perhaps it was noting the reaction of eight- and thirteen-year-old boys to the word "ass" spoken at the kitchen table at Bible story time. Perhaps it was imagining the scene laid out in the story—an animal desperately trying to do the right thing by changing course so as not to crash into an angel, and later crushing Balaam's foot against a wall (again trying to avoid angel impact), and eventually completely collapsing, all while Balaam administers angry blows to the visionary beast of burden. Whatever was going on in Grandma's mind, she began to chuckle. This, of course, got the further attention of both of us boys as well as, I suspect, Granddaddy. Despite efforts to gather herself, Grandma quickly moved past chuckling to laughter, and, even more gloriously, soon beyond laughter to laughter accompanied by tears rolling down her cheeks. Finally came the full body jiggle usually associated with Santa.

It was a wonderful evening. Actually, I credit this memory with laying the foundation for my trusting that God's purposes are both earthy and comedic even as the Creator remembers and responds to the sufferings of God's people. I also credit the family ritual of Bible story reading (with the distinct possibility of monetary gain on the side) with instilling in me a love of biblical narrative which has been "in my bones" nearly as long as I can remember.

What does this childhood recollection have to do with my focus on the Gospel according to Mark? Fast forward with me some seventeen years after Grandma's laugh to the day as a seminary student at Union Theological Seminary in Virginia (now Union Presbyterian Seminary) when I was introduced to the systematic study of Mark by Dr. James L. Mays. An ancient note I took that first day in his class reads as follows: "What is the structure of the whole? In Mark the structure is narrative and the theology of Mark is inherent in this narrative. Generally in Mark the structure/narrative is drama—the things of the stage."

How could I, as one reared listening to and engaging in biblical story, not begin on that very day in Dr. Mays's class a lifelong affair of devotion with this first-written, full narrative account in the New Testament? As one who can perhaps best be understood as almost literally dining on biblical story as a child, when my personhood was being foundationally shaped, how could I not be drawn to and fascinated by all the characters who emerge from Mark's intentionally dramatic account? The characters include the author himself, the Jesus of Mark, the followers of Jesus (the most faithful of whom are "the women"), the opponents of Jesus, the blind beggar Bartimaeus, the young man who runs away naked, and various other people in the drama, as well as the readers for whom Mark wrote, perhaps even you, dear reader, and me?

In my memory Grandma still laughs. I yet see her removing her glasses to wipe away the tears from her eyes as she laughed 'til she cried. I still feel a young boy's amazement at the communion of humor visited upon the four of us through the commotion of deep belly laughs from an adult never before seen by me to behave in such a manner. My own eyes still well up and smile when I remember.

This moment I lived with her serves to remind me what good stories do, be they Balaam's ass or *Goodnight Moon*[8] or Mark. They evoke our most sacred dreams and memories. As dreamers we are drawn toward our best imaginings of life lived in hope, not in despair or cynicism. As those who remember, we are reawakened to relationships and feelings, to laughter and heartbreak, to the richness and complexity of the human

---

8. Margaret Wise Brown, *Goodnight Moon*, illustrated by Clement Hurd (New York, NY: Harper & Brothers, 1947).

pilgrimage. And we become aware of God's part in it all—seen and unseen, "bidden and unbidden."[9]

This is why children in all their wisdom say, "Tell us a story." They ask for our best and for what their budding souls surely need. May we adults have sufficient wisdom in the face of such requests to pull up a chair or sit on a bed and reply, "Once upon a time . . ." or perhaps "In the beginning . . ."

---

9. The inscription over the entrance to Carl Jung's home near Lake Zurich, translated from the Latin, is "Bidden and unbidden, God comes."

2

"Come off it, Jesus!" A Jesus Who Grows Up

In Mark's account of Jesus, Jesus is from the beginning swept up in unexpected, ongoing transformation; his maturation is never ended, even by the tomb.

Exploring Mark's Story

As we continue our exploration of Mark's story, a brief statement regarding the Markan treasure examined in this chapter is in order. I grew up believing that Jesus, as God's Son, appeared on this earth with all his skills, talents, powers, wisdom, and loving compassion fully in place. Put colloquially, he had the full package from the get-go and needed only to reach his adult majority when he would begin to act and speak out of his inherent fullness. It was later in my faith journey—in my twenties, if memory serves—that I began to consider an alternative way of thinking about Jesus. I noticed it initially when reading and reflecting on a brief but pithy verse from Luke's Gospel: "And Jesus increased in wisdom and in stature, and in favor with God and man" (Luke 2:52 RSV).[1] Luke was describing a Jesus who grew and developed—not only physically or in the number of his earthly years, but also in wisdom and in his relationships with his fellow human beings and his God. Luke's brief verse invited me

---

1. I have taken this quotation from the RSV, since this is the translation I encountered as a young man.

to entertain the possibility that Jesus matured into his fullness as his years passed; he both made changes and was changed over his life's journey.

As I grew older and my faith journey continued, and as I was drawn more deeply into the world of Mark's Gospel, I carried with me Luke's snapshot of Jesus's growth process. I began to notice that in Mark's narrative what emerges is the portrait of a Jesus who engages in an ongoing formation process as the Beloved Son of God. Jesus grows, develops, and changes; he is transformed as Mark's account unfolds. This theme, then—the ongoing transformation of Jesus throughout his time on earth—constitutes the treasure of this chapter.

As Mark lays out his portrait of Jesus, it is accurate to say that Jesus is "born" changing and sixteen chapters later he "dies" changing. In the entirety of his work Mark leaves little room for his readers to misconstrue Jesus as a static figure, frozen in time and place and therefore unchanging and inalterable. To the contrary, as Mark develops his story, he presents his readers with numerous episodes related to Jesus's process of maturing. In this chapter, my three focal texts include some of these episodes and an evocative example of a specific aspect of Jesus's journey toward maturity found in the story of the Syrophoenician woman.[2] Taken together, the three focal texts demonstrate how thoroughly Mark embeds and develops the theme of Jesus's ongoing transformation as the narrative progresses.

Mark signals quite early that Jesus's transformation is an overarching theme. We see it initially in three consecutive Markan episodes: the baptism of Jesus (1:9–11), his wilderness experience (1:12–13), and his initial public proclamation (1:14–15).

Focal Text: Mark 1:9–15
Jesus's Transformation Begins

⁹In those days Jesus came from Nazareth of Galilee and was baptized by John in the Jordan. ¹⁰And just as he was coming up out of the water, he saw the heavens torn apart and the Spirit descending like a

---

2. I have included more than three passages for exploration here. I have done so because the passages referenced in the two groupings are tightly interwoven by Mark and I saw no helpful way to separate out a single representative from the larger grouping. Hence, I will present two collections of interrelated episodes here and a greater number of passages than I will reference in coming chapters.

dove on him. ¹¹And a voice came from heaven, "You are my Son, the Beloved; with you I am well pleased."

¹²And the Spirit immediately drove him out into the wilderness. ¹³He was in the wilderness forty days, tempted by Satan; and he was with the wild beasts; and the angels waited on him.

¹⁴Now after John was arrested, Jesus came to Galilee, proclaiming the good news of God, ¹⁵and saying, "The time is fulfilled, and the kingdom of God has come near; repent, and believe in the good news."[3]

When Mark begins to recount Jesus's baptism, he has penned only eight verses of his story. Imagine with me, if you will, that you have just settled into a favorite reading chair to begin reading Mark's Gospel. It is just about the moment when this settling is completed that Mark is off to the races. With Mark 1:9–11, Mark launches into all that begins to befall Jesus. He wastes no time in getting to his point; his immediate focus is Jesus and what he experiences in his baptism, his time in the wilderness, and his first words of Good News.

What aspects of these early back-to-back episodes point us toward a Jesus who grows and changes? Let's examine these early glimpses of the Markan Jesus.

Jesus's baptism as portrayed in 1:9–11 can be summarized as follows: an unimpressive Nazarene peasant is deluged by an astoundingly overwhelming welcome by a delighted God and is claimed as kin. A framework for forward movement in Mark's account is thus established, namely, that Jesus from Nazareth will spend the remainder of his life growing toward and moving into his identity as God's Beloved Son (child).

Jesus appears on the scene in Mark as an adult, apparently one among many seeking a baptism by John in the Jordan River. Jesus is of no special prominence or distinction, and, if anything—as a Nazarene from Galilee—would likely be considered a poor peasant from the wrong side of the tracks, to be shunned and overlooked by more upright and powerful members of his class-conscious society.[4]

---

3. I have deleted the titles given by the NRSV to each section of its translation. These captions were not included in Mark's account and I will frequently offer an alternative based on my understanding of the material under study.

4. Myers, *Binding the Strong Man*, 128. Myers outlines Jesus's lack of prominence and social standing as he comes to be baptized.

By the time Jesus walks back toward the bank of the Jordan, however, two extraordinary things have happened to him. First, he has seen the heavens torn asunder and a dove-like Spirit wing its way toward him. (The clouds being ripped apart in Mark stand as the fulfillment of the nearly six-hundred-year-old longing of the people of Israel for a fully present and saving God [Isa 64:1–3].) Second, Jesus has heard himself claimed as kin, the Beloved, by a delighted God.

At this point, Jesus may not fully understand the meaning and ramifications of his newly bestowed kinship relationship with God. In the narration of Jesus's wilderness experience, Mark hints that Jesus—when leaving the site of his baptism and certainly realizing that something momentous has just happened in his life—lacks clarity and full understanding of what it means to be a Son of God and what a Beloved Son is expected to say or do.

Being a fan of film, I find it useful when thinking of Mark's portrayal of Jesus's baptism to recall the character of Dorothy in the 1939 film version of *The Wizard of Oz*. Early in the movie Dorothy emerges cautiously from the wreckage left behind by a tornado that has uprooted her Kansas farmhouse home and deposited it—and her—in an altogether different land. As she tentatively begins to explore her new terrain, she appears both awe-struck and befuddled. Safe to say she is clear that things have changed significantly in her life. As she moves carefully and slowly into whatever awaits her, she speaks to her faithful, scruffy canine companion the absolute truth to the extent she is able to perceive it: "Toto, I've a feeling we're not in Kansas anymore."[5] In considering the universe of feelings and states of mind Jesus might have experienced immediately upon being baptized, Dorothy perhaps stands as a latter-day kindred spirit, both awe-struck and wondering what the future may yet hold.

As for my assertion that Jesus is born changing, I see Jesus's baptism functioning in Mark as his birth event. Luke has shepherds and angels (Luke 2:1–20); Matthew has wise men from the East (Matt 2:1–12); Mark has the baptism story. And by the time Mark finishes his telling of it, Jesus—no longer merely a peasant from Nazareth—has been born into a journey of discovery about being a Beloved Son of God. Birth has happened and it will not be undone. As for Jesus's initial understanding of his beginning at the Jordan River, it will be clarified, expanded, and even corrected. But undone? No, not even when he dies.

5. *The Wizard of Oz*, Victor Fleming, director (Hollywood, CA: Metro-Goldwyn-Mayer, 1939).

Continuing our focus on the three early episodes in Mark, which foreshadow his portrait of a Jesus who changes across the span of his narrative, we come to Jesus's initial journey into the wilderness (1:12–13). In Mark's recounting, the Spirit propels Jesus where the Beloved has a need to go after his grand welcome, that is, into the wilderness. Drawing on the traditions of Hebrew thought and history, Mark presents the wilderness as a place of testing, a place of being sustained by the Holy, and ultimately a place where the desert-dweller—Jesus in this case—is given opportunity for increased clarity about and comprehension of the purposes of God.

The Spirit is active in both Jesus's baptism and his movement toward the desert. It should be noted, however, that the activity displayed by the Spirit is markedly different in each episode. During the baptism, the Spirit is part of the grand welcome Jesus receives; in the wilderness, the Spirit is pictured as propelling Jesus forward in a way that is more forceful than mild-mannered urging. Jesus is driven by the Spirit, who operates here out of a firm, resolute, even tough stance when dealing with God's Beloved.[6]

Why is the Spirit here tougher and less welcoming than during the baptism? What is it Mark may hope we see by laying out these first two episodes, one after the other, and what is so important about the wilderness that Mark portrays Jesus as compelled to go there by the Spirit? Jesus is one who changes throughout the storyline, but in this desert episode, Jesus in no way appears motivated to volunteer for such change by choosing on his own to go into the desert. Rather, it is the Spirit who recognizes the need for growth that will come from a wilderness sojourn. It is the Spirit who is alert to Jesus's need to incorporate learnings beyond those that accompanied the delighted welcome and claiming at the baptism. Although the grand welcome of God's Beloved is an essential bedrock experience for Jesus, it is not sufficient; it will not prove adequate to help Jesus grow into the fullness of being the Beloved Son. In Mark's telling, the Spirit seems to know—perhaps even when Jesus may not—that more is needed. And it is to be found in the starkness of the wilderness, a decidedly sobering setting. Recognizing the need, the Spirit in effect shoves Jesus toward the desert.

What does the wilderness offer Jesus that the baptism could not? In addressing this question, it is helpful to remember the wilderness

---

6. Williamson, *Mark*, 38 (insightful discussion of the driving theme).

accounts woven throughout the Hebrew Scriptures and the historical traditions of the Israelites. Mark was likely familiar with these accounts and the prominent roles they played in the creation and renewal of Israel and her heroes. He would know of the themes presented in them—namely, the themes of testing and trial for a people (e.g., Israel) or a person (e.g., Elijah), being helped or sustained by God during the trial, and arriving at a position of greater clarity and resolve because of the time spent in the desert. Mark incorporates all these elements into Jesus's wilderness experience. Mark presents Jesus as driven to the desert to gain the maturity that comes, Mark suggests, from a period of testing, being with dark and sinister forces and "wild beasts," while also receiving the ministrations of God's sustaining agents ("angels"). The wilderness is the place—both in the Hebrew traditions and in Mark's narrative—where difficult and anguished lessons are to be learned. In Mark's view, it is a difficult and necessary path.

If the full ramifications of being a Beloved Son were not immediately grasped by Jesus in the midst of the celebration on the bank of the Jordan, the wilderness experience certainly offers itself as one means through which the meaning of being God's Beloved Son is rightly expanded. For example, the desert episode can be read as Mark's hint that being a Beloved Son will not exempt Jesus from life's difficulties and grinding moments. Being claimed as God's Beloved is not a prescription for any sort of existence of privilege or elevated standing to be coveted by his followers. Instead, as Mark's narrative unfolds, being God's Beloved will include times of breathtaking and even painful growth, maturing that comes—as it does with most of God's children—only "the hard way." It will not prove easy to be God's Beloved. In using this early reference to Jesus's wilderness sojourn, Mark advances the perspective that being so claimed is both absolutely bedrock for Jesus's formation and fraught with fearful, dark, and potentially lethal consequences. It is small wonder, then, that in Mark's presentation the newly baptized Jesus must be driven by the Spirit toward the wilderness, where an experience of the darker and sobering aspect of being God's Beloved awaits him.

Mark 1:14–15 is the third consecutive episode, early in the narrative, in which Mark establishes the centrality of Jesus's ongoing growth and maturity. In this third episode, however, Mark reveals this theme in a new way. Mark makes a stylistic shift, embedding his theme into a proclamation of Jesus, Jesus's first publicly spoken words recounted by Mark.

A brief comparison of the baptism and wilderness episodes with this proclamation episode of 1:14–15 further delineates this narrative shift.

In the baptism and wilderness narratives, Mark lays out events that happen to Jesus. In 1:14–15 the central focus is what is spoken by Jesus. The key words of the proclamation are *time*, the *kingdom* of God (come near), *repent*, and *believe* in (the good news).[7]

Mark's placement of the proclamation immediately after the baptism and wilderness scenes suggests that Jesus's declaration has been shaped by the baptism and wilderness experiences, along with Jesus's reflections and growing understanding of God's choosing him as Beloved Son. The placement here indicates that the content of Jesus's proclamation does not arise out of thin air or unadulterated inspiration; it has crystallized out of what has recently happened to him. Because of his previous encounters with the Holy, Jesus speaks with a clarity and budding confidence of a desert-dweller who has been tested and sustained. Jesus knows of what he speaks in his announcement; he has lived it.

The allusion in Mark 1:10 to Isa 64:1–3, coupled with the description of events befalling Jesus in his baptism and wilderness time, are a portrayal of the inbreaking of a long hoped-for, God-saturated epoch—one in which God/the Spirit has welcomed, driven, and sustained Jesus. Similarly, in 1:14–15, the words Jesus uses in his proclamation point to the dawning of such a season—a God-permeated time (*kairos*) and kingdom. All three scenes, then—baptism, wilderness, and proclamation—aim Mark's readers toward a new reality which is becoming possible. And, as we shall see, this new reality will challenge all other supposed realities that clamor for human allegiance.

Jesus emerges from the desert with a clearer understanding of his present identity and future direction. In the proclamation episode, Mark portrays an even deeper and more mature insight, which has ramifications beyond Jesus's own identity and path. This new dimension has to do with God's purposes for all humankind. As Jesus's proclamation makes clear, God's actions are not merely directed toward Jesus as a Beloved Child, but also toward others—in this case, Jesus's listeners. Mark portrays a Jesus who is coming to realize the possibility that what has happened to him at the Jordan and in the starkness of the desert is becoming potentially available for others. Further—and flowing from that realization—is another: that as a Beloved Son, Jesus is to call others toward the

---

7. See chapter 3, where I elaborate on these four key elements, which provide a blueprint of the kingdom of God.

realm of God. With the proclamation of 1:14–15, Jesus begins an activity that both witnesses to this deeper insight and announces the approach, proximity, and presence of God moving toward his people.

To sum up, the first two episodes of this grouping describe the beginning of a process of change and maturation wherein the Jesus from Nazareth is transformed into Jesus, Beloved Son. (The transformation is not brought to completion by baptism and wilderness, but awaits the empty tomb scene and the promise of a future Galilee meeting found in 16:1–8.) In this third episode, we hear Jesus announce, from the context of his recent experience, that there is a grand and staggering truth alive in the world; namely, that in this God-saturated, Spirit-filled time and kingdom, a way of being and living is possible for and proximate to all of God's people. This new path is intended not only for a solitary Beloved Son, but for all God's sons and daughters who have their lives turned around and trust that such a startling transformation of soul and heart is both available and sustainable in their time and in their walk upon this earth. This is a shout out of good news, indeed.

Mark carries the theme of Jesus's growth and maturity across the span of his entire work by the positioning of the next grouping of passages, which I have come to think of as the Godly Trio.

Focal Text: Mark 1:9–13; 9:2–8; 16:1–8
The "Godly Trio"—The Second Grouping

1:9–13
Jesus's Baptism and Desert Sojourn

⁹In those days Jesus came from Nazareth of Galilee and was baptized by John in the Jordan. ¹⁰And just as he was coming up out of the water, he saw the heavens torn apart and the Spirit descending like a dove on him. ¹¹And a voice came from heaven, "You are my Son, the Beloved; with you I am well pleased."

¹²And the Spirit immediately drove him out into the wilderness. ¹³He was in the wilderness forty days, tempted by Satan; and he was with the wild beasts; and the angels waited on him.

9:2–8
The Transfiguration of Jesus

²Six days later, Jesus took with him Peter and James and John, and led them up a high mountain apart, by themselves. And he was transfigured before them, ³and his clothes became dazzling white, such as no one on earth could bleach them. ⁴And there appeared to them Elijah with Moses, who were talking with Jesus. ⁵Then Peter said to Jesus, "Rabbi, it is good for us to be here; let us make three dwellings, one for you, one for Moses, and one for Elijah." ⁶He did not know what to say, for they were terrified. ⁷Then a cloud overshadowed them, and from the cloud there came a voice, "This is my Son, the Beloved; listen to him!" ⁸Suddenly when they looked around, they saw no one with them any more, but only Jesus.

16:1–8
The Risen Jesus/Promise Scene

¹When the sabbath was over, Mary Magdalene, and Mary the mother of James, and Salome bought spices, so that they might go and anoint him. ²And very early on the first day of the week, when the sun had risen, they went to the tomb. ³They had been saying to one another, "Who will roll away the stone for us from the entrance to the tomb?" ⁴When they looked up, they saw that the stone, which was very large, had already been rolled back. ⁵As they entered the tomb, they saw a young man, dressed in a white robe, sitting on the right side; and they were alarmed. ⁶But he said to them, "Do not be alarmed; you are looking for Jesus of Nazareth, who was crucified. He has been raised; he is not here. Look, there is the place they laid him. ⁷But go, tell his disciples and Peter that he is going ahead of you to Galilee; there you will see him, just as he told you." ⁸So they went out and fled from the tomb, for terror and amazement had seized them; and they said nothing to anyone, for they were afraid.

As we begin to explore this second grouping of Markan passages, I will initially consider Mark's placement of this trio of episodes and then move on to look at the content itself, which demonstrates a further broadening of the portrayal of Jesus, his ongoing growth process, and God's part in it.

Mark has arranged this second grouping of three widely separated passages at strategic points in the story—at the approximate beginning, middle, and end of his work.

- 1:9–13: This episode appears near the beginning of Mark's story. Jesus is just getting started, as it were.
- 9:2–8: This episode appears near the middle of the story and immediately follows the scene in which Jesus has made his initial statement regarding his future fate in Jerusalem (8:31).
- 16:1–8: This episode stands as the conclusion of the story.[8]

The question remains: "What connects these seemingly distinct passages?" In the content of the three episodes, taken as a whole, the reader finds a decided and deliberate focus by Mark on this portrayal of divine forces as the agents of Jesus's maturation process. In these three episodes, these divine forces are most intimately present and directly active with Jesus and his closest followers, and Mark most deftly and clearly details their influences and actions upon Jesus as he moves through his own growing up.

While at no point in the three episodes does Mark explicitly employ the word "God," he certainly sees to it that the manifestations of God's presence and activity are everywhere to be found. In the baptism and wilderness scenes, for instance, there are the heavens ripped apart, the Spirit descending, a voice from the heavens, the forcefulness of the Spirit pushing Jesus into the desert, and angels there who sustain the newly claimed Beloved Son. In the transfiguration there are dazzling changes in Jesus's clothing and a conversation between Jesus and two pillars of his religious heritage (Moses and Elijah). A voice from the clouds reconfirms Jesus's standing as Beloved Son and directs Peter, James, and John to listen to him—especially, perhaps, to what Jesus recently announced in 8:31 regarding his fate as Son of Man. In the Risen Jesus scene there is a young man, one who surely fulfills the traditional function of heavenly, angelic messengers by bearing God's tidings to God's people, in this case the three women disciples. The young man is in the tomb to witness to a sure and certain godly deed: the raising of God's Beloved. Importantly, he also announces an imminent future for the Risen Jesus in Galilee, leading his followers once again.

---

8. See chapter 9, where I outline the view that Mark ends his written account with these final eight verses.

Each of the episodes in the Godly Trio, then, describes a moment when the Divine bestows on Jesus an incremental expansion of his identity, and each gift of the Divine contributes to Jesus's advancing maturity. In baptism, God's bestowed gift is kinship. In transfiguration, there is bestowed a Godly reconfirmation of Jesus's Sonship, which has expanded to include his death and rising in Jerusalem. In the Risen Jesus scene, the already-bestowed sacred gift of life is announced, buttressed by the fact that there is no crucified Jesus to be found in the tomb.

Nowhere else does Mark invite his readers to notice the sovereign presence of God to the degree that he does in the Godly Trio. At the same time, in each of the three episodes, God is intimate in his majestic prominence. Although arranged far apart in the structure of Mark's story, this second grouping taken together stands out as a vivid, brightly colored strand woven throughout the tapestry of Mark's masterpiece. This specific thread portrays the Holy God who is as close as the air we breathe and as powerfully active as when God wrestled the chaos to birth the universe.

From the Markan perspective, then, in the Godly Trio there emerges the figure of a Beloved Son encouraged toward maturity and transforming change across his adult life, with God being the driving force in his change. God is in the beginning. God is present and active during Jesus's life journey. God is at the end. Even in Mark's concluding verse, where his readers encounter the most faithful of Jesus's followers, as they too fail and bolt in terror from the tomb, God is still present and active through the promise announced by the young man in white: Jesus is already going into Galilee and "there you will see him" (16:7). No fear, no flight, not even the silence of the women can overturn these words of promise. When even the best efforts of the most loyal and courageous come to naught, God's promise remains. I am persuaded that Mark leaves his readers with this desperate and certain hope—for the sake of the women, the absent male disciples, and even for us—that all and the worst of human fears and failings cannot undo the wispiest doings of the Most High, even a mere promise of a seemingly impossible future.

The Good News of God always seems impossible until it isn't.

In the fullness of Mark's account, there are moments of maturity and change for Jesus that occur through means other than direct, divine action of the kind suggested by the Godly Trio. Mark's readers are led to consider the possibility that Jesus matures through, for example, his own spiritual practice of prayer and reflection, or in moments when he is challenged or even corrected by other very human characters in Mark's account, or even as Jesus continues to run up against the ongoing (and apparently deepening) obtuseness of his followers, especially the Twelve.

At this juncture, I invite the reader's attention to a fine representative instance of Jesus's ongoing transformation as it is advanced through means of social interplay and challenge. Mark's story of the Syrophoenician woman (7:24–30) is one of the clearest examples Mark provides of Jesus being encountered and changed by another inhabitant of his narrative. I believe it to be one of the most arresting and powerful scenes of transformation in all of Mark. Within this story Jesus matures through the bold, incisive, and challenging speech of a courageous and desperate pagan mother of a sick child. She will not be brushed aside by a visiting healer she has chanced to hear about, even one who perhaps wants only to withdraw from the spotlight for a while to rest and recover. It is in honor of this persistent and daring mother that I titled this chapter "Come off it, Jesus!"

Focal Text: Mark 7:24–30
Jesus Changes Through Human Challenge

24From there he set out and went away to the region of Tyre. He entered a house and did not want anyone to know he was there. Yet he could not escape notice, 25but a woman whose little daughter had an unclean spirit immediately heard about him, and she came and bowed down at his feet. 26Now the woman was a Gentile, of Syrophoenician origin. She begged him to cast the demon out of her daughter. 27He said to her, "Let the children be fed first, for it is not fair to take the children's food and throw it to the dogs." 28But she answered him, "Sir, even the dogs under the table eat the children's crumbs." 29Then he said to her, "For saying that, you may go—the demon has left your daughter." 30So she went home, found the child lying on the bed, and the demon gone.

This scene portrays Jesus as withdrawing from the area in and around the Sea of Galilee, the locale where he has been exercising his ministry. He heads for Tyre, which is an unusual place for Jesus to go: "The region of Tyre, northwest of Galilee, largely gentile and despised by Jews."9 But if we trust that Mark is purposeful in denoting this peculiar destination for

---

9. Black, "The Gospel of Mark," note on Mark 7:24.

Jesus, we readers are presented with the possibility that Mark intentionally locates this scene deep in unmistakable gentile (pagan) territory.[10] Jesus is away from the usual geographical setting for his work and has instead gone into a region normally avoided by good Jews.

If Jesus can be said to withdraw geographically, it is also a distinct possibility that he has chosen to withdraw from his followers during his visit to Tyre. Although there is no definitive statement to this effect, there are several indicators of Jesus's albeit temporary separation from his disciples. First, when Jesus sets out for Tyre, his disciples are not mentioned, as they frequently are when they accompany Jesus (see 6:1, for example). Neither is their presence mentioned again by Mark until well after Jesus has departed Tyre, when he begins to conduct his second feeding of a large crowd (8:1).

Second, drawing on the work of Ched Myers, the story of the Syrophoenician woman is placed in a larger context of "the boat stories,"[11] that is, a series of stories in Mark 4:35—8:21 in which Jesus and his followers come and go in a boat, traveling back and forth across the Sea of Galilee. According to Myers, one theme of this section of Mark is that there is "growing tension between Jesus and his disciples . . . Tension is introduced when the disciples wonder out loud who Jesus might be, in the first boat story (4:41), and culminates in Jesus' exasperation in the last boat story (8:14ff.)."[12] As I understand it, the core of this rising tension is portrayed by Mark as the failure of the disciples to understand the

---

10. It should be noted that numerous interpreters take Mark to task for his geographic references, indicating his inaccuracy when naming various locations, or in laying out tortuous and unlikely routes of travel between locations. This critique of Mark is a problem mainly if one assumes that Mark is aiming for geographic accuracy when he employs such references. However, if these references serve other purposes—such as possibly here in 7:24 in which Mark may be nudging his readers primarily to note that Jesus has gone away from Galilee—this critique of Mark's poor grasp of geography is less consequential and likely not an error at all. My working assumption is that Mark's geographic references are usually not about the literal lay of the land, but rather are a way of alerting readers to other aspects of Markan thought which are associated with a particular place name or location. One of the best examples of this Markan device would be Mark's reference to Galilee in 16:7, which alerts readers not only to a specific geographic region, but more importantly to the fact that the disciples are being promised and called to a meeting with their Risen Lord back in the arena where they will carry on with their normal, daily lives, that is, in Galilee.

11. Myers, *Binding the Strong Man*, 187–90. Myers draws on the work of Werner Kelber in constructing his analysis of the boat stories.

12. Myers, *Binding the Strong Man*, 190.

meaning of Jesus's actions and teachings as they relate to Jesus's identity as the Beloved Son, and their failure to comprehend Jesus's invitation to them to live fully into the arriving kingdom of God.[13]

Jesus has apparently chosen to withdraw from the Galilean locale of his ministry, and tension is growing with his disciples, who may well not have even been asked to accompany Jesus on his trip to Tyre. It is not surprising, then, to discover yet another Markan clue about Jesus's intention to withdraw, embedded in the text of the Syrophoenician woman incident: Mark indicates in that Jesus "did not want anyone to know he was there" (7:24). With the word "want," Mark uses vocabulary that connotes a complex of meanings. "To want" is to wish for, desire, will, intend, or choose. In not wanting to be found, Jesus is exercising a firm, "set-jaw" sort of choice; he is determined to retreat, intentional in doing so, and chooses not to be found by anyone. Why he is so strongly determined to get away is not explicitly stated by Mark, but the reader can imagine that, at the very least, Jesus needs a rest after his recent heated clashes with the Pharisees and scribes (see 7:1–13) and after his discouraging and multiple attempts to help the disciples comprehend that which seems beyond their grasp. His efforts with them have come to naught. To sum up, then, in coming to Tyre Jesus chooses to disengage at least for a while. Retreat is required; rest is essential; restoration is sought—behind closed doors and away from everyone.

However, if Jesus is determined to withdraw, another person enters the story, equally determined as he, if not more so. Mark introduces us to an unknown woman and though she is given no name, Mark identifies her in several ways:

---

13. Three episodes from the "boat stories" point to the rising tension between Jesus and his disciples. In Mark 4:35–41—following Myers's analysis—the disciples' failure to understand shows itself in the question they ask each other regarding Jesus's identity (4:41). They do not recognize the God-like powers revealed in Jesus's calming the waves and the storm. And beyond that, while the words in their question focus on the obedience of the wind and sea, they apparently overlook perhaps the most central fact of the storm scene—namely that God through Jesus has acted to keep them safe and alive. Second, in Mark 6:30–52, Mark's story of the first feeding in his narrative closes with a direct statement of the disciples' failure to understand: "for they did not understand about the loaves, but their hearts were hardened." Third, in 7:17–23, the episode that immediately precedes the story of the Syrophoenician woman, Jesus comments again on the disciples' obtuseness (see esp. 7:18).

- Apparently not known by Jesus, she knows of him, having somehow gotten wind that a healer or exorcist has arrived in the area. She immediately sets out to find him.
- She is of Greek origin and specifically a Syrophoenician, and thus a non-Jewish pagan.[14]
- Beyond any other identification Mark provides her in the story, however, she is a mother of a sick, possessed child. She is propelled solely by her child's need and she will, it seems, do whatever it takes to release her child from her awful, unfree state.

Unbidden, the Syrophoenician woman dares to enter into a private home, to violate Jesus's deliberately chosen retreat, to prostrate herself at Jesus's feet, begging for the health and unbinding of her daughter.

For twenty-first century readers of Mark, this mother's behavior—while possibly brash or even somewhat pushy or rude—can be viewed as understandable and even appropriate given her daughter's condition. However, in the context of first century Palestine, her behavior leaps far beyond any such generous assessment and lands her squarely in front of Jesus in a shocking affront to him. Again, Myers: "no woman, and especially a gentile, unknown and unrelated to this Jew, would have dared invade his privacy at home to seek a favor."[15] It was just not done. Moreover, as if her actions were not jarring and unacceptable enough, Mark wants to be sure that his readers notice her very unacceptability because of who she is—as a Syrophoenician, she is a foreigner, and as a gentile, she is one of inferior religious and ethnic status. As presented by Mark, then, both her deeds and her personhood are offensive. Myers further broadens the first-century context: "the story both assumes and reflects the ethnic, cultural, and socio-political hostility between Jews and their gentile neighbors."[16] So, even as this determined mother approaches Jesus in 7:25–26, she has two strikes against her—her intemperate, disrespectful behavior and her very being as a pagan, foreigner, and outsider to Jesus's Jewish world.

Jesus's initial response to this foreign intruder who has prostrated herself in front of him, begging for her daughter's restoration, arises, I believe, from twin sources. As noted earlier, the first is Jesus's chosen state

---

14. Myers, *Binding the Strong Man*, 203.
15. Myers, *Binding the Strong Man*, 203.
16. Myers, *Binding the Strong Man*, 204.

of withdrawal and retreat. To the woman's request to heal her daughter, his first words appear at minimum coolly dismissive of her or—dare we imagine?—even biting with irritation or disgust. At the very least they leave the reader with the impression that Jesus is attempting to get this unwanted one to go away so he may continue his restful retreat. He would be done with her; he has not come to Tyre to heal, exorcise, or engage with desperately needy folks. He has come, as Mark has told us, choosing that no one find him. He responds, then, first of all, out of his prior decision to withdraw.

In 7:27 we see a second source of Jesus's response to the Syrophoenician mother. It is a source of even more difficulty for those of us reared as "believers" of various stripes, for it raises the discomforting possibilities about Jesus we may not have considered before. Here is the reader's dilemma as I understand it. This story, perhaps more than any other in Mark, demonstrates the human truth that Jesus is a product of his time. We, all of us, are shaped, impacted, and influenced—for better and worse—by the circumstances and settings in which we grow up, develop, endure, and suffer. This story reminds us that Mark's Jesus is not exempt from this broad cultural and social conditioning. Out of that conditioning Jesus can on occasion, as in this story, act and speak in ways that may strike the contemporary reader as lacking compassion or even harsh and cruel. For many of us who have traveled down the usual paths of instruction about Jesus, Mark's portrayal of him at this point poses a wrenching problem.

A close look at 7:27 reinforces this observation and invites the reader's attention to embedded prejudices that come into play as Jesus encounters this mother. In 7:27, Jesus speaks about "the children's food." In the Greek "food" is literally bread or loaves (see the RSV translation for comparison). When Mark makes mention of bread or loaves, he often does so to alert his readers to two co-existing realities, symbolized by bread.[17] The first reality is the basic human need of God's people for survival and sustenance; people must eat bread to live and their obtaining bread serves as the symbol of survival and living. The second reality, while often alluded to in a glancing manner by Mark or even hidden in

---

17. Examples of Markan bread/loaves stories and the two realities symbolized by them are, first and foremost, the feeding of the 5000 in 6:30–52 with its six references to bread/loaves. See also the feeding of the 4000 in 8:1–10 (three references) and Jesus's interrogation of the disciples regarding their understanding about these feedings in 8:14–21 (four explicit references to bread/loaves along with one implicit reference in 8:20).

the background, is the assurance that God will act or be present in such a way that the Holy will in God's mercy meet the essential, life-threatening needs of the people. It is God who sustains with bread and with much more beyond literal bread. Indeed, God will in ways beyond normal human imagining deluge the hungry, the despairing, the needy with inconceivable, life-giving help. For Mark, then, bread and loaves—both literal and symbolic—are inextricably joined with God's intent and action to meet the needs of all God's beloved children. Put another way—one consistent with Markan imagery—in the arriving kingdom of God, all will eat and be filled.[18]

Given this usual understanding of bread in the Markan narrative, 7:27 stands as the single exception to this pattern of usage. This exception, presented by Mark as coming from the very mouth of Jesus, "implies the superiority of Israel's claim upon God's blessing (food, lit. 'bread') over that of Gentiles."[19] In 7:27 the Markan Jesus does not draw on the imagery of all eating and being filled. Rather he implies gradations of those worthy of God's sustaining intent and action, with some "children" being more worthy of divine care than others—at least in the immediate moment of his encounter with this pleading mother. Indeed, when Jesus speaks directly of these lesser ones whose needs will be unaddressed in the present and who cannot expect or rely on God's merciful intent and action in the "now," he refers to them as "dogs," (7:27) an epithet sometimes characterized as slanderous or insulting.[20] Jesus's words would appear to shut down any way forward for the plea of the Syrophoenician woman on behalf of her daughter, with this shutdown also functioning in Mark's story as a putdown, a diminishment of all her efforts to help her child and indeed of all that goes into who this woman is.

Perhaps a brief pause is in order at this point—to catch our collective breath as well as to take stock of where this unusual story has brought us and to glance forward to where it will yet take us. I especially want to remind readers of the larger context here, that this story recounts another example of how Jesus is transformed and matures in the course of Mark's Gospel. In Mark 7:24–30, the agency of Jesus's transformation turns out to be the speech of a gentile woman, not a particularly godly person at all.

18. See Mark 6:42 as an example of this imagery.

19. Black, "The Gospel of Mark," note on Mark 7:27.

20. Black, "The Gospel of Mark," note on Mark 7:27. Also, Myers, *Binding the Strong Man*, 204.

Beginning with 7:28, this gentile mother utters the transformative words. The courage and tenacity that underlie her words are highlighted all the more against the backdrop of Jesus's initial reaction to her in 7:27—born as it is of his need to withdraw and his grounding as a Jewish resident of first-century Israel subject to the prejudices and biases of that time and place. At best, he has acted and spoken to dismiss her and at worst to insult and demean her. But she is neither done in nor done. Mark's intense account continues.

As we return to this story of a mother's encounter with Jesus, we begin where we left off—with 7:28. Again, it is useful to put ourselves, as best we are able, in the shoes of Mark's first-century readers, in an exercise of understanding. In my imagination, the Syrophoenician woman leaves the scene of this exchange and returns heartbroken to her stricken child. For has she not done everything that was possible to do to help her daughter? Has she not, uninvited, slipped stealthily into a stranger's home? Has she not broken into Jesus's deliberately chosen time of retreat and renewal? And, begging, has she not pleaded with this man—known to her only through the rumors spreading through the streets of Tyre—to free her possessed child? But her efforts have been rebuffed and her personhood has been belittled and shamed by the one she had hoped might help. Given her first exchange with Jesus, then, it would not be at all surprising if she had withdrawn, silenced, her face wet with tears. At least, this is what I imagine. What comes to your mind?

Instead, beginning with 7:28, this mother courageously stands her ground and argues her case further. After all, her child is in profound need—a need not yet addressed, a need the mother tenaciously keeps in her heart and mind, a need she is compelled to place before Jesus yet again, despite his initial ignoring of it. In 7:28 she again challenges Jesus with her daughter's need. To be sure, the challenge is offered with a measure of respect and a bow to Jesus's standing and authority; she addresses Jesus as "Sir." But even as she is respectful, she is also clever in her response to Jesus. She makes use of Jesus's metaphor about children and dogs in such a way that its initial meaning is turned on its head. In Jesus's metaphor, children are to be the recipients of food (read: God's sustaining favor/blessing), and dogs (read: gentiles, pagans) are lesser creatures whose hungers are not a matter of concern. In the woman's recrafted metaphor, however, the children become—even if unwittingly—the sharers of food/crumbs with the dogs who are no longer held as less worthy, but rather as fellow creatures in need of food/crumbs/God's favor. The woman's words to Jesus in her second exchange with him beckon Jesus (and Mark's readers) toward a vision of a Merciful One who provides bread to all hungry creatures, children and dogs alike. Her words to Jesus resonate with the previously mentioned Markan imagery of bread and loaves; in her recast metaphor, all will eat and be filled.

In Mark's account, the impact of the mother's challenge on Jesus is immediate. Her reshaped metaphor apparently strikes a chord within him, one that Jesus readily acknowledges: "For saying that . . ." (7:29). This time, his specific response to the words she speaks is neither dismissive nor demeaning; rather, he speaks as one who has experienced a helpful and jarring corrective. This time, he addresses the bold mother as one who has been stopped in his tracks by one of those rarest of moments when a worldview shifts, or in this specific instance, when one's prejudices are seen for what they are. In such a corrective moment, such binding beliefs begin to loosen their stranglehold and fall away; new possibilities for rightly seeing the world—and ourselves—are born, and we have the chance to emerge as wiser, freer, and more compassionate human beings.

We come then to the central message of this Markan episode—namely, that maturity once again expands for Jesus and he is caught up in yet another transformative experience. In this instance, it comes through the challenging and corrective words of a desperate and determined mother. She has seen to it that Jesus takes a second look at the need of her child over against any other culturally embedded bias by which Jesus has lived up to this point in his life. She has spoken in such a way that this second look takes place no longer through the lens of ingrained cultural, social, and religious biases of Jesus's day, but rather through the lens of a universally merciful God who knows that all the world's daughters and sons have hunger that cries out for feeding.

In 7:28 a mother speaks and consequently Jesus moves toward a broadened understanding and increased maturity. Most likely with a jolt, I suspect, it becomes clear to him that his identity as Beloved Son includes God's intention that he, Jesus, announce the immediate availability of God's good news and the arriving kingdom, not merely to the chosen few of Israel, but to all humanity. His vision and understanding of God shifts, and as a result of the words of a foreign, non-believing outsider, he continues his growth toward his fullness as God's Beloved Son.[21]

---

21. Mark's larger context for this story provides at least three indications that the words of the mother served as a corrective to Jesus, enabling him to recognize his biases and begin to shed them in order to live out of an expanded, more mature

"Come off it, Jesus!" A Jesus Who Grows Up

I close our consideration of this story with one final thought, which arises from the logic of the passage rather than any explicit statement on Mark's part. This moving story can be read as one in which two of God's children are freed from forces that bind them and keep them from their full participation in what God intends for them. A daughter is freed from the demon that renders her captive; a Beloved Son is released from his misperceptions of his fellow beings and from his limited understanding of the fullness of God's mercy and grace for all. Both are freed through the words of another—the child through the words of Jesus ("the demon has left your daughter" [7:29])—and Jesus through the words of a courageous, tenacious, and challenging woman, clamoring cleverly about crumbs. In the end, both beloved daughter and Beloved Son are set free, ever more able to move unshackled into God's arriving kingdom.

At several points in this chapter, I have interchangeably used the phrases *approaching* and *arriving* kingdom of God. I want at this point to indicate that my emphasis on the approaching and arriving kingdom is intentional and is meant to echo Jesus's first public proclamation "and the kingdom of God has come near." (Mark 1:15). I see the kingdom as in its own way dynamic, that is, not so much a static force field of some sort but a living, moving reality headed in our direction—similar to the arrival of the Spirit of an exuberant God at Jesus's baptism. This interpretation of God's near kingdom has become clearer to me through the influence of the Markan narrative. At the same time, it is likely that the following experience of the Holy also shaped my understanding of a living, approaching kingdom.

---

understanding of both God and himself as God's Beloved. The three are as follows: (1) After the mother's words, Jesus shifts from his initial reluctance to aid the woman's daughter to healing her, freeing her from her condition of being possessed (7:29–30); (2) In the two episodes that immediately follow 7:24–30, Jesus apparently shifts away from his stance of withdrawal from both Galilee and from his disciples (see 7:31, which indicates Jesus is heading back to Galilee, and 8:1, where Mark indicates that Jesus is again calling his disciples to him); (3) The episodes of 7:31–37 and 8:1–10 portray Jesus as involved in expanding his work into the gentile world. (see 7:31–37, where Jesus's circuitous route first takes him even deeper into gentile territory, toward Sidon and then the Decapolis region, and 8:1–10, where Jesus, still in the Decapolis area, conducts his second feeding of a large crowd, one presumably made up of gentiles, pagans from the predominantly gentile-populated area. As was true of the first crowd of 5000 fed near the Sea of Galilee, this second crowd fed in the Decapolis region also "ate and were filled" (see 6:42 and 8:8). Jesus has taken the Syrophoenician woman's challenge to heart and is acting accordingly.

Personal Reflection: The Arrival

When I was a child growing up in the Virginia countryside, frequently in the summer months a thunderstorm would blow in during the late, humid afternoon. When this would occur I and my friends were bright enough, despite the prevailing adult wisdom, to come in out of the rain, either into the house or, for a little extra excitement, into the barn where the grand noise of a deluge of giant raindrops on a tin roof literally drowned out all sound of small boys yelling to each other in the deafening din.

I also remember the occasional exception to my usual pattern; in these instances, I would be alone standing out on the side porch of the house waiting for the storm to arrive. My view over the side garden and rolling pasture was unimpeded for a good half mile to the far fence line marking the boundary of our property. Often there was a period of wind just prior to the storm and I learned over my youth that the wind's cessation stood as silent alert to the next phase of the approaching drama. Of course, thunder and lightning could also mark the storm's approach, but for me the ceasing of the wind was somehow even more to be wished for because of the eternal surprise of it. In the stillness I could sniff the becalmed air and smell the storm. Looking to the far horizon, a distance of a mile or two beyond the fence, I could see the storm approaching. It appeared at first as a wall of advancing silver, slowly enveloping the distant trees and even houses in its path. As it moved closer I began to hear its drumming power—first as a faint pounding on the earth but growing louder and a bit unnerving despite the smile of awe spreading across my face.

The full arrival of the storm was marked by the hissing of the leaves around the house as the large, pelting drops tore through them before reaching the dry earth. Simultaneously, the roaring from the porch roof flooded my ears. On occasion, in spite of some significant fear of the power of it all (and only if there were no lightning) I would dash quickly into the storm to have its wetness pound upon my skin and then while retreating to the porch might close my eyes and open my upturned mouth to the deluge, a pose reminiscent of a baby robin in the spring. What an experience of my smallness, my joy, my fear, my sensory exultation, my awe, my childhood God, and the power of a moment. This moment yet stays with me, no longer a child.

Perhaps the coming near of the kingdom and our entry into its reorienting realm is somewhat like stepping into an arriving summer storm. Its coming frightens and exhilarates, and certainly announces an enveloping authority beyond full comprehension, understandable best through joy, fear, wonder, and trust.

3

The Kingdom of God Is for the Birds

The kingdom of God unleashes wide-ranging changes for those who enter it; those who follow Jesus into the kingdom face the potential for both great loss and great gain.

Exploring Mark's Story

IN MARK 4:30–32 JESUS tells a parable of the kingdom of God in which he compares the kingdom to a mustard seed, which grows with an exuberance similar to Jack's beanstalk and eventually becomes a huge shrub with long sturdy branches, providing terrific habitat for many, many birds. For any self-respecting bird watcher of the twenty-first century, what pleasing and evocative images are stirred by this parable! However, as Balmer Kelly, one of my seminary professors, pointed out years ago, parables are rarely what they seem. Dr. Kelly once said, "If you read one of the parables of Jesus and don't feel a jolt, you need to read it again." His passionate belief about parables, and, in truth, about Scriptures as a whole, was that they are meant to surprise us, to reshape our understanding and perspective, and to present opportunities to reorient our lives.

Focal Text: Mark 4:30–32
Parable of Uncontrollable Growth

³⁰He also said, "With what can we compare the kingdom of God, or what parable will we use for it? ³¹It is like a mustard seed, which, when sown upon the ground, is the smallest of all the seeds on earth; ³²yet when it is sown it grows up and becomes the greatest of all shrubs, and puts forth large branches, so that the birds of the air can make nests in its shade."

The jolt of this parable is captured by John Dominic Crossan when he calls the mustard plant a "dangerous"[1] plant. There is a wildness to it, and it often takes over any area where it is planted. It can eventually bring ruin to a well-cultivated garden, even when carefully tended. Perhaps it is a cousin to the southern plant known as kudzu. There is an old piece of advice about kudzu and its tendency to overgrow anything in its path: If you need to pause in the shade on a hot summer's day, don't stand too long near the kudzu. You may never be seen again.

Not only does danger reside in the mustard seed's nearly uncontrollable growth potential; it attracts birds who damage crops—fruits, vegetables, and grains—as farmers, who were likely among the audience of this parable, can attest. Crossan sums up in eloquent simplicity: that the mustard plant "tends to take over where it is not wanted, that it tends to get out of control, and that it tends to attract birds within cultivated areas where they are not particularly desired. And that, said Jesus, was what the Kingdom was like."[2]

In Jesus's day, this teaching story, in which pesky, crop-damaging critters find safety, comfort, and even habitat to hatch their babies, would have most likely left the farmers in his audience at the very least confused and perhaps even provoked. The significant point behind the jolt of the parable, however, emerges as we recognize that Jesus is not primarily promoting the welfare of birds. Rather, Jesus speaks of the reality that change and growth are of a piece within God's kingdom. It is an out-of-control, wild, and even dangerous growth. The approach and arrival of the kingdom brings an inevitable and unmanageable reshaping of the

---

1. Crossan, *Jesus*, 65.
2. Crossan, *Jesus*, 65.

usual state of affairs, similar to the germination of a mustard seed, which foreshadows the likely demise of a carefully cultivated plot of land. The kingdom ushers in unstoppable transformation for both the individual disciple and the society in which Jesus's followers live. The coming of the kingdom accompanied by our entry into it threatens to stand the prevailing system of order on its head. The kingdom, says Jesus, has resonance with a tiny mustard seed, as it threatens to undo all attempts to control or domesticate it.[3]

In putting forward this kingdom parable, Mark invites his readers toward this surprise: that Jesus's seemingly bucolic, harmless tale about a shady resting place for birds has implications that go far beyond the world of farmers. It speaks a subversive word into the world of those in power, those who keep in place the various binding systems of order and control—leaders of the various "cultures" in which the Markan Jesus dwells, be they social, familial, religious, political, or military. A dangerous thing indeed, a mustard seed.[4]

Mark uses the mustard seed to alert his readers to the uncontrollable and even threatening changes that are unleashed in the kingdom, and the rowdy birds also play a role in the story. The birds alert the readers to a correlative reality, namely, that the kingdom of God becomes a place where the unwanted and undesirable find shelter and rest, safely beyond the punitive reach of those who would have them diminished, dismissed from their sight, or otherwise managed. By including the birds as beneficiaries of such a wild, ungovernable life force on full display as a mustard plant thrives, Mark evokes the enlivening, exuberant side of the kingdom, one we may see to this day in the gathering of loud, chattering, ebullient starlings in our backyards. The kingdom is the place where good news is extended to the unlikeliest of God's creatures. The kingdom is indeed for the birds, those feathered and those decidedly human.

For our next focal text, we consider the first public proclamation of Jesus (Mark 1:14–15) for a second time, but from a new angle, with a focus on the hearers of the proclamation.[5] The proclamation has definitive implications for its hearers as recipients of good news and potential

---

3. Levine, *Short Stories by Jesus*, 165–82. Levine presents a very different reading of this parable.

4. See chapter 4 for a detailed look at some of the threats posed by Jesus (and God's kingdom) to several established systems of order and control of Jesus's day.

5. See chapter 2 on how Jesus's recent experiences shape his first public proclamation.

entrants into the kingdom of God. Our new focus on the hearers illuminates Mark's understanding of the nature of God's kingdom and our potential participation in it.

Focal Text: Mark 1:14–15
Jesus's First Spoken Words in Mark

¹⁴Now after John was arrested, Jesus came to Galilee, proclaiming the good news of God, ¹⁵and saying, "The time is fulfilled, and the kingdom of God has come near; repent, and believe in the good news."

"The good news of God" is the central dynamic driving Jesus's proclamation. In this initial address to the people of Galilee, Jesus emphasizes the gospel of God above all else. But he follows with four key elements, represented by four words in the text (1:15)—*time*, *kingdom*, *repent*, and *believe*—that provide a blueprint for understanding what constitutes the kingdom in Mark's story.

The first key element is *time* (*kairos* in Greek). In speaking of "the time," Mark is pointing not to the passage of seconds, minutes, or days by which we currently mark our span upon the earth, but "a decisive moment appointed by God."[6] This sort of *kairos* moment is a God-sent moment or season pregnant with extraordinary significance and meaning. With his initial utterance to God's people, Jesus proclaims that a God-directed age is afoot: a season of great meaning envelopes Jesus's listeners—and Mark's readers.

The second element is *kingdom*: "and the kingdom of God has come near"(1:15). Schweizer notes that Jesus "spoke frequently of one's entering the kingdom. Therefore, the kingdom is more like an area or a sphere of authority into which one can enter, so 'realm' would be a better translation."[7] Schweizer describes the kingdom as a "realm" into which humans can journey, the defining characteristic of which is the full and authoritative presence of God. Mark suggests that this "place" of entry and dwelling is defined as available, close at hand, come near—not because humans have initially moved in its direction but rather because it

---

6. Black, "The Gospel of Mark," note on Mark 1:15.
7. Schweizer, *Good News*, 45–46.

apparently has been brought to them. The kingdom has moved in humankind's direction and not vice versa.

Third, the word *repent* directs its hearers to reorienting action so that they may live fully into the new age of transformation. As spoken by Jesus in 1:15, repent carries far richer connotations than present-day readers may realize. Repentance has to do with a turning, a shift of life's direction.

In my case, it was not until my seminary years that I learned that repenting might hold another meaning—beyond deep sorrow or regret, usually for a hurtful deed done or an irritated-to-downright-wicked or murderous thought entertained. I thought of repentance as the feeling I had when as a six-year-old child I intentionally tripped my three-year-old cousin, Jean, causing her to plummet from a couch to the hard wood floor. To be clear, this occurred not out of any childhood playfulness gone awry or because my cousin had hurt or bothered me. I did it, as best I can recall, out of pure meanness. Further, I had judged that I could do it surreptitiously and not get caught. This may have been my first conscious introduction to the reality of original sin.

It does help now to remember that I felt bad after the fact; appropriate for my age, the bad feeling came when I saw that I had hurt Jean. She fell hard. Moreover, I felt even worse when the only consequence of my spiteful action was that Jean was scolded for walking on the couch and being clumsy while I got off with no punishment. I was left feeling a bit stunned and, more significantly, fearful of my own unprovoked cruelty. Prior to hurting Jean, I had thought of myself as a "good boy" with all of a six-year old's pride and need. But this incident gave witness that my self-assessment was far from the whole truth. As best I could, I suppose, I repented, though I remained silent in my guilt. Genuine confession often takes years.

The above sort of repentance, though not hopelessly useless or errant, is only partial for Mark. Within his framework, repentance has to do with a turning, a shift of life's direction. Its primary expression has little to do with making mental lists of one's wrongdoing or feeling sorrow and regret. Repentance is a call to accept an astounding and radical reorientation of one's very core, and as such, repentance is not an easy or casual act. It is the kind of shift that causes those who repent to tremble with fear at the potential cost of the change (as in Mark 10:32). At other times, it causes those who repent to act with courage seemingly beyond human capacity.[8] Jesus's call to repent in 1:15 is a call for his listeners

---

8. See chapter 8, where we note this sort of courage in the deeds of the centurion, some women followers of Jesus, and Joseph of Arimathea, in Mark 15:39–47.

to shift soul and core. It is his beckoning to get one's life turned around, reordered, transformed.

To better grasp the meaning of repenting, imagine that you are walking down a path, going in the wrong direction, perhaps without even knowing it. Either gradually or suddenly you realize what you have been doing—moving toward a destructive or at least meaningless end point. This awareness is followed by a consequent halting in your tracks and turning around, a change in priorities or orientation. It is at this point that repentance has happened. From the Markan perspective, however, this is not the end of what is needed. Jesus suggests that a second, complementary action is called for. For even if you have stopped and turned, toward what should you now move? It is this question that Jesus begins to answer by speaking of the second task that you—the turned one—can pursue: "believe in the good news."

Fourth, *believe* in the good news. For Mark believing in the good news is the second action that you as a repentant one—one who has gotten turned around—can undertake to engage the good news. Moreover, the act of believing is aimed in a specific direction for Mark, that is, toward the good news. And just as repenting was not all that is needed in moving toward the good news, the same is true for "believing in." Jesus couples the two actions in 1:15, indicating that they stand as a complementary whole. Mark presents them together as the path a potential follower can take into the approaching kingdom.

"Believing in" should be further clarified. Believing in is an activity best understood as arising from a context of relationships. From a Markan perspective—which is in large measure reflective of the Christian canon as a whole—"to believe in" has less to do with assent to any system of affirmed content and more to do with engaging in trust.[9] Belief rests on a bedrock of reliable relationships rather than on cognitive constructs.

For example, a child believes that she will learn to ride her bike, a belief that will eventually prove true. Early in her learning process, she is sustained by her "belief system," which enables her to hold her resolve to learn despite the inevitable bumps and scrapes. The underpinnings of the child's belief are captured in her thoughts as she tentatively approaches her bike for her first official attempt to ride: "Dad says he'll catch me if I fall," and "Mom says she learned to ride her bike the same way I'm doing,

---

9. Two prominent examples of Mark's view of belief as an act of trust are Mark 5:21–43 (especially 5:35–36), and Mark 10:46–52, the story of Bartimaeus—a loud, brash, faith-filled one.

so I guess this is what I gotta do." For the child, trust is inextricably woven into her belief that she will learn to ride her bike. In her learning she becomes the personification of the biblical perspective that belief in and trusting are of a whole and involve a backdrop of reliable relationships.

Because relationships provide the context from which trust arises, the enterprise of "believing in" or "having faith" moves the believer toward a chancy, high-stakes orientation toward life since, to state the obvious, relationships do not always go well. In the example of the child and her bike, sometimes she will fall despite protective parental efforts. In relationships in general, there are disappointments, instances of (at least) emotional pain, incomprehensible betrayal, rageful words and cruel deeds, and even in the best of relationships unintentional and occasional intentional acts committed with stunning and long-lasting impact. "To believe," then, is not for the faint of heart; it involves the ferocious, tenacious courage to trust.

On the other hand, a stance of trust experienced in relationships potentially enlivens our lives. Relationships are the means by which we live into a deepening compassion wherein acts of kindness occur, vulnerabilities spoken by one are at least partially understood by another, forgiveness is sought and granted—sometimes after long periods of anguishing withdrawal and distance—and comfort and sacrificial acceptance of the other is worked at. Perhaps most delicate and miraculous, honest feedback is given and received, feedback of the sort that can be delivered only by those who deeply, carefully love. In such sacred moments wise use of truth happens, somewhat akin to the healing use of the surgeon's scalpel.

To return to the proclamation, when Jesus bids hearers to "repent, and believe in the good news" (1:15) his invitation is not toward great regret followed by intellectual assent to a list of worthy principles. Rather, it is a call for a radical turnaround in one's life and the courage to adopt a stance of trust in the rough and tumble of the human journey. As with the child and her bike, there will be the inevitable bumps, scrapes, and falls, but these will be matched by moments of a keenly felt aliveness and freedom, known in great depth. When Jesus proclaims a path toward good news, he calls his followers to turn and to trust. Jesus's language here points toward the dawn of an era and a circumstance wherein this good news can lead toward transformation and change in the lives of daughters and sons of the Holy.

There is a clear thematic connection between Jesus's initial public proclamation in Mark and the calling of his first followers. In the verses that follow the proclamation, Mark illustrates the repent and believe (turn and trust) theme when he recounts the story of Simon (later Peter), Andrew, James, and John. The first followers do indeed repent (that is, begin to get their lives turned around, reoriented), and they do indeed believe (that is, begin to place their trust) in a newly established relationship with a stranger, who calls them to an unknown and uncertain path. Moreover, this path involves the nearly unthinkable leaving behind of who they have been and how they have been living up to this point in their adult lives.[10] A repentant turning happens and a trusting in Jesus begins.

By placing the call story immediately after Jesus's announcement with its four key elements, Mark shifts from a verbal schematic of how the kingdom of God looks (1:15) to how it impacts the lives of Jesus's ordinary followers. The actions of Simon, Andrew, James, and John put flesh on the bones of Jesus's words about repenting and believing in.

In the lives of Mark's readers of whatever era, all face the possibility of transformation. Even in our time we can, in this season of the kingdom, turn and trust the One who calls. If we are up to doing so, we can lay hold to the grand good news that the kingdom of God is not about the ethereal or a pie-in-the-sky by-and-by future but rather is surrounding us on all sides if we can but see it. To find it, we are to look in the arena of human choice and action, where we will inevitably encounter the realities of courage and its failure, kindness and cruel disregard, hope and fear, and being as safe as birds sheltering in a mustard bush and being at risk in a sometimes dangerous world.

Thus far we have explored two major themes related to the kingdom of God as Mark describes it. We have considered the mustard seed parable about the kingdom, with its portrayal of risky and uncontrollable growth. We have explored Jesus's first spoken words in Mark, as they relate to God's near-at-hand realm, and as expressed in the story of Jesus's call to his first followers. I now invite your attention to a later scene in which Mark continues and expands our understanding of the kingdom.

---

10. See chapter 1 for more about the decision to leave and follow.

Focal Text: Mark 10:17–31
The Rich Man Who Cannot Leave Behind and Disciples Who Have Left Much

¹⁷As he was setting out on a journey, a man ran up and knelt before him, and asked him, "Good Teacher, what must I do to inherit eternal life?" ¹⁸Jesus said to him, "Why do you call me good? No one is good but God alone. ¹⁹You know the commandments: 'You shall not murder; You shall not commit adultery; You shall not steal; You shall not bear false witness; You shall not defraud; Honor you father and mother.'" ²⁰He said to him, "Teacher, I have kept all these since my youth." ²¹Jesus, looking at him, loved him and said, "You lack one thing; go, sell what you own, and give the money to the poor, and you will have treasure in heaven; then come, follow me." ²²When he heard this, he was shocked and went away grieving, for he had many possessions.

²³Then Jesus looked around and said to his disciples, "How hard it will be for those who have wealth to enter the kingdom of God!" ²⁴And the disciples were perplexed at these words. But Jesus said to them again, "Children, how hard it is to enter the kingdom of God! ²⁵It is easier for a camel to go through the eye of a needle than for someone who is rich to enter the kingdom of God." ²⁶They were greatly astounded and said to one another, "Then who can be saved?" ²⁷Jesus looked at them and said, "For mortals it is impossible, but not for God; for God all things are possible."

²⁸Peter began to say to him, "Look, we have left everything and followed you." ²⁹Jesus said, "Truly I tell you, there is no one who has left house or brothers or sisters or mother or father or children or fields, for my sake and for the sake of the good news, ³⁰who will not receive a hundredfold now in this age—houses, brothers and sisters, mothers and children, and fields, with persecutions—and in the age to come eternal life. ³¹But many who are first will be last, and the last will be first."

Mark continues and broadens his characterization of the kingdom in this focal text, continuing some familiar themes—the *kingdom* itself, *call*, *leaving*, and *following*—and providing a few new clues. In so doing, Mark advances our vision and grasp of God's kingdom and the complexities involved in choosing to follow Jesus by entering it.

Kingdom

Mark directly mentions the kingdom three times—in 10:23, 10:24, and 10:25. The writer does not want the kingdom to fade from the reader's awareness. Moreover, in the beginning of the passage (10:17) and near its conclusion (10:30), Mark has the rich man and Jesus refer to "eternal life." According to both Williamson and Borg,[11] eternal life in this passage is synonymous with the kingdom of God, so that the wealthy man's question about "inherit[ing] eternal life" is "about entering the kingdom of God."[12] Through these references to the kingdom—three direct and two indirect—Mark continues his narrative emphasis on the kingdom and keeps it in the forefront for his readers

Although Mark continues his emphasis on the kingdom, he hints that the reader's understanding of it should also begin to expand and deepen. A clue for this shift comes in Jesus's words to his disciples after the rich man goes away: "How hard it will be for those who have wealth to enter the kingdom of God!" In these words the reader is confronted with a new, unambiguous reality about the kingdom: the way into it can be excruciatingly difficult, at least for those with significant and capturing wealth. Entering the kingdom will not be accomplished by the snapping of one's fingers.

Call

A second ongoing Markan emphasis embedded in 10:17–31 relates to being called as a disciple. By using the language reserved for describing how a person is beckoned toward discipleship, Mark has Jesus issue a call to his wealthy questioner: "then come, follow me." These words are reminiscent of Jesus's call to Simon and Andrew, and to James and John (1:16–20). Mark's vocabulary about following in both 10:21 and 1:16–20 is the language of call and specifically Jesus's call to become a disciple. When a call is accepted and following begins, a repenting, a reorientation of one's being and way of life commences also, as it did for the first four disciples. The possibility of such a turning and core reorientation of a life is clearly presented as part of Jesus's conversation with his earnest questioner; it is a choice offered him apparently out of Jesus's love for him. It is

---

11. Williamson, *Mark*, 183; Borg, *Jesus*, 210–11.
12. Borg, *Jesus*, 211.

not meant to be ensnaring or hurtful; rather, the chance to turn through selling possessions and giving to the poor and reorienting toward heavenly treasures opens the possibility of a radically different richness for the man. Here, new life is offered to one Jesus loves.

However, entry into the kingdom and a different, richer way of being is not an easy choice to make, and Mark addresses the complexities involved in a call. For while a call is offered here, it is declined; the wealthy one refuses Jesus's call by walking away in apparent distress. This non-acceptance of a call by Jesus is the sole such example in Mark's account.[13] As a consequence of his refusal, repentance and reorientation do not happen for this wealthy person, even in a context of great love by Jesus.

With this story, Mark sets out yet again to broaden his reader's understanding of call and accepting a call. Here, Mark's story presents us with the reality that not all who are called are able and willing to accept it. Sometimes it proves too costly for would-be disciples to answer "yes" to Jesus's beckoning. This was apparently true in Mark's day,[14] and Mark invites us to recognize this truth in our own day as well. This passage raises questions for modern-day followers for which there are no certain answers: Will there come moments in the lives of those who would follow Jesus when, out of love, he calls to us, noting the specific, differing "lack" in each of us? Will Jesus touch the empty places—within or without us—allowing us to fill our emptiness through the act of following? But at those crucial points of encounter, will the paths of following and being disciples prove too costly, too frightening, impossible for us to accept? And finally, if such repentant turnings are impossible for us to pursue in those moments, what then? The question arising from the crowd becomes our own: "Then who can be saved?" (10:26).

Leaving

Mark's theme of leaving as a part of what is involved in becoming a follower of Jesus reappears in 10:17–31. It is spoken of by Peter in 10:28 and by Jesus in 10:29. Mark introduced this leaving theme during his account of the call of the first disciples (see 1:16–20). In response to Jesus's call, Simon (Peter),

---

13. Williamson, *Mark*, 183.

14. "If the civil and domestic tumult forecast in 13:5–23 mirrors the upheavals of Mark's readers, then the Gospel may have arisen in the wake of Nero's persecution of the Christians (64 C.E.) and the Jewish revolt against imperial Rome (67–70 C.E.)." Black, "The Gospel of Mark," 1915.

Andrew, James, and John leave behind foundational components of identity and orientation in their lives. They leave behind who they have been and how they have purposed their lives. For each of these first followers, leaving is a momentous event, even if not fully recognized at the beginning. Eventually their leaving reshapes their lives beyond all imagining.

In our third focal text, leaving and the costs of doing so are similarly portrayed. Peter speaks of them with exasperation, reminding Jesus of all that Jesus's followers have given up to answer his call: "Look, we have left everything and followed you." In Mark's design of this scene Peter is employed as spokesperson for those most loyal and close to Jesus. These folks are likely among those still stunned by Jesus's twice spoken words about the difficulty of entry into God's kingdom by the wealthy, who are considered to be blessed by God. While speaking for the group, it is also possible that Peter is arriving at a moment of personal clarity about his lot as a disciple, namely that his path of following has moved far beyond the leaving of nets. The fuller costs of leaving are being tallied. Indeed, everything has been left in order to follow and as the costs of discipleship are moving into sharper definition, Peter's exasperated declaration is an expression of a crystallizing reality in his mind—that losses have been involved from the earliest steps of the discipleship journey and the losses have kept mounting with very little to show for it thus far.

In his response to Peter and the other followers for whom Peter speaks, Jesus acknowledges that assuredly much has been left by those who have followed him. More than that, he specifies what Peter likely has in mind when saying "everything." Jesus speaks of houses, numerous family members across three generations, and fields, knowing as he does so that he is pointing to the cornerstones of a life lived in first-century Palestine. When followers leave their houses, they leave the security of a roof over one's head, shelter against the elements, and safety from the streets and roadways. When they leave their families, they leave siblings, parents, spouses, children—people they love and are responsible to. When they leave their fields, they leave the source of crops, which sustain their families and serve as a safety net against poverty and landlessness.

To put it somewhat differently, in his reply to Peter, Jesus in effect agrees with Peter's "everything" and proceeds to flesh this out even further with specifics that point toward the heart of the matter—namely, that discipleship involves costly losses and can place at risk the very things potential followers have relied on to secure their safety, standing, and general well-being. Some leave houses, families, or fields; for Jesus's wealthy questioner, it is possessions. Mark subtly suggests here that a wise reader would conduct a personal inventory of "everything," because the things that seem absolutely essential may be lost on the path of discipleship.

In 10:29–31 Mark again presents a message that affirms the reader's earlier understanding of leaving and illuminates a profound and nuanced perspective about it. Here, Mark's primary expansion of what it means to leave is that leaving and being disciples will touch on every aspect of followers' lives and reshape all they—and we—have held to as anchoring and foundational. Leaving for disciples is never a series of easy departures; there is a price to be paid when one leaves and follows.

Following

The "following" in 10:17–31 continues and expands Mark's depiction of discipleship in God's kingdom. Jesus's "follow me" in 10:21 and Peter's emphasis on leaving and following in 10:28 stand in continuity with other followings that appear earlier in Mark's text (e.g., 1:18, 2:14, 3:17, and 8:34). However, what is new here and expands the understanding of following is that as one follows, "persecutions" are to be expected (10:30). Jesus speaks of persecutions as part of what faithful disciples can anticipate in this God-sent season. On the one hand, Jesus says that gains and restorations will come; on the other hand, he cautions that persecutions will come—grinding hardships and difficulties with their inherent pains, brutalities, terror, and loss of courage and heart.

What are we readers of Mark to make of this? I cannot imagine that Peter and the other followers expect to hear about "persecutions" as Jesus begins speaking to them in this scene. In 10:29, he speaks to them with apparent sympathy, recognizing how much his followers have left to follow him. His words seem to offer some comfort, soothing, or even the promise of reward for their steadfastness for Jesus's sake and for the sake of the good news. Hearing these words spoken by Jesus, his disciples could indeed be forgiven should they imagine that their lives soon would open up to include greater levels of standing and security. For so long they have been viewed as unimpressive members of society, those without power or prestige. They might easily think that now is the time, the long-awaited, God-filled age that would bring all things right. But instead, Jesus adds persecutions to the mix and abruptly alters his portrayal of the path of a disciple. For Peter and his companions (and for

Mark's readers of every generation) a new reality is introduced into the decision to follow: persecutions—a reality that would indeed give pause.

Here I will take the liberty of stretching beyond the present passage of 10:17–31 for one additional verse. I believe this glance around the corner at 10:32 is justified, since it clarifies the impact of Jesus's words about persecution on his followers and expands the reader's understanding of God's kingdom. In 10:32 Mark implies that things are decidedly different for the disciples after the prediction of the persecutions is spoken by Jesus. Those accompanying Jesus on his road to Jerusalem—where Jesus has twice said he will be killed (8:31 and 9:31)—are fearful: "and those who followed were afraid." This fear can be considered as the normal human response to Jesus's announcement about his coming death in Jerusalem and the persecutions that are near at hand as part of the arriving kingdom. The disciples keep hearing talk of the potential loss of their leader, the holder of their dreams (ill-conceived though they may be), as well as of the rough roads that lie ahead for themselves (see 8:31, 9:31). In 10:32, we readers are reminded that two conflicting states of mind are true at the same moment for Jesus's followers. Some disciples remain courageous or trusting enough to follow Jesus toward Jerusalem. However, their new companion on the road is fear. They follow, afraid.

In addition to continuing his focus on God's kingdom with its familiar themes of call, leaving, and following, Mark introduces several new themes into his portrayal of the kingdom in 10:17–31. He addresses the issue of *wealth* as a surprising impediment to entering the kingdom. He presents Jesus standing at the intersection of *love* and *lacking*. He introduces the *inevitability of loss*. He closes with the paradoxical reality of an *impossible possibility*—the idea that although many things are impossible, for God all things are possible. Through these new themes, Mark again advances our understanding of God's kingdom and the complexities involved in choosing to enter it.

Wealth

In considering how disciples might reorient themselves to God's arriving kingdom, Mark is clear in declaring that those who are wealthy face a significant obstacle. Wealth is problematic, something difficult to overcome.[15]

---

15. Borg, *Jesus*, 208–11. Of particular note is Borg's suggestion that Mark's consideration of wealth in 10:17–31 may include not only the fact of being rich but also the

There are three ways Mark calls attention to the problematic nature of wealth and its pursuit. First, the rich man declines Jesus's call to him to sell what he has, give to the poor and then follow; the man walks away distressed. The prospect of taking the steps outlined by Jesus is beyond what he can contemplate and act upon. As much as he may desire to enter the kingdom, he cannot set aside what he apparently desires even more—wealth and what it has provided him in his present world. Wealth exerts a power over him and keeps him captive. He is a man possessed by his possessions and owned by what he owns.

Second, Jesus twice states to his followers how difficult it is for the wealthy to enter the arriving kingdom. Again Mark calls the reader's attention to the inherent difficulties of being rich in possessions in this life—as opposed to being the beneficiary of "treasure in heaven."

Within the context of Jesus's love and offering his wealthy petitioner a chance for a different richness in his life, I am convinced that Jesus's two declarations about the difficulties the rich face were likely said less in frustration than with a tone of sympathy and compassion. Even if this is true, however, Jesus holds to his clarity about the outcome for this man and perhaps for others holding much wealth: in not following, the wealthy can be expected to move away from the kingdom, at least in the moment. Jesus may indeed be saddened by this outcome for those he loves, but when the wealthy turn away, he honors their choices to do so.

Third, the followers react to Jesus's statements about how difficult it is for the wealthy to enter the arriving kingdom. After the first statement, the disciples are perplexed and confused. At that point, Jesus makes the second, expanded statement about this difficulty. In response to the repeated and expanded declaration, the disciples are said to be amazed, "greatly astounded." The shock of Jesus's one-two verbal jabs at those with wealth is so severe that they turn to each other, groping to comprehend what Jesus could possibly mean by making such statements.

The reactions of Jesus's followers are best understood as arising out of a religious assumption about the wealthy in first-century Israel. Borg explains:

> Wealth and possessions were central to the conventional wisdom of the time, as they are in most times and places. Obviously, it was good to be wealthy, for wealth provided both comfort

---

stance or attitude of seeking wealth "as a consuming and blinding passion" that often accompanies the acquisition of wealth. Wealth per se may not be the difficulty as much as the usual human response to it and the power it comes to hold over human beings.

and security. It was also a source of identity, a sign that one had lived right. Though Jewish voices did speak of the "unrighteous wealthy," wealth was commonly seen as a blessing from God that flowed from following the path of wisdom. In the minds of at least some, wealth was a sign of God's favor.[16]

Given popular familiarity with this view of wealth, it is small wonder that Jesus's words to his followers were dumbfounding, raising doubt about wealth as an assumed indicator of God's favor and blessing. Jesus's words apparently stirred confusion about the very path into righteousness and eligibility for God's realm. If not the rich, who was to be viewed as blessed in God's sight? Moreover, if even the rich encountered obstacles to their status as God's favored, what does that bode for the likes of fishers, tax collectors, women, and others of less note and lower standing? Who, indeed, can be saved?

I will close this exploration of Mark's depiction of the difficulties wealth presents for those who consider a life of discipleship with a perspective offered by Lamar Williamson. I offer his words because they resonate with our own age and with those of us facing the dilemma that comes from living in comparatively wealthy societies:

> After we have done our best to make this text say something less upsetting to our system of values, Jesus looks intently at us and continues quietly to affirm that life is to be had not by accumulating things but by disencumbering ourselves. Contrary to the dominant voices of our culture . . . this text proclaims the good news that the way to be really rich is to die to wealth.
> If this message does not take our breath away, if we are not shocked, appalled, grieved, or amazed, we have either not yet heard it or heard it so often that we do not really hear it anymore.[17]

Love and Lacking

A second new feature in 10:17–31, which Mark introduces as a further elaboration of what is involved in God's near-at-hand kingdom, is found as one explores the intersection of Jesus's love for his wealthy petitioner and the "lack" that Jesus perceives in him.

16. Borg, *Jesus*, 208.
17. Williamson, *Mark*, 188.

We begin by noting two features of Jesus's "loving" this man. First, nowhere else in his story does Mark mention directly that Jesus loves someone. Something new is indeed afoot here at this point in Mark's narrative, namely that the Markan Jesus answers this wealthy one out of a delineated context of love. Later in 12:28–34 Jesus will speak again of the act of loving as he lays out what he believes to be the two most prominent commandments, one being to love God with all of one's heart, soul, mind, and strength and the other to love one's neighbor as oneself.[18] In each of these three instances "loving" is in the form of a verb (*agapaō*).[19]

Second, the characterization of Jesus's love in this passage can be contaminated by our 21st-century preconceptions about what it means to love someone. Even when we appropriately set aside any notion of romantic love in 10:17–31, to love another still connotes in our day a state of significant affectionate feelings by the lover (in the broadest sense of the word) for the object of love. We conjure up a picture of at the very least heartfelt warmth for the other and frequently even more profound and intense feelings of tenderness and affection. While Black refers to Jesus's reaction to his wealthy petitioner as "affectionate,"[20] the fuller meaning of Jesus's love involves the recognition that his love includes a willingness to take action for the benefit of the man who kneels before him. Love in 10:21 is not merely a feeling. Mark's Jesus knows that love "calls for positive action in behalf of the neighbor. Jesus is the embodiment of this love, which he here extends to the man."[21] For Jesus, then, loving is in part an act of will, a deliberate choice for the benefit of another.

Jesus's love for the wealthy petitioner is mentioned after the initial exchange between the two men, and in placing love at that juncture, Mark presents Jesus as one who is beginning to *act on behalf* of the wealthy one. Surprising though it may seem to readers of our present day, Jesus's first act of love is to point to something the man lacks. This person, who has much wealth plus the benefits wealth brings, is missing something that would promote his overall well-being. Obviously, the lack is not material riches, possessions, or the security and standing bestowed by these assets; nor is it the presumed cultural, religious, and societal privilege and position that wealth connotes. To the contrary, he lives a rich and bountiful

18. Boring, *Mark*, 295.

19. Readers may have encountered the "noun" cousin of this verb, the more familiar *agape*.

20. Black, *Mark*, 226.

21. Boring, *Mark*, 295.

life by the standards of his time. But Jesus perceives a lack in him, a lack which perhaps can be best seen only by love. And possibly even more important, it is a lack that can be pointed out to the man only by love. Jesus's first loving act toward the wealthy one, then, is to speak of the man's lack and to imply a poverty that still holds this wealthy one in its grip.[22]

Inevitability of Loss

The third new feature about the kingdom, and the third new Markan emphasis in this scene, is the inevitability of loss. Loss happens. Mark's wisdom is revealed in his recognition that losses of significance and force come to everyone, including the secure, the comfortable, the powerful, and the pious. No one is exempted from loss, not even in God's kingdom.

This theme is presented in our passage through Mark's treatment of both the wealthy one and Peter and the other disciples. The wealthy man faces the losses that come with declining entry into the kingdom; in refusing to part with his wealth, refusing to give to the poor, and refusing to follow Jesus, he loses his way toward a differently wealthy, enlivened, and transformed existence. His discipleship "dies aborning."

Peter and the other disciples face different losses but losses nonetheless. In their case the losses come—paradoxically—as a consequence of exerting significant effort to enter God's near-at-hand realm. In accepting Jesus's call to follow, the disciples have lost much, or to use Peter's word, "everything." Everything includes houses, family, and fields—the very bedrock of Palestinian existence. All gone. It is not, then, only those who somehow fail or cannot stay the course of discipleship who face losses; loss comes to the faithful also, those who have taken great strides in their human efforts to gain the kingdom. Indeed, Mark presents the inevitability of loss as a sobering commentary on discipleship. In a certain way, it matters not whether a potential disciple turns away from Jesus's call or steps forward to follow it; losses will come.

God of Impossible Possibilities

With this sobering perspective on the inevitability of loss, it is with relief, I imagine, that readers are able to return to 10:17–31 for an expression

---

22. See Appendix 1 for further discussion of theological ramifications raised by Mark's focus on Jesus's love and the wealthy man's lack.

of good news: all things are possible. In this passage Mark directs his readers toward a powerful and newly emerging elaboration of the active presence of good news in people's lives. Here, Jesus's words offer a more evolved conceptualization of the kingdom and the very foundation on which God's realm rests. This belief and assurance, offered by Mark about God's near-at-hand realm (10:17–31) is the fourth and final focus of Mark's new themes about God's kingdom.

> 26They (the disciples) were greatly astounded and said to one another, "Then who can be saved?" 27Jesus looked at them and said, "For mortals it is impossible, but not for God; for God all things are possible."

What Mark accomplishes in these two verses (10:26–27) is exceptionally noteworthy. The flow of this scene up to this point has been Jesus's poignant encounter with the wealthy petitioner whom Jesus loves. In this encounter, Mark has drawn our attention to the wealthy man's human response to Jesus's call to a more meaningful and significant way of life. The central concern of this scene, then, has been human action (or inaction), intent, and capability. Moreover, even as the rich man has turned away and Jesus has issued his two declarations about the difficulty faced by the rich in entering the kingdom, his confounded disciples have focused their thoughts and comments on who can be saved. That is, in Mark's account, through the disciples' question, "Then who can be saved?" (10:26), the spotlight remains on the arena where human beings and their efforts, abilities, and standing hold sway. In both cases, with the wealthy man and with a group of disciples, what people do and what happens to them appear to lie at the center of Mark's concern in the design of his narrative.

With Jesus's words that follow the disciples' "who" question, Mark shifts the scene's emphasis. People, human beings, are replaced as the main "character" under consideration; now, and without doubt, God becomes Mark's dominant force and focus. This crucially important shift invites readers away from the disciples' question, "Then who can be saved?" to Mark's affirmation that God is the source of any and all savings worthy of the name. Indeed, even when Jesus refers to human beings in 10:27, they are presented only as aspirants to the impossible. The possibility of saving arises not with them or because of them, but because of God. It is to God that Jesus directs his disciples and it is to God that Mark points his readers.

This passage is another example of Mark (and the Markan Jesus) turning all things of any importance on their collective heads. Here, the turnover appears to be from any determination of who among the ranks of humankind is worthy or at least likely to be saved to discerning what our God will do. Neither human action nor failure to act, nor disciple-like following or lack of following, is the ultimate determinant regarding how entry into God's realm happens. Rather, in Mark's characterization of God's kingdom, it is the action of God that decides the matter. It is God who may open up his realm to rich and poor alike. It is God who determines the possibility of inheriting eternal life by both those who have given their best human efforts and those who have failed to do so. It is God alone who can see to the saving of folks, a saving that Mark's Jesus calls impossible for mortals on their own. To sum up, then, it is not through human efforts—however faithfully attempted or even successfully accomplished, or however marred by failure of courage or heart—that humankind can secure the kingdom's presence and power in the human drama. Rather, what is foundationally central and what makes the kingdom a present reality with all its possibilities for transformation and mustard-seed growth, is the character, intention and acts of God, for whom "all things are possible."

There remains one additional aspect of 10:26 and 10:27 that needs our attention in our efforts to be faithful to Mark's text. Even though these verses establish Mark's conviction that God (not human efforts or failures) is the source of saving, a completed and fully fleshed-out vision of what a "saved" life looks like is absent from Mark's account at this point. Also missing is any description of how God will act in his realm in this *kairos* season. Questions remain open at this point in Mark's narrative regarding specific acts of God that are in the offing as well as a description of what impacts living a "saved" life might produce in people. This lack of a fuller portrait of God's intended action and the impacts on the lives of those in the kingdom is consistent with Mark's practice, previously noted, of revealing his good news a bit at a time.

At the end of 10:17–31, Mark leaves his readers with this story about the kingdom of God. Realistic and cautioning about the challenges and costs of entry into God's authoritative realm, Mark invites his readers to realize an additional aspect of good news that comes with being a resident of the kingdom, namely that while all human efforts at a saving are doomed and carry with them the inevitability of impossible fulfillment, the larger human hope and possibility rests with God. God is the God of possibilities, even those that are impossible for humankind to provide for itself. God can "get done" whatever God chooses. What that will be exactly remains opaque for now in Mark's text. However, Jesus's listeners and Mark's readers can take a strong measure of reassurance that the deepest of human longings and need for saving lie—known and remembered—within the heart of God, for whom "all things are possible."

Personal Reflection: Discipleship as "Just Asking for Trouble"

As is the habit of most parents, my wife and I attempt to keep in touch with our two children though they are grown and, thankfully, walking their own paths with very little parental guidance, advice, or control at this point. Keeping in touch with our daughter and her family is easy since she lives in the same city as we do; we see her frequently. With our son it is a different matter since he and his family live in the western United States, a long way from our east coast home. Seeing the western branch of our family involves "traveling a ways," to use an expression of my grandfather.

One of the interesting and educational aspects of travel is that it nearly guarantees encountering traditions, practices, or normative behaviors different from one's own. Even when visiting close family members, certain differing ways of doing things—what I call house rules—become quickly apparent. On one of our more recent visits to our son, a situation arose during which my then three-year-old grandson announced to me with much authority and severe emphasis, "You're in a heap of trouble now!" I remember his words, but for the life of me I cannot recall which of the house rules I had broken. My hope is that it was a minor infraction; but since there are no minor infractions in the mind of a three-year-old, my pronounced state was indeed dire.

On occasion I am tempted to see my grandson's urgent words as applicable to the life of discipleship. It seems to me that any of us who attempt to live out of a faith perspective can expect trouble, though it be life-giving, enlivening trouble. To me, Mark, in addition to my grandson, seems to alert us to be on the lookout for unanticipated and uncontrollable changes if we choose to enter the arena that is, at one and the same time, ordinary, mundane, and even difficult, but also infused with the presence and activity of a loving, transforming God for whom all things are possible.

As I ponder Mark's understanding of the kingdom, prudence would seem to dictate that, for those of us who self-identify as believers, a certain caution is in order before we raise the familiar and fervent petition found in the Lord's Prayer, "thy kingdom come." Based on Markan emphases, we would be wise to consider with all due caution whether we wish to ask God for the full and unrelenting presence of the holy realm. Have we thought about what we are asking to be the primary hope and reality in our lives? With this request, we invite ourselves into God's sphere of wild, mustard-seed growth and change, the arena wherein we will be subject to the work of being remade again and again. Should the kingdom come, we can expect to be drawn toward the daunting path of becoming our truest and best selves through the unrelenting, pursuant love of God—a love that includes a divine penchant for facing us with our lacks.

And in the final analysis, in God's kingdom we will inevitably face many losses of our familiar havens, "safe" places, skewed perspectives about the world and even other people that we have counted on—in vain—to keep us somehow protected and less insecure. Indeed, if we truly find ourselves because of God's pursuant love in the midst of God's sphere of influence and activity, we will perhaps come to realize or even experience that the saving of our very selves rests with God and not our own accomplishments, wealth, standing, pious living, or any other entity to which we have given our souls' allegiance. Perhaps we should pray "thy kingdom come" not at full voice but in a whisper.

In the classic film *Zorba the Greek*, taken from a Nikos Kazantzakis novel, the main character, Zorba, attempts repeatedly to move his reserved bookish companion toward a fuller life. At one point in the film, Zorba's companion states, "I don't want any trouble." Astounded, Zorba blurts out in all urgency, "Boss, life is trouble. Only death is not."[23]

For me, Mark's Gospel raises the distinct possibility that life in the kingdom should be similarly understood. It surely does not eliminate all troubles and to the contrary tends to bring some into being, especially those that come with change and movement toward a saving. Troubles abound in the kingdom. However, it may well be, and I believe it to be so, that the holy and good news is that God—in the fullness of God's presence, character, actions, and love—abounds there even more.

---

23. *Zorba the Greek*, Michael Cacoyannis, director (Los Angeles, CA: Twentieth Century Fox, 1964).

4

Of Parents, Pigs, and Prohibited Powers

In Mark's narrative, Jesus presents those around him with redefined and liberating norms for everyday living, norms consistent with the reality of God's arriving kingdom.

Exploring Mark's Story

As MARK PORTRAYS IT, the life of a disciple involves *repentance*, that is, a life's reorientation; *believing* in the good news, that is, living a life of trust in an uncertain world; being enveloped by a *love* that faces us with our *lacks*; and *leaving* behind much that has provided our identity, security, and "shape" prior to encountering Jesus. Perhaps most challenging of all, the life of a disciple involves dwelling in the arena of God's authoritative presence, where wild and uncontrollable growth occurs, as with a mustard seed. Discipleship is an ongoing call for entrants to the kingdom to mature into their best selves. No bed of roses, this life in the kingdom.

In this chapter, we focus on other aspects of life in the kingdom that are both intriguing and liberating for Jesus's followers and by implication Mark's readers. As Mark designs his narrative, Jesus offers several redefined, alternative ways of being and acting that are open to pursuit by ordinary folks as they go about their lives. These redefined norms clash with the consensus expectations regarding how residents of Israel in the first century CE should order and conduct their lives. But as Jesus lays out unanticipated and surprising ways of being and acting for those impacted

Of Parents, Pigs, and Prohibited Powers 59

by the kingdom, Mark provides a more certain context for why he can call his account "good news." Mark makes it clear that, while daunting, moving into God's realm offers a new kind of life—a freer, enlivened, and compassionate existence. The clash between the established norms and those new norms put forward by Jesus leads potential disciples toward surprising possibilities for new life.

In our three focal texts, Jesus draws the people around him toward lives unfettered by conventions, practices, and long-held convictions of his time. In doing so, Jesus illuminates a path toward a meaningful existence open to all. Our three areas of focus:

1. Who Is Family?
2. What Does an "Alive" Life Look Like?
3. How Are Those Who Follow Jesus to Exercise Their Power, and For What Purpose?

We examine each focal text in this chapter according to a threefold framework. First, we review some of the social and cultural norms of Israel in the first century CE; second, we investigate how Jesus redefines these norms; and third, we consider how the redefined norms point the way toward the good news of the kingdom. Mark's account illustrates that, by redefining norms, Jesus offers his followers and potential disciples unexpected and liberating paths for their days on this earth.

Focal Text: Mark 3:19b–35
Who Is Family?

19b Then he went home; 20 and the crowd came together again, so that they could not even eat. 21 When his family heard it, they went out to restrain him, for people were saying, "He has gone out of his mind." 22 And the scribes who came down from Jerusalem said, "He has Beelzebul, and by the ruler of the demons he casts out demons." 23 And he called them to him, and spoke to them in parables, "How can Satan cast out Satan? 24 If a kingdom is divided against itself, that kingdom cannot stand. 25 And if a house is divided against itself, that house will not be able to stand. 26 And if Satan has risen up against himself and is divided, he cannot stand, but his end has come. 27 But no one can enter a strong man's house and plunder his property without first tying up the strong man; then indeed the house can be plundered.

²⁸"Truly I tell you, people will be forgiven for their sins and whatever blasphemies they utter; ²⁹but whoever blasphemes against the Holy Spirit can never have forgiveness, but is guilty of an eternal sin"—³⁰for they had said, "He has an unclean spirit."

³¹Then his mother and his brothers came; and standing outside, they sent to him and called him. ³²A crowd was sitting around him; and they said to him, "Your mother and your brothers and sisters are outside, asking for you." ³³And he replied, "Who are my mother and my brothers?" ³⁴And looking at those who sat around him, he said, "Here are my mother and my brothers! ³⁵Whoever does the will of God is my brother and sister and mother."

In order to unearth the treasure embedded in our first focal text, I begin with the significance of *family* in Jesus's time. In writing about family, or kinship, Marcus Borg enumerates several features that distinguish family life from what most members of "contemporary American culture" would mean by family.[1]

- A family is extended, with several generations living together.
- Being part of a family is a lifetime involvement; family members stay together (geographically speaking) over their life spans "rather than growing up and leaving home."[2]
- Family is the cornerstone of economic well-being and socialization. Family members contribute to the material security of the whole and meet most of their need for relational and communal contact from within the kinship group.
- Family members draw their core identity from who their relatives are, especially from the patriarch of the kinship group. "A man was known as son of his father. A woman was known as daughter of her father until she married, when she became known as wife of her husband."[3] An example is found in Mark's story of Bartimaeus, whose name translates as "son of" (*Bar*) Timaeus (see 10:46).
- Loyalty to one's kin is paramount. Family members are expected to put the extended family first; to do otherwise would break the

---

1. Borg, *Jesus*, 205.
2. Borg, *Jesus*, 205.
3. Borg, *Jesus*, 205.

religious obligation to one's kinship group. Higher allegiance to any other entity is seen as shameful.

Ched Myers agrees; in Jesus's day, family is the center of the social world. "The extended family structure determined personality and identity, controlled vocational prospects, and most importantly facilitated socialization. For Mark, then, kinship is the backbone of the very social order Jesus is struggling to overturn."[4]

Jesus redefines family in such a way that he promotes unexpected, freer norms of daily living for his potential followers. The actions and words of Jesus's biological family in our first focal text provide the context for Jesus's work of redefining norms. In 3:19b–35 various groupings of folks are included as members of Jesus's family. In 3:21 the family is likely the "people" who were saying that Jesus was becoming mentally unstable.[5] In 3:31 Mark refers to Jesus's mother and brothers, and in some original manuscripts, 3:32 mentions sisters as well as mothers and brothers.[6] Mark's inclusion of several groupings in his narrative serves to emphasize the extended nature of family as observed by Borg.[7] All these folks are family, and Mark's focus here is that this family—a relatively large group—is reacting as a cohesive unit, one that is sticking together in its assessment of Jesus's behavior and deciding what to do with a wayward family member, namely, Jesus.

In terms of the family's perception of Jesus at this point in Mark's story, the writer implies that they see him as deranged or "beside himself." Apparent to the kinship group at least, Jesus is not his usual self, perhaps alarmingly so; they have heard that he is not even making time to eat.[8] Whatever Jesus's family has concluded from the talk that was go-

4. Myers, *Binding the Strong Man*, 168.

5. Williamson, *Mark*, 83.

6. Note that no mention of "fathers" appears in Mark 3:19b–35. This is unusual given the authority and respect granted to fathers in the patriarchal kinship system of Jesus's day. Differing explanations have been suggested as to why Mark may have omitted fathers from his list of family members. My focus, however, is not as much on who is missing from the list as it is on the communal nature of Jesus's family; an apparently sizable number of kin are responding to Jesus's perceived imbalance, and they are presented by Mark as acting in concert.

7. Borg, *Jesus*, 205.

8. I am including Jesus in the "they" who were not eating (3:20). In part, I am led to this conclusion by a similar episode later in Mark's account which reports that the disciples and Jesus were so pressed by people coming and going that they could find no time to eat (see 6:30–31). Also, I should acknowledge that I may be too quick to couple

ing around, their concern is elevated enough that they set out "to restrain him." The word "restrain" connotes a sense of force; Jesus's family sets out to seize him, get him under control, to hinder or stop what he is doing and saying. Their plan may be to do so gently and compassionately, but when Jesus's family shows up outside the house where Jesus is staying, it is not for a social call or a pleasant family reunion. The family comes to put a stop to what he is doing.

Some scholars suggest that Jesus's kin have other motivations, in addition to concern for his health and safety. Both Myers and Williamson suggest that the family is also attempting to prevent damage to the family's reputation in the larger community.[9] Moreover, Myers notes that part of the "lunacy" the family notices in Jesus lies in his drawing the attention of powerful and opposing figures in Jerusalem, such as the scribes in this scene. A continuing provocation of such enemies was "courting disaster."[10] From the perspective of Jesus's kinship group, then, Jesus needed to be silenced and ushered back into the family fold, not only for his own safety but also for the safety and reputation of the larger group.

In 3:19b–35 Jesus begins the work of redefining the norms of kinship. When Jesus's family members arrive outside the house, they naturally enough send for him, calling him to come to them. The family's expectation—consistent with the prevailing understanding of what Jesus would do as a member of his kinship group—is that he would obediently and appropriately come to them. However, Jesus does not do so. This is Mark's first indicator of Jesus's clash with conventional family loyalty and obligation. Jesus's alternative understanding of family begins to take shape.

Mark then provides a second indicator of the emerging clash over what constitutes family. Preceding Jesus's words about family in 3:33–35, the crowd tells Jesus that his kin are "asking for you" (3:32). The word translated as "asking for" here may be more accurately rendered "searching for" or "seeking." There are ten occurrences of this word in Mark's

---

the family's knowledge that he is not eating with their view that mental instability is in the air. Because of a reservoir of psychological data collected during my years as a pastoral counselor, I could too easily see Jesus's failure to eat as an indication of mental disturbance of some significant degree just as "loss of appetite" is certainly seen as one symptom of potential mental distress in our time. Overall, however, and in keeping faithful to Mark's text, it appears that Jesus's failure to eat is more likely because of the commotion caused by the presence and activity of a large crowd in and around the house where he is staying.

9. Myers, *Binding the Strong Man*, 168; Williamson, *Mark*, 83.

10. Myers, *Binding the Strong Man*, 168.

narrative, according to Black, who identifies the following pattern: "Those searching for Jesus in Mark usually have hostile intentions."[11] I would refine Black's observation slightly, as follows: In Mark's narrative, when Jesus is searched for, he is at risk or under a threat of some sort. Sometimes the threat is to Jesus's physical well-being, and sometimes it is not. Often, as Black implies, the threat arises from his enemies. But at other times, as in our focal text, the threat is posed by his family or followers (see Mark 1:37).

The threat to Jesus here is that his biological kin, operating within the kinship system, have come to close down, silence, and take home their off-balance family member. The family is moving forward under the guidance of the norms and expectations of their culture. They may not intend harm and likely are struggling to do their best in a difficult situation. But when Jesus refuses to answer his family's call and instead speaks of others whom he pointedly claims as brothers, sisters, and mother, he redefines family as those who are kin to him through their common pursuit of the will of God.

What is at stake here is the highest loyalty of Jesus. Should it rest with his biological kin or with those connected by aligning themselves with the will and choice of God?[12] Here, Jesus places himself squarely within the community of those doing the choosing of God. He turns away from prevailing obligations and safety of the kinship system for himself, and he redefines the nature of family for both himself and those around him. Family is no longer to be established through blood or delineated by ties to a patriarch; rather it arises from doing the will of the Holy, thereby acknowledging an entirely different reality through which persons become the daughters and sons of the Holy God.

Jesus's redefined norm for kinship opens a path of greater freedom for those around him. Through this episode, Mark seems to encourage readers toward a more profound and active participation in lives of expanded liberation and aliveness.

Two examples in Mark's narrative illustrate the expansion of freedom through redefinition of the family as institution. The first new freedom is vocational and economic. Myers sees family—especially the patriarchal family—as exercising extensive control over the work a family member might engage in to contribute to the family's economic well-being. The

11. Black, "The Gospel of Mark," note on Mark 1:37. The final reference in Black's listing, 16:1, should instead be 16:6.

12. See chapter 6 for more on the close connection between will and choice.

inclinations of any male regarding the work he might choose are subjugated to the economic needs of the larger group. His hopes need not be a factor considered by the patriarch as the head of the family when determining what vocation was to be taken up by the potential worker. But Jesus—by redefining family and choosing to pursue his own vocation of being a participant alongside his new kindred as they pursue the will and choosing of God—shifts away from focus on the economics of family life as a central concern. In 3:19b–35 Jesus lives out of a new center, pursuing God's will. By not returning home with his blood kin and instead continuing on with his new family, and then a short while later returning to his work of teaching (see 4:1–9), Jesus models freedom from economic and vocational strictures of family life. In doing so, Jesus grants implicit permission to those around him to be freed from the vocational expectations of their kinship groups as well.

A second freedom emerges in this story as Jesus moves toward his new definition of family. Borg describes Jesus's view of allegiance to family as follows:

> [Jesus's] teaching clearly affirms that embeddedness in family and its conventions can hold one in bondage and prevent responding to the message of centering in God and God's passion. He saw the conventional patriarchal family as a constricting institution that demanded a loyalty inconsistent with loyalty to God. To give primary allegiance to it locked one into the world of convention.[13]

Both Jesus's words to those around him and his actions point Mark's readers to an ultimate allegiance to God. The allegiance may not be exclusive, but loyalty to the Godhead and to those doing God's will surpasses loyalty to biological kin. For Jesus's listeners, this new understanding of family, if adopted, could free them from restrictive aspects of the kinship system.

It is important to realize that although Jesus redefined family in such a way that it opened up great freedom for members of families, Jesus was not promoting a path of license, one in which his followers could disregard the family bonds that previously existed in their lives. Jesus's followers and listeners likely understood that liberation from some of the strictures of family life still left them to consider—along with the rest of us—what is the will and choosing of God that they were to do, live out,

---

13. Borg, *Jesus*, 207.

enact. Those in Jesus's redefined family are faced with whether or not to do God's will as that will relates to all others, new family and biological family as well.

Mark eventually indicates, in the fullness of his story, that the pursuit of God's will does indeed have something to do with exercising servanthood toward fellow human beings, adopting a stance of continuous and daily following of Jesus by disciples, and living out of a courage that comes as we choose to lay aside our very precious selves for the benefit of others. Consequently, Mark's vision of freedom proves to be not only a *freedom from* various restrictions but also a *freedom for* alternative and expanded ways of relating to all fellow human beings.

Focal Text: Mark 5:1–20
What Does an "Alive" Life Look Like?

[1]They came to the other side of the sea, to the country of the Gerasenes. [2]And when he had stepped out of the boat, immediately a man out of the tombs with an unclean spirit met him. [3]He lived among the tombs; and no one could restrain him anymore, even with a chain; [4]for he had often been restrained with shackles and chains, but the chains he wrenched apart, and the shackles he broke in pieces; and no one had the strength to subdue him. [5]Night and day among the tombs and on the mountains he was always howling and bruising himself with stones. [6]When he saw Jesus from a distance, he ran and bowed down before him; [7]and he shouted at the top of his voice, "What have you to do with me, Jesus, Son of the Most High God? I adjure you by God, do not torment me." [8]For he had said to him, "Come out of the man, you unclean spirit!" [9]Then Jesus asked him, "What is your name?" He replied, "My name is Legion; for we are many." [10]He begged him earnestly not to send them out of the country. [11]Now there on the hillside a great herd of swine was feeding; [12]and the unclean spirits begged him, "Send us into the swine; let us enter them." [13]So he gave them permission. And the unclean spirits came out and entered the swine; and the herd, numbering about two thousand, rushed down the steep bank into the sea, and were drowned in the sea.

[14]The swineherds ran off and told it in the city and in the country. Then people came to see what it was that had happened. [15]They came to Jesus and saw the demoniac sitting there, clothed and in his right mind, the very man who had had the legion; and they were afraid. [16]Those who had seen what had happened to the demoniac and to the swine reported it. [17]Then they began to beg Jesus to leave

their neighborhood. **¹⁸**As he was getting into the boat, the man who had been possessed by demons begged him that he might be with him. **¹⁹**But Jesus refused, and said to him, "Go home to your friends, and tell them how much the Lord has done for you, and what mercy he has shown you." **²⁰**And he went away and began to proclaim in the Decapolis how much Jesus had done for him; and everyone was amazed.

In examining the next focal text, Mark 5:1–20, we continue the threefold framework. First, we look at existing social and cultural norms; second, we investigate how Jesus's words and actions redefine those norms; and third, we examine how Jesus's redefined norms presented liberating, surprising good news to those who would choose to follow Jesus into the kingdom of God.

The purity code of the day, and the extensive role it played in people's lives, is important to our understanding of the focal text. I draw on the work of Marcus Borg to explain several features of the purity code and its ramifications for those whose daily existence was immersed in it.[14]

The first thing to understand about the purity code was its pervasive influence in the social realm. Purity has to do with various specific conditions and practices of individuals and groups. One dominant ramification of the code, even for those who work devoutly to maintain their purity, is that when impurity does occur despite all efforts, relational and social barriers are erected between the pure and the impure, the clean and the unclean. A state of ongoing impurity can lead increasingly to isolation.[15] If the conditions of impurity are severe or long-lasting enough, an impure individual may be cut off from family, friends, and the larger community. This isolation is part of the circumstance of the Gerasene demoniac in our focal text.

Several other aspects of the purity code are important in understanding 5:1–20:

- Impurity is seen as contagious; a person can "catch" it. An otherwise clean person can slip into a state of impurity merely by being in the presence of impure persons or objects. This is why unclean persons are expected to keep their distance and announce themselves and

---

14. Borg, *Jesus*, 213–17.
15. Borg, *Jesus*, 213.

their unclean condition if they are approached by others (e.g., Luke 17:11–13).[16]

- Once a person "contracts" impurity, it stays with that person until one or more prescribed purification rituals are performed. In Borg's language, impurity *clings*.[17] (Excepted are certain minor conditions of impurity that are "on the clock" and last only until evening.)

- Certain categories of people are impure by definition. All those seen as possessed by demons are referenced as having one or more "unclean spirits." Similarly, Samaritans and, Borg believes, many of the poor who cannot afford the costs associated with the purification rituals, are viewed as unclean.[18] The fact that large groupings of people are considered unclean emphasizes the deep social embeddedness of the purity code. Purity was not merely a matter of individual piety; the whole of Jesus's society was affected by life under the code.

- A violation of the purity code was not necessarily considered sinful. The code recognizes that some contact with impurity cannot be avoided and is therefore not sinful.[19] Examples are seminal discharges by men, childbearing and menstruation by women, and contact with a corpse, which was inevitable and indeed obligatory when preparing the body of a deceased family member for burial. These naturally occurring transgressions of the code can be corrected through the prescribed cleansing rites. Other violations of the code are seen as sinful, among these the eating of items prohibited in the dietary restrictions of the Torah.[20]

The purity code causes inconvenience, isolation, and suffering for people of Jesus's time, but at its foundation it has a positive purpose. The code provides a way for faithful and devout members of Jewish society in the first century CE to be in good standing and relationship with God, family, and the greater community. Ideally, as long as individuals remain pure, or repair their purity through acts of restoration, social bonds with family and others can be maintained. And purity before God can be maintained in a similar fashion. The purity system, then, can be

16. Borg, *Jesus*, 215.
17. Borg, *Jesus*, 215.
18. Borg, *Jesus*, 215.
19. Borg, *Jesus*, 213.
20. Borg, *Jesus*, 213.

understood at its center as intending positive relational standing both socially and religiously.

Jesus's teachings and actions in Mark arise from a profound immersion in Judaism. Jesus's Jewish formation probably included a familiarity with the foundational Exodus story of freedom experienced by God's chosen people, the Jews. Jesus's teachings and actions in opposing aspects of the Jewish purity code are examples of freedom in the spheres of family life, certain practices of the purity code, and the use of power. Jesus's vision of the kingdom of God is not anti-Judaism, though, but pro-freedom—meaningful freedom in any and all of the arenas where humans live their lives—social, religious, political, and economic.[21]

However, the good intentions that inform any code of behavior can become compromised or inevitably sullied by the practicalities and complexities of daily living as well as the character deficiencies built into us all. This appears to be the case here as Jesus challenges how the purity system is exercised in his day. Mark portrays Jesus as confronting a system that, instead of promoting human relatedness and community, or closer presence with God, has created nearly insurmountable barriers between many members of society. The positive goal of closer ties between God and his people has become unattainable for many, replaced by a system that offers only ongoing shame and isolation from the community and from God. The purity system has created a way of living—as with the demoniac in 5:1–20—that is not "aliveness" in any meaningful sense, but rather perpetuates an existence that Mark perceives as "death." Under the purity system, a person may become "dead" long before breathing ceases and the heart is still.

In our focal text, Mark presents a redefined norm for what constitutes "life" in God's kingdom. But first, for contrast, Mark presents a gruesome portrayal of the *opposite* of aliveness in the opening scene (5:1–13). Mark describes three interwoven features of non-aliveness: impurity, extreme brokenness, and living death.

Mark's story "create[s] a vivid picture of impurity."[22] Williamson notes that Mark sets this story in a land and among a people who are by definition impure: "Nothing about it is kosher; everything is unclean: the

---

21. Levine, *The Misunderstood Jew*. Levine offers a critique concerning how biblical commentators and theologians have misunderstood and misrepresented Judaism and the Jewish purity code of Jesus's day.

22. Borg, *Jesus*, 57.

spirit(s), the tombs, the pigs, the territory."[23] The tombs are the locale for the burial of corpses—also unclean—and they are "the realm . . . of social outcasts."[24] The social impact of the purity code is most evident in Mark's portrayal of the unclean demoniac. He is cast out, shunned, and isolated from family and the larger community. His only companions appear to be his unclean spirits—bad company, to be sure. But apparently for this man who begs Jesus not to send his spirits away (5:10), bad company is better than no company at all.

Mark uses language of brokenness to illustrate the opposite of life in the demoniac. Things exist here in a state of shatteredness, be they shackles and chains (5:4), psyches, or the demoniac's body, which is being subjected to self-mutilation. Further, absent from the man is any control over his voice, so he howls and screams (5:5, 5:7). Likewise, absent is any capacity to be at rest, so he wanders "night and day" (5:5). Also absent is any capacity to employ his strength appropriately, leaving him beyond self-restraint or helpful control by family or friends. This shattered man roams without rest in a broken land; even the name he carries, Legion, speaks of a soul that comprises numerous and perhaps warring fragments of a self, reminiscent of the shards of a broken mirror.[25]

In 5:1–13 Mark describes the demoniac as a man who is caught up in a "living death." He alludes to this condition by employing multiple markers of death. Mark describes the demoniac, in all his deathly circumstances, as

- "a man out of the tombs,"
- "with an unclean spirit,"
- living "among the tombs,"
- beyond social restraint by others who have tried extraordinary means (shackles and chains) to prevent harm to himself and others,
- beyond self-restraint as evidenced by self-mutilation, howling like an animal, and shouting in Jesus's face,

23. Williamson, *Mark*, 104.
24. Black, "The Gospel of Mark," note on Mark 5:2.
25. Borg, *Jesus*, 148–50. I refer the interested reader to Borg's helpful consideration of demonic possession and exorcisms; Borg considers the world views of both Jesus's day and our own. I view the phenomenon described in 5:1–13 as most importantly pointing to a condition in which the demoniac was incapable of exercising appropriate control over his life and actions and consequently incapable of participation in human community. For whatever reason, he was not or could not be in charge of himself.

- pursuing a life of aimless roaming without rest "among the tombs"—the third mention of tombs,
- caught up in an isolated, cut-off life,
- laying claim to a self-identity, Legion, which witnesses to his severe disintegration, and
- seeking to hold fast to the very "companions" (unclean spirits) who have done and would yet do him incalculable harm given half a chance.

Through his description of a tortured soul, considerably more dead than alive, Mark wants his readers to understand the depth of the demoniac's predicament. The man is indeed dead to anything we or Mark's earliest readers could conceive of as meaningful, purposeful existence.

The contrast between the first and second scenes of this story could hardly be more pronounced. In scene one Mark presents the demoniac, who exists in a state of perpetual impurity, shattered nearly beyond comprehension, and marked by death. In scene two (5:14–20) Mark presents a healed person—freed from the crushing sentence of being unclean with its consequent social ramifications, reintegrated in body and soul, and restored to a path of purposeful living. Most importantly, the present and future of the healed one are set out by Jesus as anchored in and enlivened by the mercy of God. It is this mercy, which has both restored the man and lies yet before him, that provides a new foundation for his life and for how he is to relate to both humankind and the Holy. No longer will the purity code be the dominant and deadly reality for his journey upon this earth. Rather, his time is to be lived under the welcoming, relational, and inclusive mercy of God.

Mark's description of the healed, restored man in scene two provides evidence of a complete reversal of the darkness of scene one.

- The newly alive one is "sitting" near Jesus. His isolation is broken; he is no longer alone. Moreover, his perpetual agitation has abated and he is able to be at rest, no longer roaming.
- He is "clothed." No longer does he tear from his body all covering, even chains and shackles. Clothed, he demonstrates a capacity for self-restraint.

- He is "in his right mind." He no longer participates in the madness of howling, shouting into Jesus's face or the darker insanity of beating and cutting himself with stones.
- He is no longer presented as among the tombs, the domain of the unclean and outcast. The tombs of scene one are no longer in the picture.
- He is no longer fractured, no longer identified by the name Legion, no longer controlled by demons. Legion and demons are in the man's past (5:15, 5:18); they are gone, vanquished, destroyed. The man, however, is present as none other than an integrated self.

An additional aspect of the aliveness of the healed man warrants attention. In 5:1–20 Mark describes four instances of begging and Jesus's response to them. Description of begging begins and ends the portrait of the demoniac of scene one and the healed man of scene two. The four occurrences of begging appear in the following verses:

- 5:10: The demoniac begs Jesus not to send away his "companions"— the unclean spirits who possess him.
- 5:12: The unclean spirits beg Jesus to allow them to possess the pigs.
- 5:14–17: A group of folks made up of townspeople, eyewitnesses to what had happened, and the swineherds beg Jesus to leave the area.
- 5:18: The healed man begs Jesus "that he might be with him."

Jesus's responses to these beggings are instructive. In Mark's text there are in effect only two responses of Jesus to these pleas, not four as we might expect. In response to the begging of the unclean spirits in 5:12, Jesus allows the spirits to enter the pigs. At the same time and with that same statement of permission, Jesus does, according to Mark, honor the plea of the man not to send his "companions" out of the country. Jesus allows the man's "friends" to stay nearby by going into the pigs. So Jesus's initial response in fact addresses both of the first two beggings.

While Jesus grants the pleas of both the man and the spirits, however, he does so for his own purposes. That is, his permission in no way allows the outcome anticipated by either Legion or the spirits. For although the spirits are not sent away, they are denied any chance of further detrimental engagement with the man. And although the spirits are allowed to enter the pigs in their hope for a new home and additional exercise of demonic control over living things other than Legion, it is doubtful that they would have envisioned that the newly possessed pigs would become the vehicles of their demise. Jesus allows the man to keep the spirits close by, but only long enough for the spirits to be eliminated. Jesus allows the spirits to enter the pigs, but only to be entombed as the pigs dash headlong into the sea.[26]

Jesus's apparent compliance with the two initial instances of begging need not be viewed as a compromise with either the fragmented man or the unclean spirits; rather, through his response, Jesus vanquishes the life-destroying forces, ridding both Legion and a portion of the Decapolis region of their deadly, demonic reign.[27]

Jesus's second response is also addressed to two beggings—that of the townspeople, who ask Jesus to leave the area, and that of the healed man, who asks to stay with Jesus. At first it may appear that Jesus acquiesces to an unreasonable demand of the townspeople even as he refuses a perfectly understandable request by the man he has just liberated.

But Jesus appears to understand that the crowd's reaction to him, and so their begging, is motivated by their fear. When they hear reports about what happened to the man (and to the pigs) and become witnesses to all that has taken place just outside their town, they start begging Jesus to leave. The fear that holds this crowd may be a response of awe in the face of something beyond their normal experience, that is, the supernatural. Or it may be fear of the magnitude of Jesus's power—a power so strong that it has restored one whose personhood lay in tatters with no capacity for self-control or peaceful living among his own. Fear may also arise because of the economic losses that have been incurred with the death of the pigs.[28] Whatever the precise nature of the fear, they want no more to do with Jesus and whatever he was up to in coming to their territory. They beg him to get out of their neighborhood, and Jesus acquiesces.

---

26. I grew up on a farm, and my family raised a few pigs each year. When I was first exposed to this story, I thought that the destruction of the pigs was cruel and horrifying beyond words. My young mind kept thinking, "But they didn't do anything wrong or hurt anybody! Why did Jesus send the bad spirits into them?" Many years later I learned to see this, as best I could, through first-century Jewish eyes. Pigs were unclean, of no value, and so could be seen as objects of good riddance. I must admit, however, I still wince when reading this text. I would never present a children's sermon on this passage.

27. Donahue, "Mark," 908. Donahue notes: "The expulsion of the demons into the herd of swine and their drowning in the sea initiates the purification of gentile territory."

28. Dowd, *Reading Mark*, 55.

As Jesus prepares to honor their plea by leaving, the healed man raises a plea of his own; he begs to be with Jesus. It is a heartfelt plea. For too long all contact with others has been with spirits who have been furthering his ongoing madness and disintegration. But while this harmful association has seemed better than no contact at all, after the exorcism, the "need" of being with his destroyers exists no longer. Rather, part of his return to sanity and clear thinking apparently includes the awareness that his true need is to be with his fellow humankind. No longer is he to dwell with those who would imprison him in a living death. No longer is he to be with those who would harm and not heal. And who better to be with than the stranger from the boat who has restored him in unimaginable ways? And so he begs to "be with" Jesus.

But to our surprise, Jesus refuses his plea (5:19). Of all the beggings laid out before Jesus in this story, this one seems most in line with Jesus's determination to restore this man. How can Jesus refuse? Mark implies that there are two reasons.

First, Jesus refuses the healed man's request because he sees far beyond what the healed one can envision for himself in the glow and exhilaration of getting his life back. Jesus realizes that the best that the healed man can imagine is to be with the one who has restored him; this is what he begs for. What could possibly seem better than staying close to his healer? But Jesus sees things differently. What Jesus sees as most needed by the healed man is restoration to human community, and most especially to his home, family, and friends. It is with his own people, who no doubt considered Legion as dead to them, that his restoration will be completed. And it is to them that Jesus directs the healed man to go. Jesus refuses his plea and sends him where he most needs to go to be fully restored.

There is a second reason for Jesus's refusal. As noted earlier, Jesus's growth in his understanding of his identity and role in the kingdom of God is a major Markan theme.[29] This scene depicts Jesus's response to the man's begging as another example of Jesus's maturation. One of the things Jesus learns in the course of Mark's account is that he is not to take on the task of being the sole proclaimer of God's inbreaking kingdom. This theme is reflected in 5:19–20 when Jesus refuses the man's plea and sends him home. Jesus sends him with instructions: tell those to whom he returns of the merciful acts of God in restoring him to life. And true to Jesus's urging, he "began to proclaim" in his home territory. With this

---

29. See chapter 2.

activity in place Jesus has entrusted the role of proclaiming to another and the story of God's mercy seen in all "Jesus had done for him" is received, leaving all who hear it to be "amazed." Jesus's refusal enables an expansion of proclamation of the kingdom.

So Jesus leaves the territory as the townspeople beg him to, but he leaves behind one who has been healed and is headed toward an even greater measure of restoration through his return home. The healed man has been readied for this journey and is directed to tell his story of what God has done for him and the divine mercy he has received. Beyond all human imagining he has returned to the land of the living, to be with his people as he needs to be and to speak to them in their need to know of a God who relates to humankind primarily through mercy and not through categories of purity. He is Legion no longer—unclean, broken, and dead. Instead, he is alive, whole, and engaging with fellow humans as he speaks about the merciful acts of God. Mark's story concludes with his conviction that God's mercy and the acts arising from it supersede all lesser understandings of God.

The story of the demoniac (5:1–20) leads Mark's readers toward a different norm for living in the kingdom. This alternative norm, if followed, leads to the subversive unseating of the purity code as a dominant convention governing social, communal, and various behavioral aspects of religious life. The purity code need no longer erect barriers between human members of society or between God and humankind. Instead, in Mark's vision, the condition of being close to God and neighbor rests with God. And through the Beloved Son, God acts despite any stain or taint by which society or societal institutions might seek to define a human being. The promise and good news of this Markan episode, then, is that what defines humanity is the mercy of God as exemplified in the actions of God's Beloved. It is a mercy that restores us to wholeness beyond what we can envision for ourselves. It is the mercy of a God who longs to open God's kingdom to all.

So what does an alive life look like? Mark would have us consider that it is a life lived within the sure and certain understanding that God's mercy and actions restore us to ourselves, to those around us in our daily living, and even to God's own self. (See chapter 7, where we explore additional features of an enlivened life.)

Good news for the unclean. Good news for the dead. Good news for us all.

Focal Text: Mark 10:32–45
How Are Those Who Follow Jesus to Exercise Their Power, and For What Purpose?

³²They were on the road, going up to Jerusalem, and Jesus was walking ahead of them; they were amazed, and those who followed were afraid. He took the Twelve aside again and began to tell them what was to happen to him, ³³saying, "See, we are going up to Jerusalem, and the Son of Man will be handed over to the chief priests and the scribes, and they will condemn him to death; then they will hand him over to the Gentiles; ³⁴they will mock him, and spit upon him, and flog him, and kill him; and after three days he will rise again."

³⁵James and John, the sons of Zebedee, came forward to him and said to him, "Teacher, we want you to do for us whatever we ask of you." ³⁶And he said to them, "What is it you want me to do for you?" ³⁷And they said to him, "Grant us to sit, one at your right hand and one at your left, in your glory." ³⁸But Jesus said to them, "You do not know what you are asking. Are you able to drink the cup that I drink, or be baptized with the baptism that I am baptized with?" ³⁹They replied, "We are able." Then Jesus said to them, "The cup that I drink you will drink; and with the baptism with which I am baptized, you will be baptized; ⁴⁰but to sit at my right hand or at my left is not mine to grant, but it is for those for whom it has been prepared."

⁴¹When the ten heard this, they began to be angry with James and John. ⁴²So Jesus called them and said to them, "You know that among the Gentiles those whom they recognize as their rulers lord it over them, and their great ones are tyrants over them. ⁴³But it is not so among you; but whoever wishes to become great among you must be your servant, ⁴⁴and whoever wishes to be first among you must be slave of all. ⁴⁵For the Son of Man came not to be served but to serve, and to give his life as a ransom for many."

In our third focal text, Jesus again proposes an alternative to the well-established behavioral and attitudinal conventions of his day. Here Mark makes clear that Jesus is specifically interacting with the Twelve, whom he assembled earlier in the narrative (see 3:13–19).

In the terminology of our day, the Twelve can be considered the leadership contingent within Jesus's larger grouping of followers. They appear to constitute Jesus's leaders-in-training, those he is preparing for whatever is to emerge after his fate is sealed in Jerusalem. In the first part of this text, Mark offers to the Twelve a reminder of the future that lies ahead for Jesus as the Son of Man; it is the third and most detailed description of what he anticipates to happen in Jerusalem, along with a hint of a yet-to-be-described rising that is to occur after three days (10:32–34).

After this reminder, the scene has to do with Jesus's dealing with this inner circle of followers—his leadership cadre. He delivers to them his last detailed instruction about what he intends for those who will find themselves in positions of increased influence, standing, and power after his death. As he does so, Jesus outlines for the Twelve a characterization of greatness of a much different sort than the prevailing model of greatness exercised by rulers outside the kingdom of God. By the conclusion of our third focal text, the Twelve have been schooled in a new paradigm for the *kairos* season. The paradigm is summed up in 10:45 as Jesus declares the purpose and character of the Son of Man as one who serves and surrenders his very core being so that others are liberated and released.

We return to our threefold framework to examine Mark 10:32–45. First, we explore the dominant understanding of greatness as practiced by the leaders of Jesus's day; second, we look at how Jesus redefines greatness in the near-at-hand kingdom; and third, we consider how Jesus's reshaped norms contribute to the liberating and surprising good news for all involved in God's kingdom. Throughout this episode, Mark has tightly interwoven the contemporary cultural and political understanding of greatness, and the powers associated with it, with a sharply contrasting understanding of greatness and the use of power in Jesus's pointed and specific instructions to the Twelve.

As a way to contrast his own understanding of greatness with the views of those considered great political leaders in the first century CE, Mark presents a scene of angry tension between James and John, on the one hand, and the other ten apostles on the other (10:32–45). The source of this tension is James and John's devious and apparently secretive efforts to maneuver Jesus into indicating that the two brothers would be appointed to hold positions of the highest prominence and influence at the time of Jesus's presumed, fantasized glory. Despite Jesus's warnings about what lies ahead in Jerusalem, James and John apparently still cling to a rosy scenario of the future, complete with images of their elevated status and increased exercise of powers from their seats on the right and left of a triumphant Jesus. As Williamson has noted, the brothers approach Jesus very much in the manner of young children attempting to secure a parental promise to do a certain thing before "the thing" has been specified.[30] Who of us who are parents has not heard a small voice ask at some point, "Dad (or Mom) will you promise me something?" Indeed, both wheedling and parental caution are time-honored practices.

The efforts of James and John fail, but when the remaining ten get wind of their ploy, the temperature starts to rise. Trouble is brewing. I would suggest that things heat up not because the ten were upset by violation of any noble principle of egalitarianism or fair play. More likely, the upset arose because the ten did not think quickly or shrewdly enough to beat James and John at their own game. Their angry reaction, then, might well have included unspoken thoughts, such as "Why didn't we think of that?" Such an unflattering view of the apostles is consistent with Mark's overall portrayal of the Twelve, this time exemplified by an angry, self-absorbed mood that infects them. At its core the heated clash reveals a struggle among Jesus's closest followers over who will assume power, prominence, and the positions of leadership in the days that come after whatever is to take place in Jerusalem. Indeed, the Twelve are caught up in a divisive and destructive moment that threatens to bear bitter, even poisonous, fruit if left unchecked.

The Markan Jesus, however, does act to check this conflict in no uncertain terms. He gathers together his leaders-in-training and speaks straight to the heart of the matter. It is important to note that in putting a stop to the disciples' heated encounter, Jesus does not forbid the pursuit of greatness. Indeed, Jesus even articulates his instructions to them in terms of greatness and its pursuit; however, he rejects the prevailing cultural understanding of what constitutes greatness. Just as he redefined the prevailing views on family and one's loyalty to it, and the purity code as the only acceptable path toward proper relationship with both God and neighbor, Jesus here confronts the dominant views of power and its uses. It simply cannot be, says the Markan Jesus, that tyrannical and dictatorial powers employed by gentile rulers stand as the model for leadership and authority in God's kingdom. Or to paraphrase Jesus, "This cannot be how you Twelve relate to each other. Not in this *kairos* time, and not in this kingdom of God. This will not do—ever."

Through references to the gentiles, Mark provides clues to what Jesus intends to prohibit in his instructions to the angry Twelve. In 10:42, when Mark mentions the gentile rulers and the powers they exercise,

---

30. Williamson, *Mark*, 192.

he is referring to "the Roman political authorities."[31] With their military might and occupying troops, they call the shots in first-century Israel. It is the Roman authorities who are considered by the larger society as the "great ones" as they exercise rule over those of lesser standing and clout; it is they, says Mark's Jesus, who "lord" their power over all lesser sorts.[32]

In 10:33–34 Mark reveals the conventional view of greatness at an even darker, more sinister level. Jesus spells out both the nature and extent of Roman power to which he as Son of Man anticipates being subjected in Jerusalem. The Romans, he says, will mock, spit upon, beat and kill. And indeed they do (15:16–39). Their "greatness" is of a violent and brutal kind; it is power held over others rather than power used on behalf of others; it is a "greatness" intended to instill fear, humiliate, and crush if necessary. Even beyond that, it contains a high degree of cruelty and sadism—the inflicting of pain for pain's sake. It is, as Myers says, a model of "leadership-as-domination."[33]

It is this norm of leadership, with its accompanying powers, that Jesus prohibits. To state this prohibition somewhat differently, in our third focal text Jesus yet again calls his disciples—in this instance the Twelve closest to him—to repent. He calls them to get turned around; to leave off from the usual and emulated model of rule, power and authority; to head in a direction away from the conventional norm woven into the fabric of the Roman empire. The ultimate logic of this prohibited manner of leadership inexorably carries its practitioners toward the lording of murderous power over others—a power as intimidating, brutal, and obliterating as it needs or chooses to be. Against such a norm, Jesus instructs his own, "not so among you" (10:43). The culturally accepted norm of intimidating and bullying others into toeing the line (and crushing them when they do not) is anathema in God's age and kingdom.

There is one additional surprise that emerges in 10:43b–45. The prohibition of intimidating and murderous powers, while essential, is not sufficient. Something is to be put in their place—something healing, something liberating. Mark invites us all toward this missing something, a crucial and definitive step forward into his full, rounded-out vision of

---

31. Williamson, *Mark*, 194.

32. The reader can see an additional reflection of this reality later in Mark's account when after their trial of Jesus and finding him worthy of death, the members of the council (the Sanhedrin) take Jesus to Pilate—the Roman authority in charge—to get Jesus's killing accomplished (see Mark 14 and 15).

33. Myers, *Binding the Strong Man*, 278.

discipleship. For not only does authentic discipleship prohibit the exercise of ruthless power, discipleship is to be most clearly comprehended and lived into as one chooses to adopt the status and function of a servant and surrender one's very life (core) to set others free.[34] Greatness in God's arriving kingdom, says Jesus, is rightly pursued when his followers choose to serve others, choose the "status" of servants and model themselves after the Son of Man himself (10:45).

And so Mark leads us to this conclusion—that being great or prominent in God's season and kingdom occurs for those whose primary role and function as disciples is to be highly attuned and responsive to the needs and wishes of others, not themselves. At base, servants and slaves are to attend to, wait on, and respond to others. They are other-focused. As reflected here in our third focal text, however, this attitude of attentiveness and response stands in stark contrast to the mindset and actions of either James and John or the ten remaining apostles in this scene. Even after hearing Jesus's detailed description of his anticipated humiliation, torture, and death in Jerusalem, James and John remain intensely preoccupied with their own desires and rosy expectations; the angry response of the other ten points to a similar orientation on their part. The needs of "the other"—in this case, their leader who is moving toward an encounter with a savage fate—appear not even to register with the Twelve.

In response to the disciples' lack of attunement to any needs that lie beyond their own, Jesus teaches his followers about two intertwined realities: that chosen self-absorption in pursuit of conventional greatness leads to great harm, and that the giving of self leads to others being set free, released. And as a final word Jesus reminds the Twelve that the very purpose and character of the Son of Man has an irreducible center: serving, even to the point of giving everything he's got—life, soul, and self—is inseparably interwoven with the setting free of others to a more meaningful existence.[35]

How do Jesus's reshaped norms about greatness contribute to Mark's vision of good news? How do Jesus's words and actions invite and urge the followers of the Son of Man toward unforeseen aliveness and liberation? In our third focal text, the reader is pointed toward at least two good

---

34. The Greek word translated in 10:43 and 10:44 as "wishes" often in Mark has to do with a person's exercise of choice in pursuing a course of action. See chapter 6 on the subject of choice in the practice of discipleship.

35. See chapter 7, where these themes receive greater attention. My treatment of serving and giving of one's life as a ransom there is expanded and given its just due.

news possibilities in the pursuit of a life of discipleship. The first is this: if we pursue greatness through being a servant, laying aside our frequent self-absorption, we have the chance to avoid, or at least minimize, the destructive tendencies demonstrated by the disciples in this episode. In 10:32–45 Mark has the Twelve start down a disastrous path toward a conventional understanding of greatness, prominence, standing, and power. While we are not told one way or another about the intentions of James and John and their plans for using any anticipated positions and powers that they hope to finagle out of Jesus, they conceivably might hope to employ them for positive, helpful purposes. However, the results of their approach to Jesus are anything but useful, helpful, or healing. Rather this pursuit of greatness by the traditional path—regardless of their intent or hopes—leads instead to secrecy, attempted manipulation of Jesus, disruption of the community of the Twelve, with rageful conflict flaring up in the group. They sow seeds of suspicion, isolation, and mistrust among the disciples. The heated atmosphere indicates that the Twelve are on their way toward adopting a life stance that inevitably leads to ruthlessness, intimidation of others, and the exercise of murderous powers.

When Jesus calls a halt to the conflict with his "not so among you" (10:43), he establishes the possibility of release from the death-inducing realities woven into the conventional pursuit of greatness. Consequently and unexpectedly, the first possibility of good news in this text arrives through Jesus's firm, "Stop! You cannot get to 'great' through intimidation and domination." Part of Mark's good news in 10:32–45, then, is that followers of the Son of Man can avoid taking that well-traveled but corrosive and deadly path; instead they can choose a path of service and self-giving as demonstrated by the Son of Man. This is not an easy choice, but for Mark it is the choice that enables his fellow human beings to move toward transformed, enlivened, resurrected existence—that is, toward good news.

A second good news possibility appears in 10:45, where the Markan Jesus invites his followers to move into a realm beyond themselves. That is, he opens up the possibility that they can model on someone—the Son of Man—who in his choices and actions steps beyond a deadening self-involvement to a life attuned to, and even given over for, others. No longer must the disciples of Jesus find themselves imprisoned by their frequently demonstrated self-absorption with all its myopic focus on their own needs and wants. This self-consumed stance—so evident in the conflict between James and John and the other apostles—can be left behind, at least on occasion. In its place reside choices, words, and actions that are resonant with the choices, words, and actions of the Son of Man.

This part of Mark's good news message, then, is that those who follow Jesus are set free even as they help to set others free. Disciples make the difficult but life-giving choice to live as servants and as self-givers like Jesus, laying aside their own needs and wants. Thus, concludes Mark, authentic followers are set free from the tyranny of self-absorption, while others are released from other circumstances of bondage. Good news: release and liberation abound.

Personal Reflection: God's Ordinary Mercy

I suppose I could call him Legion. Instead, I'll call him Roger, also not his real name.

From my vantage point as an entering ninth grader in a high school new to all of us ninth graders, everything was unknown and strange; but Roger was beyond "just" strange. He was uncomfortably strange. Physically, he was tall and gangly with a slow drawl and a deep bass voice that contrasted sharply with his high-pitched, hyena-like laugh, which burst out when something struck him as funny. He had straight, jet black hair that usually was plastered down with hair oil of some sort. His thick eyebrows were dark, as were his eyes, giving him a somewhat sinister or at least brooding countenance. Moreover, his complexion was dusky, and because he always wore long-sleeved collared white shirt and black trousers, while his classmates wore more colorful and "in" garb, Roger stood out all the more. The multiple pens and pencils he kept in his shirt pocket also didn't help; even in 1959, this was not cool. To me, even his name sounded like an old man's name. Not Bob or Tom or Sam, but Roger.

My high school class of 400 was large enough that I did not share any classes with Roger and so would only see him in the hall between classes or most especially at the end of lunch period when a large number of us gathered in a waiting area for the bell to ring releasing us to head to our next class or lockers. While Roger waited like the rest of us, he never seemed to wait with a group of friends. Indeed, he had no friends I was aware of. Since I did not see Roger in classes and so could not watch how he acted or hear what he said, I never could quite decide whether I thought Roger was "stupid" to use my limited, judgmental vocabulary from that era, or rather an awkward, repellant genius. All I knew was that he sure seemed weird. I felt pity for his differentness and at the same time hoped to avoid any close association with him so that I would not jeopardize my chances to fit in somewhere within my high school's social system.

I remember once when Roger came up to several of us, showing us a stapler he had gotten from somewhere and asking, "Do you think I'll staple myself with this?" I don't remember if any of us said anything but sure enough, Roger put his index finger—fleshy side up—on a nearby window ledge and proceeded to staple his finger. He jumped with pain, pulled out the staple, shook his hand around in an effort to relieve the pain. He finished by sucking the blood spots off his punctured finger. More than anything, I was shocked. I had no frame of reference for that sort of deliberate self-harm.

Roger's degree of strangeness attracted the bullies in our school. Several began to circle, like sharks sizing up a wounded one of their own. Showing up as we gathered at the end of lunch period, they began to pick on Roger, taunting him and knocking his books out of his hands—asking him, "What are you going to do about that, chicken?" There were, of course, three or four of them trying to provoke him into a fight. They were led by a chief bully with a reputation for meanness around the school. Retrieving his fallen books, Roger never struck back or talked back; neither did he cower or beg to be left alone or leave our gathering spot to wait somewhere else for the bell to ring. Roger endured.

As I looked on, I had conflicted feelings. I was angry at the bullies for picking on Roger; at the same time, I didn't want to draw their attention by telling them to stop or pick on someone their own size. After all, I was on the smallish side and was somewhat strange myself, it seemed to me. I lived in the "country" but came to a city school; I made good grades and so had the reputation of being an egg-head, not typically a category of folks admired by bullies. Perhaps worst of all, I was in the uncool orchestra, not the cool band, and even carried a violin case around every day. In my adolescent self-assessment, that alone emphasized my own weirdness. So while the sharks circled and attacked Roger I remained silent, doing nothing. I now realize that this stance of self-protection incurred its own costs—namely shame for not trying to stand up for Roger, and the adolescent guilt and helplessness of not living up to my own fantasies of personal bravery and fearlessness in the face of wrong or cruelty. But of course I was afraid—too afraid to do or say anything.

On occasion I felt even worse about my failings. I remember one instance when I got a charge out of an incident involving Roger. A rumor went around that someone had gotten Roger to eat a couple of squares of the laxative Ex-lax, passing it off to him as a section of a chocolate bar. At my age, I was fuzzy about how Ex-lax was supposed to work exactly, but I knew it had something to do with losing control over one's capacity to "hold it." I found myself laughing along with the others as we anticipated Roger having an accident around the time sixth period rolled around. It seemed funny at the time, but as I approach my mid-seventies the idea of soiling oneself is not nearly as funny as it was as a ninth grader.

It was years later when I received the invitation for the 45th reunion for our class of 1963. I had never been one drawn to class reunions previously, either for high school or college. The single seminary class reunion I had attended struck me as tolerable, but certainly not the "bread of life." However, the more I thought about the approaching 45th reunion, the more I felt led to go. In the objective part of my brain, high school had been a mixed, good-enough experience for me, but my heart recalled it as a mostly melancholy time, replete with numerous indicators that I never really fit in. The affective tone I carried from those years was hurt and loneliness and an awareness of my own strangeness. Given all that, I decided I had significant unfinished business related to those years, and since I was not getting any younger, now was the time to face it. While I realized, then, that I had some emotional work to attend to at the reunion, I had no specific idea of what I needed to do when I got back home to Lynchburg. I just felt the need to go.

One of the planned highlights of the reunion weekend was a large banquet held on Saturday evening. It was in that setting where I heard Roger's name for the first time in nearly half a century. The emcee for the evening was handing out numerous awards to members of our class, some "serious" but most intended to engage our humor and positive feelings as a community of folks who had gone together through the developmental passage called high school. In a moment I would never have anticipated, Roger was given an award for "Loyalty under Pressure." The emcee went on to give an outline of the events that led to Roger's award. If I heard it correctly at the banquet, this is what had happened.

Roger had been approached at some point during our senior year by some popular and mischievous pranksters in our class and asked for a favor. Would he make them a smoke bomb to put in a fellow prankster's locker near the end of the day? Apparently, Roger possessed talents in the area of home chemistry. According to the plan, no one was to be hurt; it was just to be a joke played by some adolescent boys on one of their unsuspecting peers. Roger agreed. On the assigned day, he smuggled in the smoke bomb and placed it in his own locker. The success of the venture now rested with the plotters, who were to recover the device from Roger's locker during the break between fifth and sixth periods, transfer it to the locker of their targeted friend and rig it to start smoking when the locker was next opened.

Not all good plans work out. This one began to unravel sometime earlier than fifth period when for some never-determined reason the mixture in Roger's locker began its work prematurely. Roger's locker began to smoke at a steadily increasing rate. A passing teacher alerted the office, the locker was quickly identified, and Roger was summoned to the principal's office. It was in that conference that Roger won his award for loyalty under pressure, the one presented some 45+ years later. The principal and others at the conference knew that Roger was not likely the instigator of such a clear violation of school rules.

(All of this, of course, occurred long before the national tragedies of Columbine High School; Newtown, Connecticut; and numerous others. Perhaps, it was a kinder, gentler time or at least one during which smoke pouring from a locker could rightly be assumed to be an incident of adolescent pranksterism rather than anything more sinister.)

As the conference continued, those gathered reached a quick consensus that such a violation was simply not in Roger's make-up to bring off without the collaboration of classmates. Yes, they reasoned, he was different, solitary, strange, and certainly bright enough to put together the chemical mixture, but it just wasn't like Roger to have filled a hall with smoke on his own. They began to press Roger for names of the ringleaders of the plot. Apparently during various attempts to admonish, reason with, cajole, and threaten with suspension or worse, Roger sat quietly, refusing to implicate his fellow conspirators. In those moments Roger earned the respect of his relieved partners in mischief and found his way into a community of adolescent boys who remained grateful for his loyalty long after all had grown up and turned out okay.

Pondering these events from a distance of some years, it seems to me that if this story means anything, it perhaps speaks to the quiet activity of a God who does indeed work in mysterious and merciful ways, ways beyond our capacity to foresee. In this case, for a lonely, isolated, strange, and even self-harming adolescent it is not too much to hold that God saw to it that Roger received the essential and ordinary blessing of adolescence—to belong to and find one's place in a peer group. Even if many of the rest of us were too afraid to act, to speak up on Roger's behalf, or even invite him to sit with us during lunch, the Holy worked God's mercy through a uniting conspiracy of smoke and mischief-making.

As for me, I, too, went away from the reunion with an increased sense of serenity arising from sacred mercy exercised on my behalf. Hearing Roger's story, seeing him across the banquet hall as he sat with his wife, realizing that he had traveled about a thousand miles to sit among us and be part of his high school community again—all these realities served in a way I do not fully understand to free me from the shame and guilt I had carried from years earlier. I had not realized how tenaciously the burdens from my adolescent struggles had clung to me, nor to what degree I needed to see that Roger seemed fine—as okay as the rest of us. But there he sat with whatever harm he had gone through years earlier not proving to have dictated a doomed journey. He had returned, claiming his rightful place in our imperfect but shared community. When I saw him and heard his story, something lifted from me. I was freed from an old, old bondage.

All of this naturally enough raises the possibility that Jesus's words to a man made well are yet alive and active in this era and in the *kairos* yet to come: "Go home to your friends, and tell them how much the Lord has done for you, and what mercy he has shown you" (5:19). May we all be directed toward a place of such homecoming with its accompanying, unexpected restoration and healing. Roger and I, blessed by God's merciful "Go home."

5

Splendiferous Failures

Despite everything Jesus says and does, the confusion, misunderstandings and failures of his closest followers multiply as Mark's narrative unfolds, thank God.

Exploring Mark's Story

ONE OF MY FAVORITE films is Zorba the Greek.[1] For the title of this chapter I borrow from the film's hero, Zorba, the infectious and rarely used adjective splendiferous, defined as "gorgeous; splendid: used humorously."[2] This marvelously expressive word appears in the film's closing scene when an exuberant Zorba laughs and shouts it out to his highly constricted and humorless employer, "Boss," in the context of seeming absolute disaster for both Zorba and Boss. What follows is a brief summary of that climactic scene, one that resonates with a major theme of Mark's Gospel. It is a theme that constitutes yet another surprising treasure for readers of Mark's account.

Over the course of the film, Zorba and Boss, an unlikely pair, have partnered to reopen a long-dormant lignite mine on the isle of Crete. As

---

1. *Zorba the Greek*, Michael Cacoyannis, director (Los Angeles, CA: Twentieth Century Fox, 1964).

2. *Webster's New World Dictionary*, college ed. (New York: World Publishing Company, 1959), 1407.

part of extensive repairs that must be made to the crumbling mine, the two come to rely on Zorba's rudimentary design for the construction of a system of cables, pulleys, and wooden supports, which is intended to transport logs from the top of a mountain down a long, steep slope to a delivery point near the entrance to the mine. There, the fresh timber is offloaded and fashioned to reinforce the weakened timber supports of the original mine construction. The funding for this venture has been supplied by Boss, and by the time the cable system is finished and ready for use, his financial resources are nearly depleted. Many months, hours of labor, and significant expenditures of money have gone into this scheme. The restoration of the mine rests on the success of Zorba's timber transport system.

On the day appointed to inaugurate the timber highway, villagers and workers gather near the bottom of the mountain awaiting the transported logs. Zorba and Boss are dressed in their best suits; the cable system is blessed by the sprinkling of holy water by the local Orthodox priest, and mutton is roasting on spits in anticipation of a celebratory meal upon the successful operation of Zorba's contraption. However, things do not go as hoped. After two preliminary attempts at sending logs down the cable highway, the third try brings down the entirety of Zorba's proud invention, collapsing the structure in a manner reminiscent of a long line of falling dominoes. From the launch point at the top of the mountain to the delivery point near the bottom of the mountain, everything is destroyed: snapped cables fly, wooden supports tumble, onlookers and priests flee for safety, and a huge cloud of dust erupts into the air only to slowly settle back over a scene of ruin.

It is in this moment of dust settling and beholding the aftermath of failed construction and dreams that Zorba remembers to save "the lamb," which has continued roasting, awaiting its role in the expected celebration. Zorba and Boss partake of a meal of the lamb and wine. Then, with a haunted look and in a tone of deep longing, Boss says to Zorba, "Teach me to dance, will you?" (Earlier in the movie, Zorba told Boss that it is only dancing that helps him bear the times of great pain and loss as well as times of great happiness.) So with both excitement and tenderness Zorba welcomes Boss into his life-giving ritual of the dance. In the middle of the dance lesson, Zorba turns to Boss with a huge smile across his face and shouts out, "Hey, Boss! Did you ever see a more splendiferous crash?" At this the formerly stiff and lifeless Boss bursts out with his own laughter. Tears run down his cheeks as he shouts back to Zorba, "The third time was the best. Nothing left!"

As the camera pulls away from the scene, the viewer is left with a vision of celebration, complete with lamb and wine, men laughing 'til they cry, and above all, dancing in the midst of devastation and ruin. It is indeed a scene of splendiferous failure, resurrected and transformed into the comedy of life, freedom, and in the end irrepressible dance.

As Mark constructs his narrative, he in no small way portrays Jesus's closest followers as compiling a record of splendiferous failure.[3] If anything, they seem under the spell of an inverted learning curve. As they spend more and more time with Jesus and are subject to his increasing attention in his attempt to help them grasp the realities of the kingdom of God and their place in it, their confusion and inability to comprehend increases. Even when Jesus speaks most pointedly to them and sees to it that the Twelve actually participate in some of his most revealing and compassionate acts, the mental and spiritual fog surrounding them thickens to the point of impenetrability.

Having summarized Mark's characterization of Jesus's closest disciples in such an unflattering light, I do wish to mount a small defense of these men and women. The disciples—especially the apostles and the women at the tomb—constitute one of the three major players in Mark's drama, the other two being Jesus and Mark's readers. Playing a central role in Mark's story, they are present to contribute in an unusual manner to Mark's vision of how humanity is heir to God's good news. Without the presence of the disciples with their ongoing blunders, the good news would be absent much of its Markan meaning and significance. There is a direct relationship between the failures of the disciples and the reality of God's good news.

Mark presents the disciples as progressing along in an error-rich fashion, but it should be noted that when Jesus sends out the Twelve on their trial run mission (6:6b–13), they do well. In their first attempt to follow Jesus's instructions and do the sorts of things Jesus himself has been doing in Mark's story, the apostles have significant and positive success.

---

3. Jesus's closest followers are the twelve apostles, especially the inner circle of Peter, James, and John, as well as several women disciples who were sufficiently courageous and loyal so that, while the male disciples were nowhere to be found as Jesus was being crucified, they were present for Jesus's final moments of suffering and death. Later the women go to Jesus's tomb intent on anointing his body and are the first to hear of the promise to see Jesus again in Galilee.

They proclaim the need for folks to turn their lives around (repent), they anoint and cure, and they exorcise demonic forces. At that point, as they begin to live out their commission to act in disciple-like ways, they are not failures at all. They return tired and hungry (6:30–31), but this is to be expected after their intense time of ministry. Not at all bad for a bunch of novices.

Also to the credit of the disciples, they do leave and follow when called, beginning with the call of the first of the group in 1:16–20, that is, Simon (Peter), Andrew, James, and John. These first four probably do not initially understand how much they are leaving behind (including their long-established identities as fishers and family members). Later the larger group of followers find moments to complain about their losses through their spokesman Peter (10:28). Moreover, they grow ever more fearful as they continue to follow Jesus to Jerusalem (see 10:32). Still, given all their hesitancy and growing ambivalence about travelling on with Jesus, they do continue to follow him, accompanying him until deep into his conflict with the authorities and capture in Jerusalem. The disciples eventually fail, even the bravest and boldest of them, but not without a noteworthy measure of following. And in Mark's world view, the response of following Jesus is no small matter; it can be understood in the final analysis as the only thing that matters.

However, Mark's narrative leads his readers inexorably to its concluding assessment of those closest to Jesus: despite initial and occasional moments of promise shown by them, their promise fades nearly into oblivion. As Mark has it, after the apostles arrive at their pinnacle of success on their first mission early in the story, their relationship with Jesus appears to unravel in its entirety. Even as Mark writes about the most courageous and loyal followers, the women, he pens, "So they went out and fled from the tomb, for terror and amazement had seized them; and they said nothing to anyone, for they were afraid" (16:8). By the end of Mark's account, little of the earlier promise of the disciples remains; instead, only their splendiferous failures are prominent. And *if* it were not for another promise embedded in his final scene at the tomb, Mark's portrait of Jesus's closest followers could lead his readers to conclude that all is lost. Nothing left. Perhaps for us all.

Thank goodness that the *if* above is a big one. Indeed, it makes all the difference.

By now readers may have observed my fondness for the Twelve and the women in Mark's account. My deep appreciation for them despite all they "get wrong" rests on my conviction that who they are resonates with who we are as potential latter-day followers. We, too, bumble and fail from time to time, perhaps even in splendiferous fashion. But the failing disciples are one of our surest avenues into an encounter with the good news which Jesus proclaims and Mark delineates. Their failures and the divine response to them open the way for our own hope and freedom to emerge.

Our first focal text offers a snapshot of the disciples' penchant for misunderstanding and very human failure.

Focal Text: Mark 6:30-52
Mark's First Feeding Story

30 The apostles gathered around Jesus, and told him all that they had done and taught. 31 He said to them, "Come away to a deserted place all by yourselves and rest a while." For many were coming and going, and they had no leisure even to eat. 32 And they went away in the boat to a deserted place by themselves. 33 Now many saw them going and recognized them, and they hurried there on foot from all the towns and arrived ahead of them. 34 As he went ashore, he saw a great crowd; and he had compassion for them, because they were like sheep without a shepherd; and he began to teach them many things. 35 When it grew late, his disciples came to him and said, "This is a deserted place, and the hour is now very late; 36 send them away so that they may go into the surrounding country and villages and buy something for themselves to eat." 37 But he answered them, "You give them something to eat." They said to him, "Are we to go and buy two hundred denarii worth of bread and give it to them to eat? 38 And he said to them, "How many loaves have you? Go and see." When they had found out, they said, "Five, and two fish." 39 Then he ordered them to get all the people to sit down in groups on the green grass. 40 So they sat down in groups of hundreds and of fifties. 41 Taking the five loaves and the two fish, he looked up to heaven, and blessed and broke the loaves, and gave them to his disciples to set before the people; and he divided the two fish among them all. 42 And all ate and were filled; 43 and they took up twelve baskets full of broken pieces and of the fish. 44 Those who had eaten the loaves numbered five thousand men.

45 Immediately he made his disciples get into the boat and go on ahead to the other side, to Bethsaida, while he dismissed the crowd. 46 After saying farewell to them, he went up on the mountain to pray. 47 When evening came, the boat was out on the sea, and he was alone on the land. 48 When he saw that they were straining at the oars

against an adverse wind, he came toward them early in the morning, walking on the sea. He intended to pass them by. ⁴⁹But when they saw him walking on the sea, they thought it was a ghost and cried out; ⁵⁰for they all saw him and were terrified. But immediately he spoke to them and said, "Take heart, it is I; do not be afraid." ⁵¹Then he got into the boat with them and the wind ceased. And they were utterly astounded, ⁵²for they did not understand about the loaves, but their hearts were hardened.

Our first focal text is made up of two scenes: Jesus's initial feeding of a large crowd (6:30–44), and Jesus's approach to the disciples as they cross the Sea of Galilee in a fierce windstorm (6:45–52). Connecting these two scenes, Mark inserts a series of four "for" clauses, thereby building a bridge between his feeding story and Jesus's appearance to the disciples in the storm. This "bridging" is Mark's way of indicating that the two scenes in the larger story are interrelated and inform each other.

Flashing Yellow Lights: Mark's Four "for" clauses

In 6:30–52 Mark reintroduces readers to an old friend, the "for" clause.[4] In Mark's narrative, the small word "for" (*gar* in Greek) alerts readers that something significant has either just occurred or is getting ready to appear in his story. "For" clauses function in many cases as a syntactical caution, signaling Mark's readers to pay close attention to what is transpiring in the surrounding context. Similar to the yellow road signs and flashing caution lights that assist drivers every trip they take, Mark's "for" clauses here tell readers to proceed carefully and be alert to encounter something unexpected. Of the four "for" clauses, three (6:31, 6:50, and 6:52) are readily apparent in the NRSV translation. The other "for" clause (6:48a) is easier to spot in the RSV translation: "And he saw that they were distressed in rowing, for the wind was against them."[5]

In 6:30–52 Mark uses his "for" clauses to point readers toward the prominent themes of human frailty and human failing. The context of each

---

4. See chapter 1.

5. Mark 6:48a, Revised Standard Version (RSV). In the NRSV, the gar of 6:48a is not translated as "for."

clause hints at what Mark hopes readers may uncover about the significance and depth of the disciples' intractable mindset and errant behavior.

For they had no leisure even to eat (6:31). The "for" clause here points to the twelve apostles' inability to find rest and a place to eat. They have completed their mission as outlined in 6:6b–13. They return exhausted by the energy they expended in proclaiming, exorcising, and healing. They are hungry—in part because Jesus's instructions for their mission (6:8) had included the directive that they take neither bread nor money with them, leaving them dependent on other means of being fed on their travels. After the disciples' draining trial run, Jesus detects their very human needs straight away—the need for rest and food. He leads them toward the desert.

A question for readers prompted by this "for" clause: How do the hungry find a way to eat in the barrenness of a desert?

For the wind was against them (6:48). The "for" clause here points to a windstorm that comes up and defeats all the disciples' strenuous efforts to cross the Sea of Galilee. Mark expects his readers to remember an earlier windstorm that enveloped Jesus's followers in 4:35–41. In both instances, the disciples are in peril and all of their efforts prove ineffective. And in both instances, the actions of Jesus lead to exactly the same outcome: "the wind ceased" (4:39, 6:51). Two storms; two ceasing of winds; two savings. But in battling the storm that descends on the disciples after the feeding and with their exhaustion overwhelming them, all recollection of the previous saving vanishes. Extreme vulnerability and need of the disciples is on full display, but forgotten is any recall of their earlier saving by the power of God exercised by God's Beloved.

A question for readers prompted by this "for" clause: Do the disciples ever remember their first saving during the earlier storm?

For they all saw him and were terrified (6:50). The third "for" clause again points toward the disciples' human frailty and failure. Both fear and faulty seeing are prominent here. The overwhelmed disciples see Jesus as he approaches, but mistake him for a ghost. They are terrified to the point of screaming out loud. They are afraid even as Jesus intentionally approaches them, hoping they might lose their fear when they realize God's saving presence is drawing near in their time of great distress and vulnerability. At this point in Mark's story, when they would be desperate to see any sign of hope or help on the horizon, the Twelve mis-see who moves toward them. They see no divine actor, only a ghost. Failing to see rightly who approaches, they cry out fearfully. From Mark's perspective, their need is clear—the disciples need the capacity to discern what their eyes are beholding. If they could see clearly, relief would be the outcome and their terror would fade. The reader can even imagine that terror could be replaced with the awe of being saved for a second time by the cessation of the wind.

A question prompted by this clause: Do the disciples come to recognize who approaches them and why?

For they did not understand about the loaves (6:52). The fourth "for" clause directs the reader to yet another failure to understand by the disciples. They utterly fail to comprehend what they recently lived through in the wilderness when loaves and fish were provided for all of God's hungry people, as with the manna and quail of Exod 16. The experienced reality of God's presence and merciful action to feed God's hungry people in the wilderness eludes them. Even more disturbing is the hardness of the disciples' hearts, which is linked by vocabulary to the hardheartedness of Jesus's murderous opponents earlier in Mark's narrative (3:5–6). Despite all Jesus's efforts, they cannot grasp what is truly happening or see what Jesus would have them see. With hardened hearts, the Twelve are linked with the savage opponents of Jesus. It is not too far a stretch to suggest that Mark links those closest to Jesus with the pre-eminent example of hardheartedness in Israel's history—Egypt's pharaoh in the Exodus narrative.

A question prompted by this clause: Will the disciples ever understand about the loaves and find their hearts softened?

In this focal text with its "for" clauses, Mark points his readers toward these dominant realities: (1) in God's arriving kingdom, God is at work to attend to and meet the needs of God's "hungry" people, including the disciples, and (2) in God's arriving kingdom, the closest followers of Jesus fail to comprehend the surety of God's saving presence and activity in the world as they know it.

Echoes from Hebrew Scripture Found in Mark 6:30–52

In our first focal text, Mark includes an unusual number of references to Hebrew Scripture, each of which illustrates God's relationship to the people of Israel. In each of the references, human need is expressed and God responds:

- With a deserted (wilderness) place (6:31–32, 6:35), Mark alludes to the extensive wilderness stories in Exodus, Deuteronomy, and Joshua.

    Human need: Survival and need for a home.
    God's response: God brings Israelites to promised land.

- With the story of eating in the wilderness (6:31, 6:35–44), Mark alludes to Exod 16:9–15.

    Human need: Survival and hunger.
    God's response: God provides manna and quail in the wilderness.

- With green grass and shepherd imagery (6:34, 6:39), Mark alludes to Ps 23, with its green pastures and God as shepherd.

    Human need: Need for safety, restoration, protection.
    God's response: God the shepherd is present for life's duration.

- When all are fed (6:42), Mark's allusion is to Exod 16:12, when God promises that all will eat, be filled, and know that Yahweh is the God of the wilderness wanderers.

    Human need: Survival, hunger, and knowing God.
    God's response: God supplies bountiful food so that the people will know God as their God.

- When Jesus walks toward the disciples on the sea (6:48), Mark alludes to Job 9:8, 11, 32–35, where God tramples on the sea and passes by Job, who does not see him.

    Human need: Need to recognize and speak to God.
    God's response: God later speaks to terrified Job, who then rightly sees God (Job 42:5–6).

- When Jesus intends to pass by the disciples (6:48), Mark alludes to Exod 33:17–23, 1 Kgs 19: 9–18, when God passes reassuringly close to Moses at Sinai and Elijah at Horeb.

    Human need: Discouragement and need for God's presence.[6]
    God's response: God passes reassuringly close.

---

6. See Williamson, *Mark*, 130–31 for a helpful discussion of Job 9:8 and 11, Exod 33:19 and 22, and 1 Kgs 19:11 as well as how Mark makes use of them in his narrative.

- With Jesus's declaration "It is I" (6:50) and its literal translation "I am," Mark alludes to Exod 3:13–15, when God reveals his name ("I am") to Moses as the One he can speak of to the captive Israelites as their deliverer.

    Human need: Need for deliverance and rescue.
    God's response: God brings the people out of Egypt.

- With "do not be afraid" (6:50), Mark alludes to Gen 15:1, 21:17, 26:24; Josh 8:1; and numerous others.

    Human need: Need for reassurance and help.
    God's response: God is present to reassure and save.

- With the hardened hearts of the disciples (6:52), Mark alludes to numerous instances of hardened hearts of Pharaoh and other Egyptians in Exod 4:21—14:31.

    Human need: Need to overcome hardened hearts.
    God's response: God shows Israelites and Egyptians that God is Lord and the One who sets God's suffering and enslaved people free.

Why does Mark include in this story so many echoes from Hebrew Scripture? To be sure, all of these references in one fashion or another speak of God's relationship to the people Israel. God is portrayed as the God of Abraham, Isaac, and Jacob—as well as the God of Moses, Joshua, Elijah, Job and, yes, even Pharaoh and his official advisers. It seems to me that Mark uses echoes from Israel's past to help readers understand something central about the nature and character of God. The allusions remind Mark's readers that it is precisely in moments similar to those found in 6:30–52, when there is nothing to eat and life can be snuffed out by a raging storm, when God has been most present and most active for his suffering, oppressed, and frightened people. God is a God who works like this, implies Mark: God rescues, restores, protects, calms, and sets free those caught up in desperate, crushing, or life-threatening situations.

This, says Mark, is the same God whom Jesus has announced in his first spoken words (1:15). God is the God whose age has come and whose realm is upon us, among us, available to us for entry. From Mark's perspective, then, a crucial aspect of a discipleship journey is how a follower of Jesus can grasp these new realities of God's time and kingdom and experience them, live into them, be transformed by them.

Mark implies a question of his readers: Can you, unlike the Twelve who see not God but rather a ghost, discern Who is approaching your very lives to overcome your fears and enable a more courageous and compassionate existence?

The two scenes in 6:30–52 would seem guaranteed to bowl over the disciples with their portrayal of a God who saves and restores God's people in the face of extremely adverse circumstances and overwhelming human need. Mark delineates such a saving God and suggests that such an understanding and experience of this present and active God is certainly swirling all around the Twelve for the duration of these two scenes. And potentially, it would seem that their recognition of such a God should be able to envelope and engage their full awareness and being. But is this, in fact, the case in 6:30–52? Do the Twelve come alive as the result of a deeper comprehension about Jesus and what he wants them to experience? In a word, no. And it is to a further depiction of this "no" which we must now turn our attention.

How to Feed Five Thousand Hungry People: Two Approaches

Our focal text opens as the disciples report to Jesus the activities of their successful trial run as disciples. Jesus, seeing their need for replenishment, proposes that they go together to a wilderness place for food and rest. And go they do. However, it is not long after their arrival that certain disturbing trends begin to emerge. While Jesus is responding compassionately to the large, "shepherdless" crowd teaching them late into the day, the disciples—noticing both the time of day and the starkness of the surroundings—approach Jesus and urge him to send the crowd away so that they may purchase food to eat. At first glance their approach to Jesus could be viewed as a compassionate response to the crowd's situation. However, given Mark's flashing yellow light to readers with his "for" clause ("For they had no leisure even to eat"), it is certainly possible that any seeming "compassion" of the disciples could in reality consist mainly of their own hunger needs. The disciples followed Jesus into the wilderness expecting food and rest and they have received neither.

This less than charitable interpretation of the disciples' state of mind appears more likely given their opening words to Jesus in 6:35–36. They speak to Jesus as if the lessons from their religious history as God's chosen people are lost to them. For what better place is there for a crowd of hungry Israelites to be fed and sustained than the wilderness? The disciples need only remember their past as recounted in Exodus 16. For there, did God not feed his hungry children in the stark and inhospitable wilderness with quail and manna? Also, the disciples speak to Jesus as if the learnings from their recent mission have failed to register. For were they not protected and sustained on their travels, even though they took no bread/loaves to eat or money with which to provide for themselves? When speaking to Jesus, then, the Twelve demonstrate a failure to recognize that they are urging Jesus to send the crowd away from the very sort of place and circumstance in which God will most surely act to provide for and feed God's people. They also seem to forget their own recent journeys, during which they were sustained despite carrying neither food nor money. Rather, they made it through by relying on God and those to whom they proclaimed.

Following the disciples' approach to Jesus and urging him to send the crowd away, Jesus's conversation with them again exposes the disciples' lack of comprehension. Jesus says to the Twelve, "You give them something to eat" (6:37). Williamson suggests that Jesus's words are born out of his confidence in the disciples,[7] given their recent successful mission. However, this assessment is arguable especially in light of the disciples' ironic expectation that the people should be sustained by using their own money to secure food when they, the Twelve, had been provided for even though they had no money to purchase food on their mission.

It may not be possible here to determine whether Jesus's words—"You give them something to eat" (6:37)—are prompted by his confidence in the Twelve or by his wariness of their motivation in urging him to send away the hungry crowd. Be that as it may, what can be said is that the disciples' response to Jesus's directive that they see to the feeding of the crowd erases all doubt regarding their lack of understanding. Their words betray a failure to grasp the sacred possibilities of what can happen when God relates to a people—here, God's own people—in need. Moreover, when the core followers reply to Jesus in 6:37b—claiming in effect that what he wants them to do is beyond them and, if truth be told, an impossible if not ludicrous request—the disciples' failure to comprehend is as stark as the desert that surrounds them.

When Jesus replies to the disciples' assertion of the foolish impossibility of their providing food for the crowd, he demonstrates his ongoing

---

7. Williamson, *Mark*, 126.

capacity to recognize the godly opportunities presented by a hungry people gathered in a wilderness. While the Twelve see only a desert locale that provides little if any hope of addressing the needs of a hungry crowd—to say nothing of their own hunger needs—Jesus sees the stage set for God to sustain and feed God's people yet again. Jesus takes a God-trusting approach to what is to come as he moves forward to meet the needs of the crowd.

In taking this approach, Jesus remains constant in his efforts to help the disciples see what he sees and to recognize for themselves what in truth is unfolding before them in the new kingdom's time. Jesus does this in good pedagogical fashion: he sees to it that the Twelve actively and fully participate in what Mark places next in his narrative—the actual feeding of the five thousand.

Kelber comments on the high level of the disciples' participation:

> In reading the feeding story one should observe, as always in Mark, the role played by the disciples as much as that of Jesus. Their involvement in the feeding goes far beyond giving Jesus a helping hand. They are commissioned to feed the people (6:37), they are to look for food (6:38), they are instructed to make the crowds settle down in order . . . and they do feed the people, distributing the bread among them (6:41). More than the disciples helping Jesus feed the people, this is a case of Jesus showing the disciples how to feed the people. It is not sufficient, therefore, to note that the feeding story reports Jesus' feeding of the people.[8]

And so the five thousand are fed. It is an event that portrays a kingdom moment beyond all human imagining. It reveals Jesus's compassionate concern for and response to God's people. It shows his constancy with the Twelve as he leads them through a hands-on learning experience when they feed the people, an experience re-enacting God's feeding of the wandering Israelites in the wilderness. But a question remains at the conclusion of the feeding. Has the significance of all that has occurred and in which the Twelve participated been internalized by them to any degree greater than previously? This unresolved question invites readers toward a closer look at scene two of our focal text: (another) stormy sea, Jesus's response to it, and the disciples' response to Jesus.

---

8. Kelber, *Mark's Story of Jesus*, 35–36.

Another Storm: Fear and Failing on the Sea of Galilee

In scene two (6:45–52), which recounts the story of a second storm (see 4:35–41 for the first storm), Jesus separates himself from his close followers. He compels the disciples—presumably including the Twelve—to return to their waiting boat and start out across the sea while he goes to speak his farewell to the crowd. After this, and still on land, he goes to pray.

In the following few verses that describe the disciples' attempt to cross the Sea of Galilee, Mark answers the question that was left unanswered at the close of the first feeding. Fresh from their time of participating with Jesus in evidencing the inbreaking of God's kingdom as God's hungry people are fed in the desert, have the disciples understood the import of this event? Mark's narrative seems to imply to the contrary that their actions give testimony to an altogether comprehensive failure. It is a failure to see, hear, and remember. A few words about each of these failures are in order.

Failure to see (6:47–50). The disciples set off on the Sea of Galilee as Jesus directs them. Soon, however, trouble develops. Strong, overpowering winds spring up and although they row strenuously for what Mark indicates is a lengthy period, they are apparently getting nowhere and the disciples are at significant risk of perishing. At this point, Jesus, who has noticed the disciples' distress from his vantage point on land, begins to make his way toward them. In doing so, Jesus's approach serves as an allusion to Hebrew Scripture. Similarly to how God is described in Job 9:8–11, Jesus strides across the water toward his disciples and they, echoing Job's failure to see God, do not rightly see who is approaching them. They see a ghost, not God, and are terrified, believing the approaching figure is up to no good. In seeing events in this way, the Twelve also do not realize that Jesus intends to come to them and pass close by them for the purpose of reassurance and demonstrating God's saving presence in their time of peril. Jesus's passing by is similar to God's passing by Moses on Mount Sinai and Elijah on Mount Horeb. Completing his portrayal of the faulty vision of the disciples during the storm, Mark leaves no doubt as to who did not rightly see: "for they all saw him and were terrified" (6:50).

Failure to hear (6:50b). After Mark describes the disciples' errant seeing, he addresses their inability to hear rightly. The issue is therefore broadened to include not merely what the Twelve see, but also whether they really hear what Jesus says to them. Jesus speaks three short sentences in 6:50b. In these few words, there are again deafening echoes from

Hebrew Scripture in two of the three: "it is I"[9] and "do not be afraid." These echoes are meant to reassure the disciples and counter their fears as they affirm the protective presence and saving power of the God of Israel. However, there is no response or apparent hearing by the disciples at this point and so Jesus—now identified by Mark as bearing the Holy name "I am"—follows up his words and steps into the boat with them.

Failure to remember (6:51). It is at this point in this scene that Mark presents the hazardous situation of the disciples in a manner that would seem certain to evoke their recall of an earlier indelible experience, that is, the earlier storm in 4:35–41. Mark's portrayal of the second storm parallels the first. In both, Jesus responds to the need of the disciples with the result being the same (identical in the Greek): and "the wind ceased" (see 4:39 and 6:51). It is instructive to note how Mark writes of the disciples' response to their second saving from a storm. They are utterly, exceedingly astonished. I can imagine one of Mark's readers responding to the disciples' state of being astounded with, "How come they're amazed? Shouldn't they have seen this coming and realized, based on their earlier experience with Jesus and storms, that this dilemma would turn out like the first storm? Identically, even?" But all memory of the initial storm and its saving outcome is forgotten, or perhaps more charitably, has been swept away by the terror that enveloped the Twelve. And so, they end up in a state of astonishment, not one of recall.

Mark's Exclamation Point

Mark completes our focal text forcefully. Its power is compressed into a partial sentence: "for they did not understand about the loaves, but their hearts were hardened" (6:52). Through a "for" clause, Mark calls his readers' attention to the very center of this text. He makes it crystal clear for his readers that Jesus's followers did not comprehend in the least the significance of what they experienced with the feeding and the storm. They grasped nothing. Their sight, their hearing, their remembrance all failed. If readers have any sympathy for Jesus's close followers—as I believe Mark encourages us to have—it yet remains true that it just does not go well for them after the people are fed, the wind from the storm dies down, and they stand amazed. Their comprehension and discernment fail them. Utterly. Exclamation point.

9. An alternative translation is "I am."

I believe Mark intends to stun his readers with this ending for this text. For here, at the very end of this lengthy account wherein Jesus has been expending much energy, making vigorous and multiple attempts to instruct the disciples and move them deeper into the reality of God's arriving season and kingdom, Mark reveals something that even Jesus has not yet come to recognize regarding his closest followers. That is, that the numerous blunders of the disciples and their failure to understand, is in truth, says Mark, *impossible* for the Twelve to avoid. Why? Because "their hearts were hardened" (6:52).

Black describes hardness of heart as a condition of "stubborn obtuseness."[10] This being the case, it is no wonder things went over the disciples' heads, did not sink in, were forgotten, or failed to register. And—says Mark—since these close followers were caught up in a state of mind/soul wherein access to the larger significance of events was closed to them, they were not capable of understanding about the loaves or much of anything else Jesus was hoping to teach or show them. In such a state of mind (and heart), the Markan disciples are true kin of Egypt's Pharaoh in Exodus (see e.g., Exod 4:21—14:31). Again and again, Pharaoh found his heart hardened in his dealings with the captive Israelites, Moses, and even the great I AM. The disciples—Mark tells us—could not have understood Jesus or all they had recently gone through in both the wilderness and at sea. Like Pharaoh, their hearts had been hardened.[11]

After encountering 6:52 and letting the full import of its ramifications "soak in," somewhat befuddled readers of Mark might well raise several crucial questions and/or comments at this point of our exploration. Chief among these might be the following: What in the world is Mark up to at this point in his narrative design? For not only do the disciples fail but they are *destined to fail* because of their hardened hearts.

---

10. Black, "The Gospel of Mark," note on Mark 3:5.

11. Mark's primary concern in 6:52 is that his readers recognize that Jesus's closest followers were in a state wherein their "hearts were hardened." But Mark offers no specific indication on how the disciples arrived at this state of "stubborn obtuseness," to use Black's words ("The Gospel of Mark," note on Mark 6:52). By contrast, in the Exodus account of Pharaoh's heart problems, Pharaoh is sometimes said to harden his own heart (Exod 8:15, 32; 9:34), and at other times it is clearly Yahweh who causes Pharaoh's heart to harden (Exod 4:21; 9:12; 10:20, and 14:4). Mark seems not especially interested in who produced heart difficulties in the Twelve; rather he indicates that the brittle and unyielding state of being is where they find themselves despite all Jesus has done and all they themselves have experienced up to this point. In such a condition, they are incapable of right seeing, hearing, or remembering.

Even beyond that, not only do Jesus's efforts to help the Twelve prove ineffective, but—if Mark is to be believed—all his hard work with his disciples is destined to flop. So, in addition to portraying close followers who fail, is Mark also presenting his readers with a portrait of Jesus who fails? That is, at this point in Mark's story, does Jesus stand before us as one unable to infiltrate the disciples' brittle and unyielding state of hard-heartedness? And if the disciples are to be judged as "in the dark" here, is Jesus also to be thought of as in the dark? Is there something *he* has yet to understand about his dealings with the Twelve? Is there something he is missing as he works diligently but without success to help his key followers, see, hear and remember?

At the conclusion of our exploration of 6:30–52, readers may imagine Jesus pondering such as questions as, "What do I need to do to get through to my leaders-to-be? What am I missing that could help them move into and experience the reality of the kingdom of God? Do I need to rethink what I've been doing and somehow change it and do something different?"

The first feeding story leaves Markan readers with significant questions yet to be answered. In doing so it propels readers forward to a subsequent Markan story, a second feeding in a desert place. There we glimpse Jesus's ongoing growth and development as the Son of Man as Jesus shifts direction and broadens his understanding of what it means to be God's Beloved Son.

Focal Text: Mark 8:1-21
Mark's Second Feeding Story

⁸In those days when there was again a great crowd without anything to eat, he called his disciples and said to them, ²"I have compassion for the crowd, because they have been with me now for three days and have nothing to eat. ³If I send them away hungry to their homes, they will faint on the way—and some of them have come from a great distance." ⁴His disciples replied, "How can one feed these people with bread here in the desert?" ⁵He asked them, "How many loaves do you have?" They said, "Seven." ⁶Then he ordered the crowd to sit down on the ground; and he took the seven loaves, and after giving thanks he broke them and gave them to his disciples to distribute; and they distributed them to the crowd. ⁷They had also a few small fish; and after blessing them, he ordered that these too should be distributed. ⁸They ate and were filled; and they took up the broken pieces left over, seven baskets full. ⁹Now there were about four thousand people. And he sent them away. ¹⁰And immediately he got into the boat with his disciples and went to the district of Dalmanutha.

¹¹The Pharisees came and began to argue with him, asking him for a sign from heaven, to test him. ¹²And he sighed deeply in his spirit and said, "Why does this generation ask for a sign? Truly I tell you, no sign will be given to this generation." ¹³And he left them, and getting into the boat again, he went across to the other side.

¹⁴Now the disciples had forgotten to bring any bread; and they had only one loaf with them in the boat. ¹⁵And he cautioned them, saying, "Watch out—beware of the yeast of the Pharisees and the yeast of Herod." ¹⁶They said to one another, "It is because we have no bread." ¹⁷And becoming aware of it, Jesus said to them, "Why are you talking about having no bread? Do you still not perceive or understand? Are your hearts hardened? ¹⁸Do you have eyes, and fail to see? Do you have ears, and fail to hear? And do you not remember? ¹⁹When I broke the five loaves for the five thousand, how many baskets full of broken pieces did you collect?" They said to him, "Twelve." ²⁰ "And the seven for the four thousand, how many baskets full of broken pieces did you collect?" And they said to him, "Seven." ²¹Then he said to them, "Do you not yet understand?"

Our second focal text—Mark's second feeding story (8:1-21)—is similar in structure and content to the first feeding story (6:30-52). John Dominic Crossan describes the second feeding story as "a deliberate doubling"[12] of the first. In both stories, the plot centers on a large group of hungry people who are sustained in the wilderness through the actions of Jesus and the disciples. In both stories,

- the crowds seem to be in dire need;
- Jesus has compassion for the people;
- the disciples are unable to imagine meeting the need of the crowds for bread in the wilderness;
- Jesus asks an identical question of the disciples: "How many loaves do you have?";
- Jesus communicates with the Divine through prayer or blessing;
- the disciples participate in the feeding; and
- the crowds eat their fill and baskets full of extra food are left over.

Mark's intention for both stories is to portray a God who is present and active in the lives of people who find themselves in a situation of need—a need sometimes so desperate that they are at risk of falling exhausted in the desert, likely succumbing (8:3). In the face of such need, God sees to it that his kingdom advances, providing those in need a saving they cannot secure for themselves.

Along with these similarities, however, the second feeding story differs from the first in several important ways, including the setting. While the first feeding is conducted "in a Jewish milieu,"[13] the second takes place in decidedly gentile territory. Werner Kelber asserts that the feeding of this gentile crowd is the culmination of a central Markan theme, namely that the arriving kingdom of God is as available, accessible, and welcoming to non-Jewish people as to the Jewish populace of 6:30–52.[14] By placing the second feeding in gentile territory, Mark shows that the kingdom of God, the sphere of God's presence and activity, is inclusive of all.

In the second feeding story, Jesus focuses his attention on the disciples earlier and more keenly than during the first feeding. After the disciples failed to "understand about the loaves" in the first feeding, Jesus has become more aware of their obtuseness, and he undertakes renewed and more direct efforts to awaken their capacity to understand and see

---

12. Crossan, *Jesus*, 174.
13. Kelber, *Mark's Story of Jesus*, 35.
14. Kelber, *Mark's Story of Jesus*, 36–40.

what is happening right before their eyes. He speaks aloud to the disciples about his compassion for the crowd, not leaving it to his disciples to make deductions about it (as in 6:30–52). He pointedly directs their attention to the dire situation of the hungry crowd, spelling out the weighty consequences of sending the crowd to their far-distant homes. And at the end of the feeding, Jesus "immediately" (8:10) gets into the boat with his disciples, remaining with them instead of separating himself.

The Disciples' Persistent Lack of Understanding

Despite Jesus's intensified efforts, however, the disciples are apparently unchanged in any positive sense.[15] Their question, "How can one feed these people with bread here in the desert?" (8:4), suggests that hearts remain hardened and comprehension is still beyond them. If anything, the disciples come across as even more dense than in the first feeding. During the first feeding, the Twelve had implied that it was impossible for them to feed the hungry throng. Here in the second feeding, their increased sense of the impossibility of the task leads them to say that no one can accomplish this. Williamson captures this deepening intransigence of the disciples, who "had recently participated in the miraculous feeding of five thousand people in another desert place ... [However,] the incredible dullness of the disciples is precisely the point the feeding of the four thousand intends to make."[16]

After the second feeding, Mark inserts a short interlude[17] that describes a run-in between Jesus and Pharisees, who show up at moments when the disciples are especially vulnerable to becoming unsettled as they try to follow and understand Jesus. A familiar Markan formula is at play here, namely that when the Pharisees are close by, the disciples' attempts to hear, see, and remember Jesus's teachings are diminished. The disciples get rattled.[18] Mark uses the interlude with the Pharisees to focus on his dominant theme at this point in his narrative: that the experience

---

15. Williamson describes the disciples' response in 8:1–21 as one of "friendly dullness" (*Mark*, 146).

16. Williamson, *Mark*, 141–42.

17. Some see Jesus's encounter with the Pharisees in 8:11–13 as a distinct scene in Mark's story (e.g., Williamson, *Mark*, 141–43).

18. Mark 7:1–23 is a prime example of the Pharisees' disturbing effect on the disciples. Note especially the disciples' lack of understanding in 7:18 after they witnessed the Pharisees' engagement with Jesus.

of the second feeding fails to increase the disciples' capacity for sight, hearing, and understanding. By bringing the Pharisees into the middle of Jesus's ongoing efforts with his disciples, Mark foreshadows another in a long line of discipleship missteps.[19]

In 8:14–21 Mark returns to the dialogue between Jesus and his disciples. Once again they are in a state of confusion and limited comprehension. They have forgotten to bring loaves. Mark seems to suggest that they intended to bring a greater store of supplies than in their past travels, but it slipped their minds, bothered as they were by the unsettling presence of the Pharisees. They do have "one loaf with them in the boat" (8:14), but they have not even mentally registered the presence of that loaf.

For Jesus, the residue of conflict with the Pharisees still seems to weigh on him. He appears worried for the well-being of his disciples, warning them to be wary of "the yeast of the Pharisees and the yeast of Herod" (8:15). Clifton Black identifies yeast here as "a symbol of pervasive corruption hidden within human beings."[20] When Jesus speaks of yeast, he refers to the corrupting influences of the Pharisees and the Herodians, perhaps especially those influences capable of "infecting" the disciples. But his warning falls on deaf ears. Jesus's words have no meaning for them beyond their own immediate focus on having "no bread" (8:16) for their upcoming trip. Their tenacious dullness remains intact.

When Jesus hears members of his core group speak of having "no bread," the patience Jesus has maintained in enduring the disciples' oft-demonstrated dullness evaporates. Twice now, he has taken the Twelve through the saving event of feeding a desperately needy people in the starkness of the desert; twice now, Jesus has given thanks and called the attention of the disciples to the presence and activity of God; twice now he has recruited the disciples to actively participate in distributing a meager supply of loaves and fishes; and twice the disciples collected baskets full of leftovers which witness to the sustaining abundance of God's kingdom. Twice now. But a flash point has been reached between Jesus and the disciples and Jesus erupts with a barrage of nine questions placed squarely before the disciples.[21] Perhaps the last of them best captures the deep poignancy

---

19. I assume that the disciples witnessed the encounter between Jesus and the Pharisees (8:11–13). There is context to support this assumption: Jesus and his disciples travel in the boat together, and Jesus mentions the Pharisees to the disciples after the confrontation.

20. Black, "The Gospel of Mark," note on Mark 8:15.

21. Myers refers to Jesus's outburst as a "tirade." As for Jesus's emotional state

and emotional distress of the whole. As it echoes in the air, silence is the disciples' only answer for "Do you not yet understand?" (8:21).[22]

Jesus's Newly Emerging Self-Understanding

With the conclusion of Jesus's stinging confrontation of his disciples in 8:21, Mark is preparing his readers for a shift of great magnitude and importance, a shift that lays the foundation for the remainder of Mark's Gospel and thereby constitutes one of Mark's richest buried treasures. The shift invites readers toward an expanded understanding of Jesus's purpose and identity; from this point on in Mark's narrative Jesus is to be most rightly seen by Mark's readers as the Son of Man who is to suffer, be killed, and rise (8:31).

The doorway to this more expanded view of Jesus is provided through Mark's intricate weaving together of the record of nearly complete failure by the disciples in the first half of his narrative and Jesus's evolution in his self-understanding and growing maturity that emerges in the second half of Mark's Gospel. Prompted by his followers' inability to understand, Jesus comes to internalize something new about himself in the aftermath of the two feedings. His self-awareness is birthed out of the nearly deafening silence of his followers in the face of his questions to them. While they manage two one-word answers about the number of baskets involved in the feedings, they give no other reply. In that silence, Jesus begins to recognize that no change is likely in the Twelve. There will be no dawning comprehension, nor seeing, hearing, or remembering on their part. All his efforts have proved insufficient to break through to them.

But as Jesus recognizes that his disciples likely cannot change, he begins to understand that he must change. Something previously unanticipated is required of him. Something that can soften his followers' hearts, opening them to God and their fellow earthly sojourners. He must walk a new and different path. It is a path to be followed in light of his more

---

at the point of asking these questions, interpreters offer various conclusions, such as exasperation similar to Moses's exasperation with Israel in the wilderness (Myers, *Binding the Strong Man*, 225); anger (Kelber, *Mark's Story of Jesus*, 40); and dismay over their ongoing misunderstanding (Williamson, *Mark*, 146).

22. The power carried by these questions can be understood by reading the entire set out loud. Try to imagine what it was like for Jesus as he spoke in such a manner and at such length to his disciples. Similarly, try to imagine what it was like as a disciple to hear these questions asked of you—relentlessly, one after the other.

mature self-awareness as the Son of Man who models service and giving of self for the setting free of others (10:45). So the journey of the Beloved continues and its destination is dangerous Jerusalem, home to Jesus's most ruthless adversaries.

The shift in Jesus's self-understanding, purpose, and direction marks the turning point of Mark's narrative. It is of crucial importance to the remainder of Mark's Gospel. It is Mark's vibrant and transformative treasure, waiting for readers to unearth and claim as their own.

Jesus's Core Followers and Their Splendiferous Failures

Occasionally in this chapter, I have hinted that the record of splendiferous failures by Jesus's disciples, most clearly delineated in Mark's two feeding stories, is something that Mark's readers could and should celebrate. Even at the close of the second feeding when it is clear to Mark's Jesus as well as Mark's readers that in the then-present moment of 8:21, there is for the disciples no dawning awareness about God and God's arriving kingdom—even then the bumbling hardheadedness and hardheartedness of Jesus's followers stand as something we can be grateful for. I hasten to add, however, that such a thankful attitude proves possible, it seems to me, only if readers find themselves in one of two circumstances. That is, readers are resolutely trusting of Mark to make good on his intention as implied in 1:1—to ultimately present a vision of the reality of God's good (as opposed to disheartening) news. Alternatively, the readers' circumstance includes a basic familiarity with what lies ahead in the second half of Mark's account. Sustained either by such trust or such advance knowledge of what is to come, thankfulness could be part of the readers' state of mind as they arrive at the end of the first half of Mark's story. So, despite all that readers have observed about the disciples in Mark through 8:21, we come to the point of reiterating the surprising treasure of this chapter: that even as the words, deeds, and attitudes of the Twelve coalesce into a seemingly ever downward and darkened path, Mark invites his readers to view them through a lens of gratitude.[23]

23. Kelber arrives at a different perspective on the disciples than the one I am advancing here. His assessment of the disciples based on their consistent record of failure is that, "Far from experiencing a change of heart they betray, contradict, deny, and in the end abandon the suffering and dying Jesus . . . There is no way that the disciples can become the leaders of the Kingdom of God" (Kelber, *Mark's Story of Jesus*, 87). Kelber further argues that "the disciples never do return to Galilee" following Jesus's

The question remains, however: how can this be,[24] given all we readers have come to know about the Twelve by the end of the second feeding episode? With this question in mind, I will now shift from hinting at the contributions of the disciples to Mark's good news to more explicit statements about their essential and positive place in Mark's narrative.

A more clearly delineated portrayal of Jesus's inner circle can begin with this general statement: Mark's presentation of the disciples—and their consistent and repeated failure in their attempts to understand Jesus—contributes to Mark's suggesting for his readers an incomplete but nonetheless significant vision of the life of faith. To put it slightly differently, Mark's portrait of the disciples accomplishes the furtherance of his viewpoint about what it means to follow Jesus. Mark shaped this vision in several ways.

First, the portrait of the disciples as representative of those attempting to follow Jesus opens a path for us latter-day readers of his Gospel. For like the earliest followers of their charismatic and peculiar leader, we too falter, fail, and blunder in our daily pursuit of following, of living into "the faith." An assumption here, as well as my experience as a believer (in the most general sense), is that those of us who attempt to the limits of our understanding and abilities to pursue a life of discipleship during the span of our lives have an awareness of moments or periods of time when we also stumble or even much worse. Some basic, simple examples:

- Our courage fails us when we could speak up in settings where cruel, slighting, or bullying words are being spoken.

- We set out to be helpful to someone only to realize later that our words and efforts have proved hurtful, shaming, or patronizing to the one we intended to help.

- In a class or after-dinner discussion we hear ourselves saying things like, "Well, I know we're supposed to turn the other cheek, but I won't be doing that more than once, I tell ya."

---

death. While I agree that the disciples are dismal failures and that Mark's indication of whether they remain in Jerusalem or instead return to Galilee is inexact, I lean toward an interpretation wherein they do return to Galilee and recommence their very human following of Jesus. I would envision that most assuredly their multiple failings would continue as would Jesus's relentless patience, forgiveness, and ever challenging call. See chapter 9 for further discussion of this line of thought.

24. Note that our question, "How can this be?" is not one foreign to people of faith. See Luke 1:34.

- Or, in relationships most dear to us, we find ourselves—sometimes subtly, sometimes not—speaking/acting in a savage, vengeful manner, such moments often being rationalized by thoughts or words such as, "I'm doing/saying this for your own good, you know," or "Well, if you hadn't started it, I certainly wouldn't have," or "Oh, come on. That didn't hurt. I was just kidding. Geez, you're sensitive."

Mark's portrayal of the disciples, then, impacts us in three ways. First, it holds up a mirror to us, facing us with our less-than-attractive side, and at the same time, paradoxically, offering us hope. The disciples help us know that similar to them, we are among the throng of God's children, far from perfect and capable of repetitive blunders and even of inflicting significant hurt. But like Mark's "original" followers, even after such efforts that genuinely disappoint or harm others and also ourselves, a path remains open to us—one which, thankfully, we still can choose to follow, even though we, too, are afraid (see Mark 10:32). This is good news.

Second, the errant steps of the Twelve emerge as a prerequisite for Mark's central theological understanding of the good news. After the two feedings, the mature Markan Jesus comes to comprehend and indeed grow toward a new identity as the suffering, self-giving, and rising Beloved Son of God/Son of Man. It is not enough that Jesus be healer, teacher, challenger of oppressive conventional norms, calmer of storms, and feeder of thousands; it is imperative that he also move toward becoming the Son of Man who comes "to serve, and to give his life [self] a ransom for many" (10:45). In Mark's story it is precisely the ineptitude of the core followers, the collapse of their discipleship, that leads Jesus to speak of and claim his newly necessitated and realized persona as the Son of Man. Jesus sets a new course; he incorporates a clearer, more mature identity, and all this arises from the unintentional but relentless failure of discipleship. The significance and meaning of Mark's Gospel is profoundly altered as Mark invites his readers to focus on a Beloved One who chooses to serve, up to and including the surrender of his very life/self so that others are set free—even, it is to be hoped, wayward, captured, and hardhearted disciples.

Third, Jesus's shift invites a new direction for the disciples themselves. In the second half of Mark's story, the scope and meaning of "following Jesus" changes. "Following" becomes clarified and refined. As Jesus pursues his new direction to Jerusalem, endures suffering to the point of being killed, and then rises (in some manner yet to be spelled out by Mark), the disciples also are invited toward service and self-giving. The new discipleship stance and way of being—implies Jesus—will help others become free, enlivened, and capable of personal courage not previously known (see 8:35 and 10:45). A new way of following is open to those who would accompany Jesus as he walks this new path, which holds the potential for becoming the distinctive way of living for both Jesus and his disciples. It is the way (road, path) Jesus speaks of in the central paradox of Mark's good news: "For those who want (choose) to save their life will lose it, and those who lose their life for my sake and for the sake of the gospel, will save it" (8:35).

Thus Mark goes on record with his vision of a way of discipleship that, if pursued, bestows (1) an existence of meaning, (2) a being enlivened during one's days upon this earth, (3) the courage to engage and endure the world's bankrupt and idolatrous systems of power and security, and (4) at least on occasion, the capacity to lay down one's life/self so that others become free from the many prisons they (and we) find ourselves inhabiting.

"Yet": A Future Beyond Failure

Mark concludes the first half of his story with Jesus's anguished and haunting question to his closest followers: "Do you not yet understand?" (8:21). Earlier I commented on the overall sense of distress that is reflected in this question, especially when it is placed in the context of the complete list of nine questions Jesus directs at his disciples. But even with the exasperation, dismay, challenge, anger, or incredulity carried by Jesus's final question, "yet" can be viewed as an embedded ray of hope, pointing toward a future still to be realized. Perhaps the most crucial aspect of the "yet" is that it signifies that the Jesus of Mark's story has not given up on his followers; his efforts with them will continue. No doubt, by the time the second feeding is completed, he has a clearer understanding of what he is up against in his efforts to reach them. But he is not finished with them; he does not give up on them, even when they seem impervious to all that God would bestow on them. He persists, doggedly, as he travels toward Jerusalem and matures as Son of Man.

Williamson describes this moment (8:21) as follows:

> For if, in one sense, Jesus' final question functions as a statement reproaching the disciples' present incomprehension, in a deeper sense it retains the interrogative force of an invitation. "Do you

not yet understand?" is an invitation to read on in the Gospel, and in our lives to stay with Jesus till we do understand.[25]

The splendiferous failures of those closest to Jesus lead Mark's readers toward news that is both surprising and good indeed: that redemptive and compassionate living will not be lost to any darkness or brokenness we latter-day and stumbling disciples will inevitably bring into the world, at least not as long as God and God's Beloved have anything to do with it. The path to continue our faltering, unsteady but enlivening discipleship remains open to us. It beckons, invites, and encourages us forward. It remains available for our ongoing exploration and—dare we choose it—pursuit.

Personal Reflection: Waiting for William

In September 1989 I wrote the following reflection, which seems germane to the theme of "yet" noted in Mark 8:21. I had recently returned from a trip to the United Kingdom where I had accompanied my then-seventy-four-year-old mother on a visit to one of her favorite places—the Lake District in northern England.

> But those who wait for the Lord shall renew their strength, they shall mount up with wings like eagles, they shall run and not be weary, they shall walk and not faint. (Isa 40:31)

Perhaps it began several years ago when I found myself standing in the pulpit of Second Presbyterian Church, Richmond, Virginia, preparing to read the Scripture lessons for the day. As I looked out at those in the pews I heard myself inviting them to listen. "Be expectant," I said and realized I was smiling slightly. "Be expectant and listen for the word of God." And at some level, I think I knew that it had happened again—that phenomenon that many of us who stand before God's people experience from time to time, and that is that a word spoken by us to God's people ends up being the Spirit's word to us who speak. "Be expectant," I had said to others and found myself being invited by the Holy into a life orientation of expectant, non-anxious waiting, anticipation with a smile.

About six weeks prior to my trip to Great Britain—a trip during which I was to accompany my seventy-four-year-old mother—I went

---

25. Williamson, *Mark*, 146.

with Lyn, my wife, to see *Field of Dreams*.[26] It was a powerful movie for me and I was certain it was one vision of the coming of the Kingdom of God and what Communion of the Saints looks like. I found myself weeping at the end. Certainly, some of the tears arose out of the moving scene when son and father are reunited in a game of catch. I cried because I have no memory of catch with my father. I ached to do what Kevin Costner's character was doing on screen and the tears came.

For several weeks after seeing *Field of Dreams*, I kept saying to myself that I wanted to go see it again. It had touched me. But I kept forgetting, kept thinking I couldn't go during work hours, kept thinking I couldn't go because Lyn likes to see movies only once. Yet, when I drove home there it stood on the movie marquee at the local mall: *Field of Dreams*, always beckoning, a mute Siren. Then, one afternoon about a week before my mother and I were to leave, I decided I was going to go and see, just like some shepherd who had been given something, someone to go look for.[27] At the end of the movie I knew why I had been drawn back to it and I went home and told Lyn, "I think I know why I had to go see that movie again." And with the hair rising on the back of my neck out of fear, mystery and anticipation, I added, "I'm going to meet my father when I go to England." It sounded silly to put into words; how could it be that I would meet one William Hill, dead some thirty-eight years? Foolish indeed. But I found myself expectant, waiting, certain, and calm.

In the days prior to the trip, I occasionally wondered how it would happen. Would I get Mother to speak more of Dad, something I'd never had much success in enabling to happen? Would I encounter him through a greater sharing of family history? Or would it happen in some other manner I could not even begin to guess? Finally, I decided I had no idea; I would just try to keep my eyes and ears open so as not to miss him when he showed up.

I could have made a thousand guesses and never picked the right answer because it happened in a way beyond all probability, just like when a king is born and placed in an animal's feeding trough. I have never been a wanderer in art galleries to speak of and the world of modern art has never done anything for me. Mother, however, wanted to visit the

---

26. *Field of Dreams*, Phil Alden Robinson, director (Universal City, CA: Universal Studios, 1989). Movie includes the oft-quoted line, "If you build it, he will come."

27. My references to a shepherd given someone to look for and a king placed in an animal's feed trough after birth are allusions to Luke's account of Jesus's birth (Luke 2:1–20).

Tate Gallery in London, a place she had been before. It seemed to be the thing she most wanted to do in London, and so we went one morning. When we got there, she was doubly delighted to discover that there was an exhibit of Paul Klee's work on loan from the Metropolitan Museum of Art in New York City. I didn't know Paul Klee from a hole in the ground, but she had studied about him years ago in an art appreciation course and wanted to see his work. And being the dutiful son who had given over the morning to escorting his mother, I went along with the idea. Besides, I was still getting used to British money and two pounds sounded cheap enough. We wandered around the exhibit for approximately forty-five minutes. It was interesting enough for modern art; there were touches of humor, humanity, and poignancy here and there. As I approached the last wall of Klee's work, I moved in front of a painting titled *Clarification*[28] and immediately it held me. As I stood there, my heart began to beat faster. Calm presence, serenity, and shalom entered me, or I entered them. They seemed to exist in the space between me and the painting also. After the briefest of moments, I knew this was it: Dad was with me, conveyed through the medium of modern art of all things. I sat down on the bench opposite the painting, looking at it, seeing it, experiencing his thereness. I don't remember needing to cry or wanting to shout. I was just with him and it was good, the eighth day.[29] We were quiet. No words were spoken, no visions seen. Yet, there we were together: Communion of the Saints, a "mystic, sweet communion."[30]

Later in the trip I realized I had time to squeeze in another trip to see him on the morning I was to leave London and decided to do so. I had some anxiety about it all. Would he be there this time or would I decide it had all been an illusion? I didn't think so, but I wondered. When I arrived much of the same experience reoccurred. Again, there was a calmness and serenity I had felt in my soul when I sat looking at the painting. As I looked at it more carefully this time to note colors and details, I began to believe that the work itself must be Klee's statement about the human and divine connectedness and separateness, how these worlds are separate and yet resonate with each other in grace-filled ways. The longer I was there, I began to believe that maybe it was not my biological father whom I was encountering so much as it was my Heavenly Father. I finally

28. Paul Klee, *Clarification* (Oil on canvas, 1932).

29. Genesis 1 and 2. "Good" and "the eighth day"—allusions to one of the accounts of God's creating the universe, matter, and all life.

30. Samuel John Stone, "The Church's One Foundation" (Hymn, 1866).

decided that even if father with a small "f" had not been there, certainly Father with a big "F" was and that was more important, I told myself. Again I left with a sense of serenity and mystery, with my knees a little weak from it all. But I was not as certain of Dad's presence and tried to tell myself that was okay.

About an hour later I was riding the Aerobus back to Heathrow Airport for my flight home. As I rode along I was watching the scenery and pondering the trip as a whole. We were driving up a street full of small shops and I glanced up ahead. There in front of me for a full three to four seconds, in letters three to four feet high above a storefront was a name, the name: William Hill. I grinned and laughed out loud. What fun it is to be covenanted with a playful God! It was as if God were saying to me in a teasing, rib-poking sort of way, "Okay, Hunter. I thought I gave it a pretty good shot at the Klee exhibit, but you seemed to be wavering about that a bit, so here you go. You shouldn't be able to dismiss this one too easily. It's certainly not abstract art, just plain English letters. Of course your Dad was there in the Gallery; we were all—the three of us—there together. Remember? Communion of the Saints? Anyway, how's this for a finishing touch to your journey?"

I remember an early mentor, Doug Oldenburg,[31] saying long ago that he could envision a laughing God. I could not then and could not for years. But it seems to me that on August 8, 1989, God played with me on a red bus, in a foreign city, when I expected it least. And like Sarah, I laughed.[32] It was without doubt the perfect finishing touch, O Spirit One. Praise be to you, O Spirit, God of Abraham and Sarah, of unnamed shepherds and Mary, mother of Jesus, and of William and Hunter. Be expectant. Be expectant, indeed.

As I complete this chapter, I am hopeful that readers will realize my deep appreciation and even affection for Jesus's disciples, most specifically the inner circle of the apostles along with certain women followers. With Mark's help they have over the years captured both my mind and my heart. They remind me of me, an example of which is my experience at the Tate.

---

31. Douglas W. Oldenburg served as minister in the Presbyterian Church, USA, moderator of the denomination's General Assembly (1998), and president of Columbia Theological Seminary in Georgia (1987–2000).

32. Gen 18:1–15, 21:1–7. Sarah breaks forth in laughter at the "nonsensical" idea that at ninety years of age she could both enjoy sex with her husband and bear a child from this union. She had been childless and laughed at because of it all her life.

In my understanding of what happened there—although others may assuredly view this event quite differently—I was beckoned into a moment of sacred mystery. It happened not because I am in any unusual way special or deserving, but rather because God is good and caring, and possessing a decidedly advanced sense of humor. My lack of any special piety or other distinguishing attribute is evident in the account of the episode itself, for within a few days of its occurrence, I was having second thoughts about the whole experience and convincing myself that it was of diminished significance if not altogether illusory. So, like the disciples I had eyes that failed to see and ears that did not hear; and riding on a bus back to Heathrow Airport, I found myself backing away from the fullness of the moment.

Then, however, came the "yet" moment—the moment when I glimpsed the reality that God remains at work with us and, in truth, "on" us. The "yet" leaped out from seeing my father's name, William Hill, whose abiding and healing presence I had begun to dismiss—not able to grasp and hold the sacredness of the moment. Yet, God in his playful mercy refused to let me get away with any such dismissal. With what I believe to be a Spirit-inspired glance down a London street, I again was placed in the presence of William Hill. How could I not laugh about such a wily and persistent God, filled with an abundance of "yets" and ready to use them on behalf of all God's children on the occasion of their need?

One further note of postlude. A year or so after returning to the States, I happened to be glancing through a copy of Newsweek magazine. By chance, I noticed an article (or perhaps it was even a brief letter to the editor) that made a reference to betting odds being established on some upcoming event in the United Kingdom. I cannot recall the exact nature of the future occurrence; perhaps it had to do with which name might be adopted for a royal baby or, alternatively who was the betting favorite to finish atop the English Premier (Soccer) League. I cannot remember with certainty. What I do recall is that Newsweek cited the source and establisher of the odds—the prominent British betting and odds-making institution, William Hill. What icing on the cake for me—to discover that God had made use of a legal betting parlor as the foundation for my "yet" moment.

I conclude this chapter, on the disciples and their failings, then, with this personal conviction. If we latter-day pilgrims choose or even stumble our way into a discipleship stance of following, we will most assuredly fail—sometimes in petty or unintended ways and sometimes magnificently and maliciously. However, the God whom Mark opens to us remains at work on our behalf, hoping to reach us ever more profoundly. Mercifully, then, there are "yets" in our present and sacred hopes to be birthed in our futures. In the midst of our times of wayward wandering and incomprehension, God's "yets" remain. Always.

6

Choosing Not to Choose

In Mark's narrative the facing and making of choices is a central concern; often choices are about nothing less than life and death.

ABSENT ANY LEGAL CONNOTATIONS, the exercise of what I think of as "grandparental due diligence" has evolved over my several years of being called "G"—the name I've been assigned by my two grandchildren. My initial impressions of what grandparents do no doubt had their genesis in my early years and were heavily influenced by the fact that I was raised mostly by my maternal grandparents from age five to seventeen. In the earliest of those years I heard my Grandmother Anna speak about "seeing what the rest of the family is up to" or "wanting to keep up with the kids and grandkids." I learned that these words would soon be followed by activities such as telephone calls, taking a Sunday drive to visit the nearby relatives, and letters to those far enough away to be too expensive to call. (I am well aware that all of these activities are now considered "quaint.") Best of all, from my point of view, these words could also indicate that a large family reunion was in the works. At those gatherings I could count on there being numerous cousins to play with, a looser set of rules to abide by than usual as well as less adult supervision, and lots of good food to eat with little expectation that I would finish my vegetables or stop after having one small dessert. In the present age, seeing how the folks are doing or keeping up with the grandkids has been expanded—or, depending on one's perspective, reduced—to tweeting, texting, sharing one's Facebook page, skyping, and the sending of electronic greeting cards of all sorts. Phone calls are usually made only to the less technologically adept members of the family, "yours truly" included.

Given my history and personality, my favorite modality of grandparenting involves, whenever possible and affordable, the old-fashioned practice of bringing grandparent and grandchild into each other's actual presence. In my mind, such real life, face-to-face meetings offer a fuller and more nuanced picture of what's going on than any of the electronic options. While the information sent over the various electronic highways is certainly welcomed when in-the-flesh meetings are not feasible, my preference remains to visit our two grandchildren or have them visit us. On a recent visit to the western branch of our family, my wife Lyn and I had such a memorable face-to-face meeting with our grandson, Andy. Since this meeting resonates with the theme of this chapter—the centrality of choosing in Mark's good news—it is a good place to begin.

Lyn and I had arrived at our son's home the previous evening and were sitting in the den after finishing our breakfast. The parents had left for work and the day lay wide open for us three—Lyn, grandson Andy, and me. This was the first time in several months to be with Andy and we had long looked forward to our stay as a time to reinforce our shameless tendency to spoil him to the best of our grandparental abilities without any parental override anywhere in sight. (As an aside, there is an old saying in which I find much wisdom: "The reason grandparents and grandchildren get along so well is that they share a common enemy.")

As we sat in the den that morning, there was one problem Lyn and I had not anticipated as we finalized our plans to head out the door with Andy: Andy was still minus his shoes and socks and was deeply engrossed in play with his toys. Lyn and I were aware that the toys needed to be picked up before we left the house so that when the parents came home, it wouldn't look like we had let loose a tornado in the house. At the same time, we did not want to start our much-anticipated day by getting into a power struggle with Andy over breaking off his play to pick up his toys.

Lyn addressed our dilemma quite cleverly, I thought, when she proposed the following: "Andy, it's time to head out, so you've got a choice to make. You can put on your shoes and socks before you pick up your toys or you can do it after. Your choice." Andy stood up from his play and, collecting his thoughts for a moment, he looked at us both in a cool, disdainful manner. With a slight cocking of his head to one side he announced his firm choice: "I am choosing not to choose."

Exploring Mark's Story

In Mark's narrative drama—just as in the above snapshot from the drama of everyday life—the issue of choice occupies an important role in how the writer's story develops. In our dealings with Andy, prepared as we were with a full agenda of grandparental plans, Lyn and I felt stymied by this ordinary crisis over choice. For Mark, in contrast, the dilemmas arising from moments of choosing are of much greater consequence, and Mark weaves problem-laden scenes into the design of his Gospel at strategic moments. At these crucial moments, significant issues arise over whether and how a choice is made, either by Jesus, his disciples, or others in the story.

Choosing is no small matter for Mark—rarely a simple exercise of thought that works its way toward some semblance of rational decision or conclusion. Rather, Mark's account offers his readers a surprise, one often overlooked in his Gospel: that the act of choosing is to be understood as encompassing one's whole being. Consequently, when a person's choice is exercised in the face of a critical moment of decision, such choosing calls for the putting of one's whole heart and soul into the decision at hand. Alternatively and equally probable from Mark's point of view, a person can decide *not* to choose, thereby backing away from a compelling moment of truth. Mark's vision of choice, then, includes at its core the ability for someone—that is, anyone—to choose and act upon a most profound "yes" or "no" even in the kingdom of God. Choosing matters in Mark. To quote Shakespeare, "And thereby hangs a tale."[1]

The three focal texts in this chapter highlight Mark's emphasis on choosing and the exercise of will. The first two texts focus on choices that Jesus faces—one very early in his time in Galilee and the other much later, just before Jesus's arrest. The third text centers on the darkly ruthless choices made by several of Mark's most sinister characters.

In chapter 2, I noted Mark's use of the Greek verb *thelo*. This expanded look at *thelo* is necessary since the meaning of Mark's concept of choosing—along with the subsequent exercise of one's will that accompanies a choice—is the foundation for this chapter.

---

1. Shakespeare apparently found this expression quite useful as it appears in several of his plays, including *As You Like It*, *Othello*, *The Merry Wives of Windsor*, and *The Taming of the Shrew*.

- *Thelo* is translated in the NRSV by several words: to wish, to want, to intend, and to choose.
- In occupying a central place in the Markan narrative, the first feature of *thelo* is that it points Mark's readers to the incalculable significance of choosing as well as how the characters in Mark's story can and do make their choices—for good or for ill.
- The meaning of *thelo* in Mark goes well beyond any nonchalant whimsy of a wishful longing or vague aspiration. Rather, in Mark *thelo* connotes a vigorous longing, an internal aching for something with "everything you've got"—a determined yearning that leans toward an action or movement in a definitive direction. For Mark, *thelo*, to wish, to want, to intend, to choose, points toward crossing over from the realm of unrealized hope to accomplished reality.
- In sum, *thelo* points Mark's readers toward the drama of whether and how those who live in his pages choose. In choosing, they wager their core beings on a particular vision of reality.

Focal Text: Mark 1:35–45
Jesus Makes a Difficult Choice

³⁵In the morning, while it was still very dark, he got up and went out to a deserted place, and there he prayed. ³⁶And Simon and his companions hunted for him. ³⁷When they found him, they said to him, "Everyone is searching for you." ³⁸He answered, "Let us go on to the neighboring towns, so that I may proclaim the message there also; for that is what I came out to do." ³⁹And he went throughout Galilee, proclaiming the message in their synagogues and casting out demons.

⁴⁰A leper came to him begging him, and kneeling he said to him, "If you choose, you can make me clean." ⁴¹Moved with pity, Jesus stretched out his hand and touched him, and said to him, "I do choose. Be made clean!" ⁴²Immediately the leprosy left him, and he was made clean. ⁴³After sternly warning him he sent him away at once, ⁴⁴saying to him, "See that you say nothing to anyone; but go, show yourself to the priest, and offer for your cleansing what Moses commanded, as a testimony to them." ⁴⁵But he went out and began to proclaim it freely, and to spread the word, so that Jesus could no longer go into a town openly, but stayed out in the country; and people came to him from every quarter.

The theme of choosing is introduced quite early in Mark's story as Jesus is in the midst of taking his first steps towards engaging God's people. Prior to Jesus's initial choosing, he has secured the services of his earliest followers, taught at the local synagogue in Capernaum, and accompanied Simon (Peter) and Andrew to their home. These actions have demonstrated for those around Jesus several abilities not normally expected from a young rabbi, just starting out: he possesses an authority that amazes the members of the synagogue; he silences and controls a demonic adversary, freeing a man from its control; he restores Simon's mother-in-law to full health, and by the close of the day, all of Capernaum has gathered outside the house pressing Jesus to heal and exorcise deep into the night.

With all these events as context, Jesus approaches, albeit unknowingly, his first moment of decision and choice.

Jesus in Capernaum: A Success or Under Threat?

John Dominic Crossan makes a case that our initial focal text is best viewed through the lens of societal and familial expectations about the work of healers in Jesus's time.[2] According to the accepted norms of the day, Jesus's actions would likely lead his contemporaries to identify him as a healer or exorcist of unclean spirits. Jesus has done what healers do to begin to establish themselves: gathered a group of followers to assist him in his work (1:16–20), enhanced his reputation and demonstrated his abilities by teaching and exorcising in the synagogue, leading to his fame spreading in the region (1:21–28). And he has healed Simon's (Peter's) mother-in-law as well as a multitude of sick and possessed residents of Capernaum (1:29–34).

Crossan asserts that because all these occurrences have coalesced around Jesus, members of the Mediterranean culture Jesus inhabited would expect him to take the additional necessary steps to establish a *healing practice* in the city of Capernaum. Jesus would locate himself in Peter's family home—the site of his recent remarkable and plentiful successes. Having stationed himself there, Jesus would await the further spread of his fame as a healer and exorcist through "the peasant grapevine."[3] When his reputation had increased to a sufficient degree,

---

2. Crossan, *Jesus*, 99–101.
3. Crossan, *Jesus*, 99.

Peter and other members of his family (who would be known to others in the area) would begin to shepherd all those seeking Jesus's services into the city. Once established, this work could be expected to support Jesus, his disciples, and various family members who were helping "broker" Jesus's services.[4] Our first insight, then, is that prior to 1:35 Mark's readers have naturally begun to view Jesus as a healer.

While Mark's contemporaries would likely expect that Mark's narrative is moving readers toward viewing the work of Jesus as healing and exorcism, *this is not the course Jesus follows.* Jesus heads in another direction. We begin to see this other path emerge when, in the middle of the night, Jesus leaves behind Simon's familial home and the exhilarating successes of the day to settle into a secluded, quiet place seeking communion with God through prayer. In the full Markan narrative there are three instances when Jesus "withdraws to pray alone"[5] (1:35, 6:46, and 14:32–39). Mark implies that these moments of prayer are Jesus's way of seeking help with the pressures and complexities presented by each situation. In 1:35, Jesus goes off on his own to be with the Holy. In this moment of quiet as Jesus is communing with God, Mark—ever the dramatist—has Simon and his companions interrupt Jesus's prayer time and, perhaps unintentionally, further complicate Jesus's situation.

The motivation of Simon and his companions as they set out to find Jesus is somewhat subtly stated by Mark. However, the NRSV translation begins to hint at the underlying truth about their actions—they are hunting for Jesus (1:36). Clifton Black makes a similar observation by calling attention to Mark's vocabulary of "searching" or "looking for". He enumerates ten instances in Mark's narrative that indicate that Jesus is being "searched for" or "sought." (The NRSV translation of the Greek is rendered variously, most often as "asking for" or "looking for.") Black asserts that "those searching for Jesus in Mark usually have hostile intentions."[6] I would further posit that in each of the "searching moments," Jesus is at risk or under a threat of some kind, either from his enemies or from those close to him. But what is the nature of the threat Jesus faces in 1:37?

Kelber suggests that the action of Simon and the others is an act of pursuit that arises not out of loyalty or concern for Jesus, who has gone

---

4. Crossan, *Jesus*, 100.
5. Williamson, *Mark*, 56.
6. Black, "The Gospel of Mark," note on Mark 1:37. As noted earlier, Black's list of ten occurrences of Jesus's being "sought" or "searched for" contains an incorrect reference to 16:1. The reference should be to 16:6.

missing in the night, but rather that they "wish, understandably enough, to repeat the glory of the past day."[7] Simon and the others hunt for Jesus, hoping to return him to Capernaum because they expect to profit from his healing talents. By having Jesus continue to employ his obvious and recently demonstrated gifts in Capernaum, they could all earn a respectable living doing a respectable thing right in Simon's hometown. And from the disciples' and the accepted societal perspective, this is how it is supposed to go, isn't it? Those who heal as many as Jesus has are supposed to become healers.

However, when his pursuers find Jesus and speak to him, saying "Everyone is *searching for* you" (1:37), Mark's readers are presented with a scene that signals the need for Jesus to be wary of a risk from those who seek to return him to town. In Jesus's reply to his pursuers' self-interested invitation to revisit the successes of the previous day and continue the promising and economically advantageous course that began to open up for them, Jesus demonstrates that he has rightfully discerned the threat he is under. Turning aside their vision for the future, he begins to spell out what he has prayerfully discerned as vital for the coming of the kingdom in the days that lie ahead.

With his words and actions in 1:38–39, Jesus demonstrates that he will not allow himself to be lured back to Capernaum. In contrast, he affirms that his ministry will be an itinerant one. He will be on the move, traveling widely and certainly not stationary in a single, specific location. He will travel to towns and geographic regions far beyond Capernaum's boundaries. He expects his work to reach a greater number of people, not to deal only with a single localized population. He himself will go out, making his way toward other folks, not expecting or requiring them to come to him. And most important, Jesus will claim his identity and shape his actions as one who is primarily focused on proclaiming. Note that Mark twice emphasizes that Jesus is intent on proclaiming (1:38–39) and uses a "for" (*gar*) clause to highlight Jesus's proclaiming identity and activity: "for that [proclaiming the good news message] is what I came out to do" (1:38). At the same time, we need only glance at 1:39 to see that Jesus does *not* forsake the activities of healing and exorcising; he continues these practices. But in 1:38 he reaffirms his initial orientation as a proclaimer (see Mark 1:14) and reclaims his primary identity in the face of competing and compelling pressures.

---

7. Kelber, *Mark's Story of Jesus*, 22.

And so, Jesus turns away a serious threat at the beginning of his ministry. It is not a threat to his physical safety, but rather to his understanding of what makes for the furtherance of God's arriving kingdom and the proclamation of the good news to people who need to hear it. So, Jesus—the one so recently claimed as God's Beloved—endures and overcomes the threat to his mission brought on by his successes. He sets a course toward the "the neighboring towns" intent once again to "proclaim the message there also, for [*gar*] that is what I came out to do" (1:38).

But then a leper approaches, speaking of a choosing Jesus can make. And the words of a country music classic come to mind: "Hello, Trouble. Come on in."[8]

A Complicated Choice: To Heal a Leper

What can be said of the leper who steps into Jesus's path in Mark 1:40? Mark introduces the leper in the following context: having arrived at a place of greater clarity after his prayerful encounter with God, Jesus is traveling throughout Galilee, visiting various towns and villages and actively engaging people through his reclaimed mission of proclaiming and exorcising. At this point, with Jesus in figurative mid-stride, the unclean stranger shows up and brings Jesus's journey to an abrupt and unanticipated halt.[9]

Several aspects of the leper's approach are noteworthy. First, it is the leper who approaches Jesus—a clear breach of the purity practices of Jesus's day. Second, the leper approaches Jesus "begging" (1:40). For Mark, when someone adopts a begging posture with Jesus, a sense of helplessness, powerlessness, and even near collapse is implied; those begging Jesus are desperate (e.g., 5:10, 5:12, 5:17, 5:18, and 8:22). Third, while the leper begs, his words to Jesus connote a longing and even a partial certainty. He speaks his conviction: "you can make me clean" (1:40). He shows no hint of wavering or uncertainty about Jesus's power or ability to act.

However, what is at issue here is not Jesus's power or ability to restore, but whether Jesus will choose to do so: "If you choose, you can make me clean" (1:40). There is a decision to be made and the making of it cannot be compelled by the leper or assumed by Mark's readers. It is a choice only Jesus can make.

---

8. Orville Couch and Eddie McDuff, "Hello Trouble," 1962.
9. See chapter 4 about the purity code and its impact on those who lived under it.

So it is that Mark brings us to a moment of decision for Jesus. Just when things have been going along smoothly and successfully; just as Jesus has reclaimed his primary identity and vocation as proclaimer, despite the expectations and pressures to the contrary; just after he has prayerfully escaped the sirens of growing fame and security—here a further dilemma arises in the person of an unclean, impure leper. The leper kneels before Jesus as a solitary, isolated man, an outcast living on the fringe of his society. With his impurity and the boldness of his words, he stands as an impediment in Jesus's way. As we shall see, life has just gotten much more complicated for Jesus. But Mark is never one to imply that being God's Beloved is easy.[10]

As Mark presents this scene, there are several layers of complication for Jesus. When the leper appears, blocks Jesus's path, and speaks about a choice Jesus faces, Jesus is compelled to consider whether he will touch and make clean the one positioned at his feet.[11] One problem is that Jesus's newly reaffirmed plans for proclamation may be at risk if he chooses to touch the leper. Under the strictures of the purity code, if Jesus, an observant Jew, were to touch the leper, he himself would become contaminated. He would then remain unclean until a priest determined him to have been restored to purity. Such a determination would likely be made after social isolation for a lengthy period of time, thereby delaying Jesus's plans. Although Jesus's touch might prove restorative to the leper, it would in the same moment prove contaminating to Jesus. In forcing isolation and delay upon Jesus, his touch would endanger his plans to proclaim the good news.

---

10. I have remained indebted over the years to Dr. James L. Mays for planting in my mind and spirit the interpretive seeds of this text, Mark 1:35–45. Many of the themes I raise in this exploration grow out of Dr. Mays's instruction of a young seminarian years ago as I listened and marveled as he taught. It is largely through his teaching about this specific text that I first began to envision the possibility that ancient and dusty languages and cultures could carry the power and depth to enliven and inspirit readers into every present age.

11. As readers consider the role of the leper as he enters the story in Mark 1:40 and more especially why his presence and few words constitute such a dilemma for Jesus, brief mention of two pieces of background can guide exploration. First, certain aspects of the purity code underlie this encounter between Jesus and the leper; see chapter 4 for discussion of the purity code. Second, in Mark the act of healing frequently involves physical touch between two parties. This practice is without doubt part of the intense drama played out between Jesus and the one who begs and kneels in front of him in 1:40.

Another layer of complication emerges when readers note that if Jesus is contaminated after touching the leper, he will be isolated *from the very people he needs to be with*—those whom he has identified in his prayer time as most immediately needing to hear about the inbreaking of God's kingdom. Jesus urgently wants those living in "the neighboring towns" (1:38) to hear his message, but it will not happen if he is cut off from them.

A third layer of complication arises around the issue of need. Embedded in the declaration of the leper to Jesus is an implied question: "Whose need will you choose to meet—mine or yours?" If Mark had presented the leper as a more talkative sort, I imagine the leper might have said,

> What will you choose, Jesus? I see the fire of clear purpose in your eyes and your firm intent to proclaim God's good news to as many as possible. As for me, I kneel before you as an isolated and solitary man with no special standing or attractiveness. The only thing I have left to call my own is my very real need—the need to be made clean and restored as a member of my human community, free once again to live with my family and friends. Without doubt, your need, your drive, your motivation differs from mine. But I ask you—to whose need will you attend in this moment? Will it be your understandable and even noble need to proclaim to the many? Or will it be my need to be restored? I am certain, Jesus, that if you choose, you can make me clean. But what will you choose? For whom will you choose?

The interruption by the leper is beyond troublesome to Jesus. Who the leper is and what he does and says threaten to throw all of Jesus's prayerfully conceived plans into disarray. Depending on his choosing, Jesus could face contamination and delay, being cut off from those he most needs to go to, and having his identity and function as the proclaimer subverted. And perhaps worst of all is that he faces a choice between two very legitimate needs—his own and those of another of God's children.

There is no easy choice here. No easy choice at all.

Jesus Responds with Pity or Anger? A Variant Reading

At the point in Mark's story when Jesus is preparing to respond to the leper's words and choose, we pause to consider a technical issue, a "variant reading," that emerges in 1:41. This illuminating step will help us to grasp the richness of Mark's story, not only as it relates to how things turn out for the leper, but also as it relates to what Jesus learns from this encounter and the maturity that comes to him as a result of it.

I begin with an introductory explanation I found in the *HarperCollins Bible Dictionary*:

> The originals of the books that comprise the Hebrew OT [Old Testament] and the books of the Greek NT [New Testament] have not survived. We do, however, have very old copies of the original books, which are called "manuscripts" (MSS) because they were handwritten. Moreover, both OT and NT books were translated into other languages of the ancient Near East and copies of these early translations, called "versions" (VSS), are available to us. Through the science of textual criticism, biblical scholars have been able to establish rather accurate texts for both the OT and the NT books. These are available to us today in printed editions.[12]

The term "variant reading" is used when referring to a circumstance encountered by biblical scholars and translators in their work. In studying multiple copies of ancient manuscripts or versions grouped together because of similar but not identical texts, researchers have uncovered and catalogued the differences that exist between the documents. These differences are known as "variant readings." Most textual variations are minor and can be easily accounted for. For example, a "scribal error" is thought to have occurred when a copyist of an older and deteriorating manuscript made a mistake in hand-copying a "fresh" identical copy of the older document.

Markan materials are those documents widely believed to be authored by Mark or closely associated with Mark. Variations are found in these multiple Markan documents, just as with other biblical manuscripts, and most variations are inconsequential or easily explained. But in Mark 1:41 scholars have identified a variant reading of greater than normal significance and impact on the writer's intended direction for this story of Jesus and the leper. Some Markan documents (or "ancient authorities") indicate that in his response to the leper's words, Jesus was "moved with pity." This reading appears in the NRSV translation of 1:41. However, according to Black, "Other ancient authorities read *anger*."[13] Moreover, Black adds, "Pity . . . appears in most ancient manuscripts, though the

---

12. "Texts, Versions, Manuscripts, Editions," in *HarperCollins Bible Dictionary*, 1113.
13. Black, "The Gospel of Mark," textual note *o*.

harder, variant reading *anger* (text note *o*) may be the original."[14] In 1:41, then, the task faced by students and scholars has been to figure out which of the two readings—pity or anger—is the more authentic rendering of Mark's story.

The matter is unresolved among scholars. Both pity and anger are considered responsible alternative readings of Mark's work, and each reading has its supporters.[15] What is beyond dispute is that it makes a profound difference to the story's meaning whether Jesus responds to the leper from pity or anger. What is at stake here—near the very beginning of Mark's story—is how the reader comes to view Jesus, his words and actions, as well as what transpires for both the leper and Jesus over the remainder of Mark's story. Although our focal text, taken from the NRSV, shows the word pity at 1:41, I make sense of the episode by reading it through the lens of the anger variant.[16]

14. Black, "The Gospel of Mark," note on Mark 1:41.

15. A concise but illuminating look at the complexities involved in the analysis and interpretation of 1:41—one that considers both readings—is found in Williamson, *Mark*, 58–61. Williamson's commentary on this passage serves to reassure readers that decisions about important differences located in various biblical manuscripts and versions are considered thoughtfully and carefully. Every effort is made to eliminate the personal and or religious biases of those studying and making judgments about biblical texts. Obviously, complete agreement between scholars is not always the outcome in such cases, but decisions about textual variants as well as other issues in the arena of biblical scholarship are not carelessly or lightly made. Williamson's discussion reflects such care. To my albeit limited knowledge no scholar dedicated to the study of ancient texts has based their decisions about Mark 1:41 on a flip of a coin!

16. An additional clue that helps make sense of 1:35–45 is a passage much later in Mark's narrative, 14:3–9, the story of Jesus's anointing in Bethany. While this account lies outside the direct focus of this chapter, it is worth noting that the two passages, 1:35–45 and 14:3–9, are the only Markan stories that mention both "leper" and "anger." Taken together, these texts signal Mark's readers to consider the widely separated scenes as related. Employing our metaphor of Mark's Gospel as a tapestry where various thematic threads weave their way throughout the entirety of Mark's literary structure, one thematic thread woven into these two accounts is Jesus's process of maturing. These two stories outline a progression in Jesus's self-understanding and further realization of what a Beloved Son of God is to do in his time on this earth. The greater level of maturity and understanding Jesus demonstrates in 14:3–9 emerges as readers note something Jesus has learned since his encounter with the leper of 1:35–45, namely, that God's purpose of proclamation will continue long after Jesus's approaching execution. His physical presence may cease, but proclamation of the good news will continue in the self-giving deeds of those like the woman who lavishly anoints him. By 14:9 the Son of God is admittedly as good as dead; with the anointing, he is prepared for burial and can go to his tomb, trusting God to finish God's work of proclamation begun in him.

Let us return to our analysis of 1:35–45, at the point in Mark's narrative where the leper suddenly appears and poses a dilemma about choosing for Jesus. It is a choosing fraught with trouble. If Jesus chooses to cleanse the leper, the outcome for Jesus appears likely to be an interruption and delay, perhaps lengthy, to his recently clarified and reclaimed purpose, mission, and identity. If Jesus chooses not to cleanse the leper, the outcome for the leper is a lost chance for restoration to a meaningful life.

The central observation Mark invites us to make in 1:41 is that, even while angry, Jesus gives answer to what it is he will choose; he exercises his will to move toward this contaminated and contaminating one, touching him and saying, "I do choose. Be made clean!" (1:41). But why is anger essential to this specific instance of choosing? The anger need not be seen as a hostile reaction toward the leper himself; rather, Jesus is angry at the situation in which he is confronted with a hard, hard choice. He must choose between his own legitimate needs and those of the man who begs before him. When the leper approaches him and speaks, all of Jesus's resolve and forward movement is at risk again. There is much in this meeting for Jesus to be angry about.

The Dilemma of Doing God's Will

With our first focal text, Mark presents Jesus as beginning to wrestle with a profound theological (and personal) question: what guides him as he seeks to live out the will of God on this earth? In the first half of 1:35–45, it appears that Jesus has successfully answered this question and has set off on a sacred journey of proclaiming to the many who need to hear of God's good news. All this is a noble enterprise, discerned and blessed in a time of prayer. At the same time, his chosen path is radically at odds with the norms of the day, which push Jesus toward identity and function of healer rather than proclaimer.

Through the leper, Mark presents Jesus's dilemma of doing God's will even more keenly. His story invites readers to ponder, along with Jesus, the following question: When seeking to live out God's will, what is one to do when the need of another clashes with one's own—for example, when the need of the leper to be cleansed conflicts with the essential need of the Beloved Son who is destined to proclaim? The answer is incarnated by Jesus in Gethsemane (our second focal text) as he again wrestles and prays, and finds his own profound longing to live caught up in yet another excruciating moment of decision. But it is here in 1:35–45 that Mark plants a seed about choosing whose need is to be met. This seed will grow to fruition in Mark's emphasis on giving one's self for the sake of another as the highest expression of doing God's will.

I want to share an image that has taken shape for me during the time I have spent with this passage. It falls within the realm of speculation, so I offer it cautiously. I imagine the leper as he kneels before Jesus, begging. I hear him speak his words about choosing and his conviction about what Jesus can do. I see an intense flash in Jesus's eyes as he reaches to touch this man. I hear his words: "I do choose. Be made clean!" (1:41). And I imagine that Jesus speaks in a low growl, through clenched teeth.

Jesus Drives the Healed Leper Away

We have followed Mark's buildup to Jesus's choice in 1:41, and our natural expectation might be that in 1:42 the leper is immediately made clean. But Mark does more than that; he not only portrays Jesus as choosing to heal the leper, but also surprisingly portrays him as acting in a manner that indicates Jesus's desire to be rid of this man. Quickly.

Note what happens in 1:43–44:

- Jesus "sternly" warns the cleansed man (1:43). (Or, literally, "snorts" in his presence.)
- Jesus drives the cleansed man away. The Greek verb translated in the NRSV as "sent away" (1:43) is the same verb used by Mark to describe Jesus being driven by the Spirit into the wilderness (1:12), as well as Jesus driving buyers and sellers out of the temple (11:15). The verb connotes a determination and forcefulness with which the sending away occurs.
- Jesus drives him away "at once" (1:43). Mark notes that the driving away happens immediately. There is no pause between the cleansing and Jesus telling the man to move on.
- Jesus directs the cleansed man to "say nothing to anyone" (1:44) except the priest. (The priest, as previously mentioned, is the one authorized under provisions of the purity code to declare leprosy gone after an unclean person has undertaken a course of ritual sacrifices.[17] Going to a priest would thereby open the way for a person

17. See Williamson, *Mark*, 60–61, for a brief but helpful description of the

cleansed of contamination to be restored to family and community.) It can be argued that Jesus here proposes silence for the healed one as the best way out of the mess Jesus finds himself in, brought to full flower by the choice he has made.

Although Jesus has chosen to cleanse this man and has done so purposefully and emphatically, he now wants this man out of his sight and hearing. He seeks no further contact and does not invite him to follow as a disciple as he recently did with others (see 1:16–20). He does not linger in conversation with the cleansed man, reflecting on the meaning of his recent experience. Jesus wants to be done with him and so sends him, drives him, compels him on his way.

In my interpretive judgment, Jesus's actions in 1:35–45 make more sense when Jesus's motivation is interpreted as anger rather than pity or compassion. Jesus chooses to cleanse the leper, but he appears far from pleased or tender in the doing of it. Rather, in 1:43–44 Jesus's irritation, frustration, anger seem to hang in the air. Jesus does not relish the choice he has made. If Jesus is motivated by anger, his actions can be interpreted as a last-ditch—even frantic—effort to preserve his own recently reclaimed identity and practice as proclaimer. It is possible that Mark portrays Jesus as scrambling to come up with a plan to salvage his mission, which seems on the brink of collapse after his meeting of the leper. In my reading, such an interpretation does justice to the text. Jesus has no time to get bogged down by an absolutist compliance to the purity code and no desire to be sent into isolation. To the contrary, Jesus is on fire to move forward. He is bent on proclaiming.

And so, apparently on the spur of the moment, Jesus handles the dilemma brought on by his touch, which cleansed the leper but contaminated Jesus. Jesus directs the cleansed man to go quickly and quietly to a priest and be declared free of leprosy. Just prior to sending him to the priest, however, Jesus admonishes him firmly to "say nothing to anyone" (1:44). If the restored one can just hold his tongue, Jesus can continue on his way proclaiming; with no talk circulating about any meeting between the two, Jesus can maneuver his way around the restrictions called for by the purity code. It is a plan that could lead to a good result for both parties. The leper would get what he needs because of Jesus' choice and Jesus could continue on his way proclaiming.

---

importance of such ritual cleansing.

The problem is the plan begins to disintegrate, Mark implies, almost as soon as Jesus and the leper are out of each other's sight. The leper simply cannot just "say nothing," keeping the lid on his good news. Certainly this is understandable, for his life has been handed back to him; he is now fully restored—religiously, socially, and culturally. How can he keep quiet when such an event has taken place? And so, the leper, who apparently does not seek out a priest, goes out and begins to "proclaim it freely, and to spread the word" (1:44). He is too enlivened and exuberant to do otherwise.

Proclamation Happens Despite All

Predictably, consequences follow. Jesus is no longer able to go to towns and villages but instead has to relocate himself to the country, that is, the desert places. Just as Jesus feared, he has now become the one isolated, cut off from those to whom he had hoped to proclaim. With this development, a Markan reversal appears to be complete: the restored one goes out and proclaims while the contaminated Jesus goes into isolation in the desert.

Jesus would not have expected people to gather in the desert to be proclaimed to—not in such a desolate place and in the presence of such a recently contaminated teacher. But, Mark says, the unexpected does happen. Mark closes out 1:35–45 with a jaw-dropping stunner, in the form of a simple, concise statement the import of which can be easily overlooked: "and people came to him from every quarter" (1:45).

What are the implications of these few words?

- Despite all that failed to go as expected in 1:35–45, Jesus ends up surrounded by the very people he had hoped to be with—those who most need to hear the proclamation of God's arriving kingdom and their place in it.
- Despite Jesus's inability to come to the people, the people come to him. They come not just from the local surroundings but from far afield.
- Despite Jesus's expectation that he would be proclaimer, it is another who proclaims because he just cannot help himself. And although the leper's proclamation, one that he could not contain, creates trouble for Jesus, it also inspires others in their own dire straits to go, see,

hear and be with this Jesus. For here is one who has had the courage to choose, choosing not exclusively or even primarily to meet his own needs, but choosing to attend to and meet the needs of others.

Mark leaves us, then, with this surprising conclusion to 1:35–45. As first narrated in 1:14–15, God's purpose that the good news be proclaimed is accomplished in our first focal text, despite all obstacles placed in its path. Proclamation does not happen in ways the Markan Jesus imagined, for he is not the sole proclaimer here, but happen it does. In this seminal story, placed near the beginning of Jesus's Galilean journey, proclamation by the restored one is set in motion as the freeing result of a difficult and rending choice faced and made by God's Beloved. And as Mark's narrative unfolds, this first episode of choosing plants the seeds for other choices of self-giving for the sake of "the other." The significance of choosing in Mark's Gospel is firmly established by Jesus's costly and angry reply, "I do choose. Be made clean!" (1:41).

Choosing—even angry choosing—matters in Mark. Both lives and being enlivened depend on it.

Focal Text: Mark 14:32–42
The Costly Choosing of God

³²They went to a place called Gethsemane; and he said to his disciples, "Sit here while I pray." ³³He took with him Peter and James and John, and began to be distressed and agitated. ³⁴And he said to them, "I am deeply grieved, even to death; remain here, and keep awake." ³⁵And going a little farther, he threw himself on the ground and prayed that, if it were possible, the hour might pass from him. ³⁶He said, "Abba, Father, for you all things are possible; remove this cup from me; yet, not what I want, but what you want." ³⁷He came and found them sleeping; and he said to Peter, "Simon, are you asleep? Could you not keep awake one hour? ³⁸Keep awake and pray that you may not come into the time of trial; the spirit indeed is willing, but the flesh is weak." ³⁹And again he went away and prayed, saying the same words. ⁴⁰And once more he came and found them sleeping, for their eyes were very heavy; and they did not know what to say to him. ⁴¹He came a third time and said to them, "Are you still sleeping and taking your rest? Enough! The hour has come; the Son of Man is betrayed into the hands of sinners. ⁴²Get up, let us be going. See, my betrayer is at hand."

Our second focal text, later in Mark's narrative, takes place immediately after the Lord's Supper and before the betrayal by Judas. Of all the moments of high drama and suspense in Mark's narrative, the portrait of Jesus wrestling in Gethsemane is second in intensity and importance only to the resurrection scene at 16:1–8.[18] Here in 14:32–42, Mark brings Jesus to the crucible wherein he faces the choice that matters most to both Jesus and Mark's readers, including us. It is the moment that Jesus as the Son of Man has been foretelling ever since he began to be clear and specific about his own end—that in Jerusalem he expected to be killed and afterwards undergo a "raising," an outcome still ill-defined. All of us can only wait and watch as Jesus confronts his most costly choice of all. His life, his physical existence on this earth, hangs in the balance. This moment in Mark's account will either validate or give the lie to Jesus's courageous teachings and intention to fulfill his identity as the Son of Man. As his enemies close in and his disciples flee, will Jesus find the capacity to live true to who he is to be: the one who trusts God enough to undergo great suffering, be killed, and be raised?[19] The Gethsemane episode "raises the question whether Jesus will live out the truth of the Gospel of the Kingdom which is contingent upon his suffering and death. The Kingdom itself is at stake in Gethsemane."[20]

Choosing and Betrayal

To understand the profound significance of the issue of Jesus's choice in Gethsemane is to realize that 14:32–42 is part of a recurring theme of betrayal. Several questions about betrayal emerge from Mark's narrative:

What Does Mark Mean by Betrayal?

The Greek root word Mark uses is translated by the NRSV as "betrayed"[21] or "handed over."[22] (The RSV sometimes translates the Greek as deliv-

---

18. See chapter 9 for a detailed consideration of 16:1–8.
19. See the three passion predictions: 8:31, 9:31, 10:33–34.
20. Kelber, "The Hour of the Son of Man," 46.
21. See e.g., 3:19, 9:31, 14:10, 14:11, 14:18, 14:21, and 14:41.
22. See e.g., 10:33 (twice), 15:1, and 15:15.

ered or "delivered to."[23]) This word connotes not only an act of disloyalty or broken trust but more vividly an act that indicates that Jesus's physical body and welfare are placed in the literal hands of a variety of his enemies. When Jesus is betrayed, what is at stake is not merely a matter of bruised feelings or emotional and psychologically distressed states of mind; rather, his person is given over to others who act on Jesus's body in physically assaultive, pain-inducing ways.

Who Commits the Betrayal?

Mark leaves no doubt that Judas Iscariot is foremost among Jesus's betrayers. At first mention, Mark names Judas as "Judas Iscariot, who betrayed him" (3:19).[24] Mark further indicates Judas's status as the driving force behind the betrayal by noting that Judas "went to the chief priests in order to betray him to them" (14:10). Moreover, making the matters crystal clear for his readers, Mark has Jesus refer to Judas as "my betrayer" (14:42). In addition, though, Mark implicates a vast array of others who participate in the process of handing Jesus over, passing him on to a variety of other adversaries. Each of the adversaries contributes to and escalates the brutality and humiliation enacted on Jesus. Consequently, readers are enabled to recognize that Jesus's betrayal is progressive and cumulative, beginning with his being handed over by Judas "into the hands of sinners" (14:41),[25] that is, a crowd sent by the chief priests, scribes, and elders to arrest Jesus and bring him to them. These authorities in turn, after a midnight trial that includes the "whole council" (14:55), hand Jesus over to Pilate, a Roman (gentile) with life-and-death powers. Pilate in turn, when he is finished with Jesus, hands him over to crucifixion through the agency of his military troops under the command of an unnamed centurion. The centurion sees to the execution, the culmination of the betrayal. And so, from Mark's perspective,

---

23. See RSV translation of 10:33, 15:1, and 15:15.

24. Borg and Crossan suggest that Judas Iscariot is singled out as the betrayer because of his position as one of Jesus's inner core of disciples. Of all of Jesus's adversaries/enemies, he is the only one who is "one of the twelve" (*The Last Week*, 106–7).

25. In light of Jesus's compassionate regard for "sinners" as seen in Mark 2:15–17, the sinners mentioned here need not be viewed as an especially heinous group of folks. Rather, it is possible that Mark's construction of this arrest scene could be his ironic indication that even those to whom Jesus was consistently attentive and compassionate were among those handing Jesus along—as did others—toward his passion.

the betrayal—the progressive handing over of Jesus from one group to the next—originates with Judas but does not end with him.

Who is Betrayed?

The obvious answer is Jesus. But to say that and nothing more is to risk overlooking Mark's sharper focus here. For it is not merely Jesus as Mark's main character in the story who is betrayed; it is Jesus in his identity and being as the Son of Man. In our focal text, Jesus says as the moment of arrest is upon him, "The hour has come; the Son of Man is betrayed into the hands of sinners" (14:42). Prior to this statement in the section of material known as the Way (Road) of Discipleship (8:22—10:52), Mark makes seven references to the Son of Man.[26] Three of these lie at the heart of the three forecasts Jesus makes regarding his own fate—8:31, 9:31, and 10:33. In these passion predictions, there emerge only three explicitly stated commonalities. There is Jesus's self-designation as the Son of Man. There is reference to the Son of Man as "killed." There is reference to his rising again after three days. Even prior to the Gethsemane passage, then, Mark lays the foundation for his readers that it is Jesus as the Son of Man who is to be executed and after three days rise. It is this being-killed-and-rising Jesus who is the betrayed one. No "other" Jesus can fulfill Mark's narrative design or his christological framework.

What is the Human Purpose Behind the Betrayal?

The human purpose that lies as substrate for the betrayal is the collective efforts of many to kill Jesus. Mark uses two different verbs to delineate this purpose, both of which carry the meaning of ending someone's life.[27] From early in his narrative, then, Mark indicates that the moti-

---

26. These seven are found in 8:31, 8:38, 9:9, 9:12, 9:31, 10:33, and 10:45. These seven make up half of the fourteen instances when Mark has Jesus self-designate as the Son of Man.

27. Verses containing forms of these two verbs are 3:6 (where the NRSV translation is "destroy"), 8:31, 9:31, 10:34, 11:18, and 14:1. Note also that those gathered for Jesus's trial include the entire Jewish council (the Sanhedrin) and that "*All of them* condemned him as deserving death" (14:64, emphasis added). Later, the chief priests stir up the crowd gathered before Pilate and the crowd shouts twice for Jesus to be crucified. Readers can safely assume that members of the crowd knew that crucifixion was a death sentence for Jesus and was a form of execution as cruel, painful, slow, and

vation driving the betrayers is the prospect of Jesus's death. In Mark's account, Jesus is handed over for the explicit purpose of execution.

Choosing: The Two Ways

One important Markan theme, the choice between two ways of being, holds particular relevance for the Gethsemane episode. I draw on the work of David Rhoads, who describes Mark's vision of the Two Ways, that is, two orientations by which humans may live their lives.[28]

Rhoads points to a significant moment in Mark's story, at 8:31–33, where there is a brief but compelling glimpse of Jesus—the Son of Man—who chooses in Gethsemane to walk the path toward execution. This foreshadowing emerges at the precise point where Mark pivots the direction of his Gospel. It comes when Jesus makes his very first declaration that he is to suffer at the hands of his adversaries and then be killed (8:31–33). Upon hearing Jesus's prediction, Peter makes vigorous efforts to stop Jesus from talking in what the disciple believes to be a fevered or nonsensical manner, especially in light of Peter's just declared affirmation of Jesus as the Messiah (8:29). But Jesus turns the tables and stops Peter from speaking, pointedly saying to Peter, "You are setting your mind not on divine things but on human things" (8:33). With these words, the Markan Jesus delineates two clashing life orientations, the Two Ways, and he foreshadows that he and those who follow him will inevitably and continually confront these two ways of living. When the clash of orientations comes, choices will need to be made between the "things" of humankind and the "things" of God. With his account of Peter's rebuke, then, Mark suggests that more life-shaping choices lie ahead.

The first Way is characterized by self-orientation and a self-serving approach in all matters. The goal of this Way is to obtain and perpetuate "status, power and security."[29] It is a fear-driven approach to life and its ultimate expression occurs when its followers remove or destroy any obstacle or person that stands in the way of a goal. The disciples are susceptible to the first Way.

---

humiliating as any Rome had devised. It was a process intending not only to end a life, but to obliterate, negate, and crush both body and soul, as well as intimidate onlookers.

28. Rhoads, "Losing Life for Others," 358–69.
29. Rhoads, "Losing Life for Others," 360.

The disciples have a strong desire to serve themselves. In contrast to self-serving values that will lead only to a life of competition and domination, Jesus is showing them relationships of mutual serving. But the disciples see honor as worth, power as privilege, wealth as blessing, and security as salvation. For that culture, serving was not noble or honorable but the work of slaves and women. So rather than serve those below them, they want to secure their own privilege and honor.[30]

In contrast, the second Way is characterized as "God-centered."[31] In enabling such a way of living, Mark indicates, God draws to God's self those willing to set aside their own interests and needs as well as the pursuit of security, power, and status. While anxiety and fear may be experienced by followers of the second Way, trust in God can supply the courage to hold these fears at bay, at least on occasion. This second Way is to be lived in the manner of a servant or slave, or as Rhoads puts it, "to be one who gives up the status and power that one has, or feels entitled to, on behalf of those with less power and status."[32]

In my view, Mark further implies that the outcome of this selfless path is twofold: that those attended to and cared for will be set free, and those who choose such a path of service and self-giving will find themselves saved, made whole, possessing the courage and capacity to live meaningfully—certain of God's enveloping benevolence and challenging presence, and assured of their own standing as Beloved sons and daughters.[33]

In the Gethsemane passage Jesus faces a stark choice reflective of choosing between the Two Ways. In the Garden, he will either exercise his will to choose self-preservation in its most literal form, or he will choose to trust God and remain God-dependent in the most extreme, vulnerable, and excruciating circumstances of his life. In Mark, then, choosing between the Two Ways, that is, the things of God and the things of humankind, is not for the Jesus of Gethsemane a choice between abstract conceptual constructs. Rather, as the most prominent and consequential choice Jesus faces and makes in Mark's narrative, his choosing is indeed a matter of life and death. And not just anyone's life and death, but his very own.

30. Rhoads et al., *Mark as Story*, 127.
31. Rhoads, "Losing Life for Others," 363.
32. Rhoads, "Losing Life for Others," 362.
33. Borg, *Jesus*, 191–223. Borg offers an additional exploration of the two ways.

The Crucial Choice: Jesus's Struggle in the Garden

In beginning our closer look at the Gethsemane account, readers are to recall that immediately prior to their accompanying Jesus into the Garden, the disciples had sworn loyalty to Jesus and vehemently declared that they would even die with him if necessary (see 14:26–31). They refuse to hear of Jesus's prediction that they will all soon abandon him, predicting instead their own courage to stand with him.

Jesus's Purposeful Search for God

Jesus has a specific purpose for going to Gethsemane: he needs to pray. In Mark's account when Jesus withdraws for a time of solitary prayer these are moments of great consequence. In each of these prayer-filled times, Jesus finds himself subject to mounting pressures and complexities that arise from his life situation. Here in 14:32–42, Jesus appears to have realized that he is to be betrayed by one of his trusted inner circle and that this handing over will in turn lead to being abandoned by the remainder of his core group despite their oaths to the contrary. Even more traumatic is his recognition that he is moving ever closer to his own passion and death. As Jesus enters the Garden, then, and as he has done in the past, Jesus seeks a profound and personal dialogue with God. With such an engagement he hopes to wrestle through the agonizing difficulties that are closing in on him.

In moving into the Garden to commune with God through prayer, Jesus does so in three steps. Initially, not yet ready to be alone, Jesus takes with him the full complement of disciples. Soon, however, he selects the three he is closest to—Peter, James, and John—to accompany him deeper into the Garden. It is with these three that he begins to speak of his debilitating distress and grief. Then, even as Jesus prepares for his third movement even deeper into the Garden for his time alone with God, he remains reluctant to separate completely from them and asks that they remain nearby, staying alert during his period of struggle. Mark presents Jesus as both moving ever closer to his time with God and at the same time needing some measure of companionship and human connection to surround and undergird him as he prays.

Jesus's Solitary Prayer: Agony, Pleading, and Trust

Mark leaves no doubt that Jesus's time in Gethsemane is one of agonizing, even crushing intensity. In the presence of the three accompanying disciples Jesus becomes "distressed and agitated" (14:33). Myers writes that with this vocabulary, Mark is indicating a time of "profound inner turmoil" for Jesus.[34] He adds, "The language of 14:33 is very strong: he 'shudders in distress' . . . and 'anguishes' . . . Jesus is facing his 'destiny' not with contemplative detachment, but with genuine human terror. There is no romance in martyrdom, only in martyrologies."[35]

The words Jesus uses to speak to the three as he moves farther into the Garden show the depth of his suffering. While the NRSV reflects the grief that sweeps over Jesus in 14:34, the Greek text points readers to an additional reality—that this anguish and sadness is penetrating Jesus's very "soul."[36] When Jesus pours out his most profound anguish, saying that his soul (i.e., his very center) is close to dying, Mark has led his readers to a portrait of Jesus "shaken to the core,"[37] or as Kelber puts it, Jesus is "on the verge of retracting his passion predictions and close upon disavowing his vocation as the suffering Son of Man."[38] At no previous moment in Mark's account has Jesus been as vulnerable, near the point of abject depletion. In Gethsemane, he has come to the full existential awareness that his determined and divinely affirmed journey to Jerusalem will likely mean the death of him.[39] Unless the impossible becomes possible.

In 14:35 Mark summarizes Jesus's prayer, and in 14:36 he provides a word-for-word account of it. Then, with 14:39, Mark helps his readers realize that Jesus is offering up the identical prayer for the third time as he prays. Jesus's struggle is so ferocious that he finds his prayer pouring from his being over and over, mantra-like. Moreover, the choice between the divine things and human things appears to be doing battle in Jesus's

---

34. Myers, *Binding the Strong Man*, 366.

35. Myers, *Binding the Strong Man*, 366. Kelber comments similarly: The two verbs Mark employs for distressed and agitated "portray a Jesus who is overcome by anguish and horror in the face of death" (Kelber, "The Hour of the Son of Man," 43).

36. Black, "The Gospel of Mark," note on Mark 14:34.

37. Myers, *Binding the Strong Man*, 366.

38. Kelber, "The Hour of the Son of Man," 44.

39. I view Mark's story of Jesus's transfiguration in 9:2–8 as God's affirmation of the path Jesus has set for himself in his first passion prediction, 8:31—9:1.

mind, heart, and soul in this crucial moment. A reader may even imagine a shroud of internal conflict and tension over the prone Jesus, his body pressed hard against the earth where he has thrown it.

As for the content of the prayer, several themes stand out.

The cup and the hour. In 14:35, 14:36, and 14:41, Mark uses both the "cup" and the "hour," metaphorically to refer to Jesus's suffering and death, which is hard upon him. Mark makes clear that Jesus neither seeks nor desires such an end but trusts that it is possible for God to bring about an outcome that avoids his suffering and execution. He prays with his whole being that the "hour" pass and the "cup" be removed. Kelber observes succinctly: Jesus's "request for the passing of the hour and the removal of the cup has every indication of a desire to bypass the cross."[40]

Abba, Father. The first word Jesus prays is *Abba*, an Aramaic word meaning Father. Mark's use of *Abba* here heightens the pathos and poignancy in the Garden. Borg notes that this is the only use of *Abba* in the gospels and that in Jesus's day, it was used by children to address their father. He adds that *Abba* "is much like the English 'papa' or 'dah-dah.' But it is not simply the language of children; it was also used by adult children to address their father. The word is relational, familial, and intimate."[41] I see an additional layer of meaning in *Abba*. In my work as a pastoral counselor, I observed that in moments of extreme psychological distress and vulnerability, people often find their thinking and vocabulary reverting to an earlier time in their lives. In such moments, there is the distinct possibility that a verbal reaching out to or calling for a parent or close sibling can occur. Such a phenomenon is also well attested in film and literature where young soldiers *in extremis* call out for their Mama or Papa.

I and you. Mark includes verbatim Jesus's prayer to his *Abba* Father, the concluding portion of which is "yet, not what I want, but what you want" (14:36). He uses the personal, intimate, emphatic pronouns[42] here, both the "I," which refers to Jesus, and the "you," which refers to God.[43] In emphasizing the "I" of Jesus and the "you" of his *Abba* God, Mark reminds his readers that the two characters whose presence is

---

40. Kelber, "The Hour of the Son of Man," 43.
41. Borg, *Jesus*, 129.
42. Rhoads et al., *Mark as Story*, 10, 34.
43. I am indebted to John Carroll of Union Presbyterian Seminary in Richmond, Virginia for first alerting me to the importance of the pronouns in this passage. Carroll also alerted me to various resources on Mark and offered support and encouragement for my work. He provided the kind of shot in the arm a writer needs from time to time.

quintessentially required in this poignant and tension-filled scene are Jesus and God. All others have for the moment been moved to the sidelines. Jesus prays to live, hoping to avoid the suffering and dark end that awaits him. God, the source and advocate for all things divine, moves through his Beloved Jesus to offer the world One who is willing to give self for others, thereby enabling the possibility of liberation for all who choose to follow a Way similar to Jesus's. In 14:36, then, Jesus and his God are emphatically and fully present. We readers can only await the outcome of their intense communion in the Garden. Much hinges on it.

In the midst of Jesus's ongoing and urgently repeated prayer in our second focal text, we come to a second occasion wherein a costly choice faces God's Beloved. It is no accident that this Gethsemane choosing resonates with the emphasis on choosing (*thelo*) in our first focal text. In his meeting with the leper in 1:35–45 Jesus confronts a sudden and unanticipated choice to be made, one that is exquisitely difficult and even angering. Here in the Garden emerges a choosing with even higher stakes. In Gethsemane, Jesus is keenly aware of what his "I" wants, what his *ego* would choose; he desires to live, and he wants to avoid the cup and the hour. From our usual human perspective, he could hardly be faulted for choosing ongoing life over suffering and execution.

Jesus Chooses God

However, in this second crucible of costly choosing, of even greater meaning and importance to Jesus than life itself is that he chooses God, aligning his will with the "divine things" of God. Setting aside his own will, he chooses not to choose any path of self-survival or self-preservation that would distance him from God. To the contrary, he gives himself, trusts himself to the Holy and will follow the Divine into whatever his future holds, as frightening as this may be. In this most intense of moments, then, Jesus chooses the you of God, laying aside any I-directed choice of self. His focus is on his *Abba* Father; Jesus's future, his life, his core being now rest completely with his God: "yet, not what I want, but what you want" (14:36).

This verse underscores that choosing occupies a central role in Mark's narrative. As Mark portrays it, Jesus's struggle and anguishing in the Garden reflect the Markan perspective that choice can be exercised from within one of two divergent frameworks. From within the framework of self-preservation and security, out of which we humans live most of the time, Jesus could have been expected to choose to keep living, to keep teaching his disciples and others about God and God's kingdom, to keep breathing in and out, holding fast to a seemingly safe and vibrant life until there came a more distant and natural close to his days on earth. But instead, and after much grief, agony, and terror—and, yes, growing courage also—Jesus chooses the God-centered orientation, a Way characterized by laying aside the self so that others may be made free. In the Garden Jesus chooses not self but alignment of his whole being with God and whatever divine thing God may have in mind for the revelation and dissemination of good news to humankind.

Jesus Moves Toward Judas and the Kingdom Moves Ever Closer to Humankind

I now invite your attention to the end of our focal text, Jesus's closing moments in the Garden, when he proceeds from his time of prayer to his initial, resolute steps toward the "hour" he had hoped and prayed to avoid.

First, Mark shows the failure of Peter, James, and John, who are unable to stay awake even though they were singled out by Jesus to accompany him more deeply into Gethsemane. Moreover, even though Jesus has poured out his soul sickness to them, asking them to remain nearby and alert during his time of communion with God, these three prove unable to comply—not only once but three times. In falling asleep they unwittingly take their first steps toward undoing their recent vows never to desert Jesus or deny him even if that should lead to dying with him. Their impassioned words and firm resolve are overcome by weak flesh and heavy eyes (14:38 and 40). Their good intentions have proved bankrupt and they can think of nothing to say.

Second, Mark shows that Jesus's choice to align his will to that of his *Abba* Father is clearer by the end of the prayer than it was when he began. His growing clarity and resolve is demonstrated as the Gethsemane episode draws to a close. In 14:41 the Markan Jesus acknowledges and claims as his fate that the hour of his betrayal and passion "has come" to him, the Son of Man. Moreover, the episode culminates with Jesus rallying his disciples, moving with them to approach the betrayer Judas, for he "is at hand" (14:42). The time has indeed arrived. Jesus leaves behind the Garden, walking resolutely and courageously toward his passion.

Third, the Greek word that conveys "at-hand"-ness appears in two disparate Markan verses. In 1:15 it is the kingdom of God that is at hand, and in 14:42 it is the betrayer who is at hand.[44] Kelber sees Mark's vocabulary in the two verses as constituting an "inner connection between the arrival of the Kingdom and that of the passion."[45] In making this link, Mark presents the possibility that the arrival of the kingdom of God and Jesus's movement into his passion and execution are of a whole. Not only does Mark not separate these two crucial strands of the Good News, but he knits them together through the at-hand-ness of both the kingdom and Judas. The result is that the scope and meaning of the kingdom of God are magnified in Gethsemane and in the coming passion of the Beloved.

Gethsemane confirms, then, that the laying aside of self and choosing to give self—though this takes the form of suffering and execution—lies at the heart of following Jesus into the kingdom. For Mark, there is no good news that excludes chosen self-giving. As Jesus has said earlier in Mark's account, "For the Son of Man came not to be served but to serve, and to give his life [core, soul, self] a ransom for many" (Mark 10:45).

By the time Mark brings the Gethsemane episode to a close, he has carried his reader from one realm into another. Prior to his time in the Garden, the Markan Jesus has with some frequency put into words his expectation that what lies ahead of him is suffering and being killed. By the conclusion of his time in the Garden, Jesus has moved from the arena of what has been spoken to what he will now live out; he enters this new realm as he gathers his disciples and begins his walk toward his betrayer. The betrayer is that very individual whose at-hand-ness clarifies what living into the at-hand-ness of the kingdom of God entails.

By the time Jesus leaves the Garden, his fierce, depleting, and fearsome struggles are behind him. Resolution has emerged through his choosing to lay aside any I-directed orientation and trust God and whatever "divine things" will arrive in his future. With this resolution as the foundation for the remainder of Mark's Gospel, Mark has moved Jesus from prayer to passion, from words to action. However, Mark's haunting question remains: "Dare we follow such a One, or are we to be found among the ranks of his earliest followers with weak flesh and heavy eyes?"

44. NRSV uses the translation "has come near" in 1:15 but offers "is at hand" as an alternate translation. Black, "The Gospel of Mark," textual note *j*.

45. Kelber, "The Hour of the Son of Man," 45.

Choosing matters in Mark; it poses for us issues of living and dying. In one form or another choices will arise to face us all, perhaps driving even us toward our own places of anguish and prayer. The personal struggle of Jesus in Gethsemane evokes our own. And whose will and which Way will we choose?

Focal Text: Mark 6:17–29
Dark Choices, Darkly Made

17 For Herod himself had sent men who arrested John, bound him, and put him in prison on account of Herodias, his brother Philip's wife, because Herod had married her. 18 For John had been telling Herod, "It is not lawful for you to have your brother's wife." 19 And Herodias had a grudge against him, and wanted to kill him. But she could not, 20 for Herod feared John, knowing that he was a righteous and holy man, and he protected him. When he heard him, he was greatly perplexed; and yet he liked to listen to him. 21 But an opportunity came when Herod on his birthday gave a banquet for his courtiers and officers and for the leaders of Galilee. 22 When his daughter Herodias came in and danced, she pleased Herod and his guests; and the king said to the girl, "Ask me for whatever you wish, and I will give it." 23 And he solemnly swore to her, "Whatever you ask me, I will give you, even half of my kingdom." 24 She went out and said to her mother, "What should I ask for?" She replied, "The head of John the baptizer." 25 Immediately she rushed back to the king and requested, "I want you to give me at once the head of John the Baptist on a platter." 26 The king was deeply grieved; yet out of regard for his oaths and for the guests, he did not want to refuse her. 27 Immediately the king sent a soldier of the guard with orders to bring John's head. He went and beheaded him in the prison, 28 brought his head on a platter, and gave it to the girl. Then the girl gave it to her mother. 29 When his disciples heard about it, they came and took his body, and laid it in a tomb.

Mark 6:17–29 may seem to be an odd choice for our third focal text, since it appears at first glance to have little to do with either Jesus or his disciples, the characters who usually receive the bulk of Mark's attention. In this specific passage John the Baptizer could certainly be viewed as the main character, but he "is overshadowed by the flamboyant characters surrounding his death."[46]

46. Williamson, *Mark*, 122.

Choosing Not to Choose 147

This focal passage is an account of dark choices, darkly made. In this sinister scene, our understanding of choice is broadened to include the perspective that choice can be exercised malevolently.

This unusual text contributes to Mark's emphasis on choosing.

- On four occasions in this text, Mark employs the Greek verb *thelo*, translated in the NRSV as "want" or "wish," signaling a choice. These multiple uses of *thelo* weave a web that captures three different characters in the story: Herod's dancing daughter (Herodias), Herod's duplicitous wife (also named Herodias in Mark's story) and Herod himself. Choosing is exercised by each of these three.

- Choices are not only for Jesus, the Son of Man, to make. In this scene, Mark shows that choices are not Jesus's alone to face. They also arise for others.[47]

- In Mark, choices can go either way; they can lead toward good or toward the kind of harm that leaves us shuddering at their cruelty and viciousness. In the other focal passages for this chapter, our exploration of "choice" has centered on two crucial choices Jesus made, and in each case these choosings can be said to have turned out positively. In one instance, the proclamation of the good news has been advanced and in the other Jesus's will has become more closely aligned with God's "divine things." Both are worthy outcomes. But our third focal text recounting John's death serves notice that not all choices lead toward the good. Some are conceived and executed in a setting and manner most repulsive and cruel.

- It is abundantly clear that all the choices in 6:17–29 are exercised in the first Way, that is, from within a life's orientation of self-saving and self-serving.[48] Certainly, Mark is aware that this Way can manifest in a variety of human actions from seemingly petty to brutal. The example of Herod and the two Herodias women lies at the extreme brutal end of a spectrum of human choice and action.[49] These three characters act in pursuit of the first Way—to obtain and

---

47. Pilate and the crowd present readers with additional examples. See Mark 15:6–15, especially 5:9 and 5:12.

48. Rhoads, "Losing Life for Others," 360.

49. The extremity of choice and action shows itself again in the cries of the crowd, "Crucify him!" (see Mark 15:6–15).

perpetuate "status, power and security."⁵⁰ Each of the three will allow no obstacle to get in the way of self-interest and self-satiation, even when the obstacle can be removed only through murder.

Let us explore more thoroughly the choices depicted in 6:17–29.

Choosing and the Fate of John the Baptist

Mark's first use of *thelo* comes in 6:19. John the Baptist has been proclaiming that King Herod's marriage to Herodias, his brother's wife, is illegal under Levitical law. While these pronouncements by John are likely irritating and even angering Herod—leading him to imprison John—the more prominent driving force behind John's arrest is Queen Herodias, who is—in John's eyes—still Philip's wife. Her reaction to John goes far beyond anger to a burning desire to see John dead. She wants him annihilated and silenced permanently. Mark portrays Herod, however, as having a more ambivalent relationship with John, both fearing him and in some way drawn to his teachings. Out of this ambivalence he has protected John, holding Herodias's venomous rage in check. But Queen Herodias is a woman who holds a grudge. She knows how to bide her time.

Herod decides to throw himself a birthday feast and invite members of Galilee's upper crust to celebrate with him. In the context of this celebration, Mark again presents his theme of choosing.

Entering the revelry in 6:22 is the other Herodias, the young dancer.⁵¹ She entertains Herod and his guests by dancing in such a way that Herod and his elite courtiers are well pleased. Herod speaks to young Herodias, addressing someone Mark presents as far closer in age and maturity level to a child than an adult woman.⁵² In speaking, Herod's character places Mark's theme of choice squarely before his readers: "Ask me for whatever you wish [choose] and I will give it" (6:22). With these words Herod begins to dig a deep hole for himself, one he deepens when he swears an oath in front of his assembled guests reaffirming his promise to the young girl. He then further complicates his situation by expanding

---

50. Rhoads, "Losing Life for Others," 360.

51. While this youth is referred to in 6:22 as Herod's daughter and in 6:24 as daughter of the adult Herodias, her loyalties and emotional ties to her mother dominate her allegiances.

52. Mark highlights the youthfulness and immaturity of Herod's daughter by indicating at three points that she is a "girl" (see 6:22 and 6:28 [twice]).

his promise of a reward for her dance to include "even half of my kingdom" (6:23). As noted by Clifton Black, these words are borrowed from the story of Esther, an honored and favorite heroine in Hebrew Scriptures.[53] A brief look at Esther's story is, therefore, in order.

Esther's story, in the Book of Esther, is the tale of a young Jewish queen who saves the lives of all Jews living under the rule of Esther's husband, King Ahasuerus of the Persian Empire, a man of singular power and wealth. As the story develops the king is unaware that Haman, his right-hand man, has hatched a plot to annihilate all Jews throughout the empire. Told of this plot, Esther risks her life to spare her people by appearing uninvited before the king. Such an unbidden appearance before Ahasuerus so severely violated Persian court protocol that it carried the penalty of death. With no little trepidation, Esther approaches the king and he grants her permission to come forward and speak. In a series of conversations between Esther and the king over the next few days, Ahasuerus—out of his love for Esther—asserts on three separate occasions that whatever petition she has to present to him will be granted "even to the half of my kingdom" (Esther, 5:3, 5:6, and 7:2). Eventually, Esther—revealing to the king for the first time that she is Jewish—asks the king to spare her life and the lives of her people, who are close to the time appointed by Haman for their destruction. Her petition is granted, the Jews are saved, and the archvillain, Haman, is put to death.

With Mark's allusion to the story of Esther in the Hebrew Scripture, the question arises, "What purpose might it serve for Mark, amid his own vivid and darkly captivating story about Herod, to insert reference to yet another dramatic life-and-death account, reaching back hundreds of years into Israel's past?" I think it is Mark's intention to present the striking contrasts between the female characters of royal standing who inhabit the two stories. On the one hand, you have the young Herodias and her vengeful mother, and on the other, you have the young Jewish Queen Esther during a period of Israel's exile. On the one hand, a daughter and a mother collaborate and make choices that set in motion a gruesome execution of a hated enemy. On the other, Esther risks losing her life to bring rescue to her people, God's chosen. (Her actions constitute a strikingly close parallel to Mark's characterization of Jesus as the Son of Man who lays down his life to set others free.) As a concluding contrast, you have a young girl who acts out of an apparent adolescent enthusiasm for

---

53. Black, "The Gospel of Mark," note on Mark 6:23.

mayhem and murder. Her portrayal is eerily like that of certain teenage girls in Salem, Massachusetts, who cried "Witch!" In contrast, Esther is a courageous young woman whose energies are expended in the service of securing life. Given such divergent stories, I am persuaded that Mark wants his readers to recall Esther by remembering her example, standing in sharp contrast to the two royal Herodiases of Mark's account. Esther acts for life; the two Herodiases deal in death.

We now return to Mark's story, at the point where Herod has promised to give up to half of his kingdom as a reward to the young Herodias for entertaining at his birthday party (perhaps in her "birthday suit"). She goes to ask the queen for guidance about what she should request from Herod. Queen Herodias, who has been waiting for such a moment for a long time answers immediately, "the head of John the baptizer" (Mark 6:24). This is a woman who knows her own mind and she makes her long wished-for choice out of a vengeful clarity.

But while the Queen's immediate and chilling response no doubt aims her daughter toward a clear course of action, the young girl Herodias makes her own enthusiastic contributions to John's fate. It is she, after all, who exercises her own "choosing" in this episode; it is she who says to the king, "I want you [choose for you] to give me at once the head of John the Baptist on a platter." Actively involved in the plot against John and with a final flourish that goes beyond anything suggested by her mother, she asks for the Baptist's head "on a platter." Mark invites us to see that the young and girlish character operates out of a darkness that is not merely a reflection of the Queen's. In addressing the king, young Herodias declares her own choice, and it is not the stuff of sweetness and light.

The fourth "choosing" is Herod's. To be more precise, Mark's fourth use of *thelo* points to a choosing Herod refused to make. Myers suggests that the throng of courtiers, military officers, and leaders of Galilean society who attend Herod's celebration are to be viewed as incorporating "the murderous whims of the ruling class of Galilee."[54] It is with these elite that Herod surrounds himself on his birthday. With her choice of John's beheading, the girlish Herodias stands front and center representing this larger assembly with all their whims. When Herod is confronted by his daughter's request—one he has already sworn in the presence of his guests to grant—he succumbs to "peer pressure" (or perhaps more accurately the "peer identity") present in the banquet hall. Although Herod

---

54. Myers, *Binding the Strong Man*, 216.

feels bad (i.e., grieves) about what is transpiring, in the final analysis "he did not want [choose] to refuse" young Herodias (6:26). As Myers observes, Herod acts not to save life but "to save royal face."[55]

As in our previous focal texts, Mark's theme of choosing holds central place in his narrative. Here again, choosing matters in Mark, as does refusing to choose. Markan choices are shown once again to be the stuff of life and death.

Choosing in Mark—Conclusions

Across the span of his sixteen chapters Mark both envisions and elaborates what is involved when choices are faced and made. Drawing from the richness of our three focal texts, I offer some conclusions about Mark's understanding of choosing.

- As indicated by the presence of some form of the verb *thelo* in multiple texts, choosing is centrally important in Mark's account. Whenever readers come across a moment in the narrative when a choice is faced and a decision is to be made, readers can anticipate that a complicated and perplexing moral or spiritual dilemma is likely a significant component of the episode.

- Choosing in Mark is no easy matter. Compelling traditions, practices, or consequences—be they social, religious, or the natural human desire to live and seek security—provide the context for decisions. Choosing is a difficult enterprise for many in Mark's narrative.

- Choices can be exercised for good purpose or ill.

- A choice made (or sometimes not made) is often the expression of one of two clashing life orientations—the Way of self-focus, self-preservation and self-aggrandizement, or the Way of self-giving. Those who choose the first Way seek to secure and maintain status, security, or power that can be directed against others. Those who choose the second Way elevate their attention and level of response toward meeting the human needs of others; they set aside their own legitimate needs and aspirations as of secondary importance.

---

55. Myers, *Binding the Strong Man*, 216.

- When a self-giving choice is made, the result for "the others" whose needs are attended to and addressed involves gaining freedom of some kind.

- When a self-giving choice is made, the result for those who lay self aside is often an unanticipated experience of being enlivened, made whole, or transformed.

- Living one's life from a stance of self-giving is perhaps the closest possible human approximation to doing God's will.

- Markan acts of self-giving involve a radical trusting of God with whatever the future holds, including life and death. Those who give their very hearts, souls, and cores to God maintain a life-stance of trusting and believing that God's purposes will be fulfilled on this earth—that is, that the proclamation of the good news of God's presence, beneficence, and loving of God's people will be accomplished. In the final analysis, God will see to it that nothing will subvert or defeat this gospel.

Personal Reflection: Choices—I Hide, God Seeks

For as long as I can remember, I have sought out a certain distance in relationships. This trait even shows itself in situations most would consider non-threatening or even pleasant. Consider, for example, my frequent practice of waving at neighbors while rarely taking (literal) steps to engage in friendly chitchat. Similarly, take my reaction when Lyn, my wife, and I receive an invitation to a party. My immediate response is to hope we have a conflict in our schedule that will free us to decline. If no such conflict exists and we "really should go," I start to calculate how late we can choose to arrive and how early we can choose to leave without being rude.

Thankfully, this isn't the whole story about me. One of the things I genuinely enjoy is bantering with harried check-out clerks in the grocery store or with customer service representatives over the phone, the ones who sound as if they have had a morning of being chewed out by angry or rude customers. In such settings I like to use wit and humor to lighten their load a bit. There is also the reality that I spent thirty years of my work life as a minister and pastoral counselor who, on a daily basis engaged with others as they moved through personal crisis and distress. This work was not for the faint of heart for either client or me, and a meaningful degree of connection came to exist in many of these relationships. In the counseling setting, then, I chose to move toward a form of closeness, albeit of a professional kind.

There is a specific incident from decades ago that highlights the ambivalence I carry about personal closeness and distance. I have often thought of it, gradually coming to understand that I revisit it because it so well captures my human desire and struggle to be both close enough and distant enough to feel emotionally safe.

I was a seminary student, completing my final year at Union Theological Seminary in Virginia (now Union Presbyterian Seminary). During the previous year, I had participated in one of the seminary's yearlong internship programs and spent the time in a setting quite different from anything I had ever experienced—as a "political intern" in an office on Capitol Hill in Washington, D.C. Built into this experience was the opportunity to observe and learn about the political process as well as how persons engaged in high-stress work situations were impacted by them.

This program proved an educational introduction to a world beyond the seminary's boundaries, preparing me to understand more clearly some of the pushes and pulls that my future congregants would live through in their work lives. Concurrently, my "education" was being broadened in another significant arena since I was "learning through" my first year of married life.

When I returned to the seminary campus in the fall of my final year I was surprised that I felt off-balance, like a stranger in a strange land. It dawned on me that the year away had involved much more than separation from familiar surroundings; the time away had been accompanied by a significant degree of personal change that had arrived largely unnoticed. No longer was it a simple adjustment to slip back into the known and secure cocoon of being a student, something that had been a primary role and identity for me for eighteen consecutive years.

No longer was I a single male student living on the second floor of the men's dorm, and no longer was I "hanging out" with the other students. I was a married student, living in the married student's apartments, which were at some remove socially and emotionally from my former stomping grounds. I wanted to spend less time with my friends and more time with Lyn. This time was not only wanted, it was necessary as Lyn and I were learning to shift our individualistic orientations toward attending to our wants and aspirations as a couple. And at this early stage of things we had not truly understood that "compromise" could be more than an unfortunate, often grudging concession each of us had to make; we held little appreciation that "compromise" could instead rise to the level of gift, given out of a deep regard for the personhood of one's life partner.

The specific incident occurred at the intersection of these changes and adjustments with the ongoing traditions of the seminary. In those days, chapel was held three or four times a week, and faculty typically officiated, but students were sometimes asked to lead worship. I was asked to deliver the sermon at an upcoming service, and although I had never spoken from the chapel pulpit, I accepted. Soon a sense of dread set in as I imagined my admired and respected mentors and teachers gathered just a few feet in front of me, evaluating my every utterance. I recalled the words of a classmate who had led worship for this august gathering earlier in the year. Keenly aware of the intimidating environment, he looked out from the pulpit and began his sermon with these tremulous words: "I can think of a thousand other places I'd rather be right now."

As I began to consider what I might say in my sermon, certain anchoring realizations crystallized and helped ground me. For one, I knew that the blunt truth was that my style of preaching left much to be desired and that my demeanor in the pulpit resembled that of a deer caught in the headlights. Second, if I were to have any chance of reaching listeners, I would need to speak out of heartfelt conviction or vivid experience. I had learned that authentic speech arising from a place of deep meaning in the speaker could compensate for poor delivery. Third, I knew that the transitions in my personal life were the realities about which I could most genuinely speak. But I did not want my chapel message to be an exercise in autobiography or self-absorbed navel-gazing. Rather, it was to be a sermon—a group of words, thoughts, feelings, and story that would carry a word of good news and freedom for those gathered, in the language of my Reformed religious heritage, "to hear the Word of God read and expounded."

As the time for my chapel appearance grew nearer, I became convinced that the common ground for my soon-to-be listeners and me was our life together in the seminary community. The emphasis on community had been a constant theme over my years at Union. Even prior to being a student there, I had heard the phrases "the seminary community," "community life," and "our seminary family" on a visit to the campus. These words were spoken in a serious and near-reverential tone, suggesting that community was of utmost significance, something all members of the student body lived and breathed.

However, when approaching my time to speak in chapel, I found myself reflecting on how my understanding of "community" was changing. I had grown uncomfortable with fellow students who spoke passionately and glowingly of "our seminary family." Such terminology seemed to imply a stronger level of connection with my seminary colleagues than I felt. Besides, I already had a family—not a perfect one but certainly one whose loyalty and connection surpassed any I had experienced on campus. To use a southern expression, my family and I were "bound by blood," usually for better and on occasion for worse.

My ideas about community were changing for other reasons, too. In Washington, D.C., I had lived for a season in a markedly secular environment. This time away had caused me to envision community as including members of "tribes" quite different from my own. And as I grew into marriage, I was learning that being part of a couple altered both my ties to the community and my understanding of it.

So I put my thoughts to paper and wrote a sermon. In decent Presbyterian fashion, I fashioned three main points related to "community." First, while all of us had been formed and nurtured by the "seminary community," we would soon be exposed to other communities and worldviews that would challenge our understanding of community. Therefore, expect and prepare for change to come; it would shake us, but it would also open doors to a larger and potentially more vivid world. Second, although other communities would likely feel foreign, strange, or even unnerving, it was possible and likely even wise to reach toward the newness presented by these communities. To cling too tightly to what we have known and even found sacred in the past could cause us to miss out on the newness God might have for us in the present. Third, our ongoing journey would be permeated by a yet-with-us God, one who is steady and insistent in God's promise to accompany God's people into whatever unknown lies ahead. We would be okay and even more than okay; God is leading us toward a new and even—one might affirm—resurrected life.

I was initially satisfied with what I had drafted. Overall, it seemed a caring attempt to prepare my classmates for what I believed comes to all of God's beloved—change. Within a short while, however, I found myself thinking of a specific person, someone on the seminary campus whose words and demeanor grated on me. I now recognize that my feelings about this person at the time revealed more about myself—my youthful pettiness and judgmentalism—than it did about her.

Then, however, I saw her as one of those among us who spoke too glowingly and gushingly of the "seminary family." She pressured all in her hearing to acknowledge that our Christian community was unique and always to be characterized by undying mutual devotion and cloying closeness. When she spoke of community and family, her words did not ring true but seemed to me born of a desperate neediness rather than a connection to anything healing and freeing. When she was near a group of folks, she would nudge her way into the center of the interaction, willing with all her might to belong, to insinuate herself into the literal middle of things. Then there was her laugh—a loud, anxious high-pitched expulsion of air that reminded me of a whinnying horse. I was put off by her large, garish eyeglasses with their massive circular lenses. And her fingernails were chewed to the quick. In her occasional interactions with me, she stood too close, unaware of my need for physical and social distance.

In sum, I was not fond of this woman. I wanted to avoid her at every turn, much to the delight of my darker angels.

Over the years I have found myself drawn back to the memories of this chapel episode, convinced that it has much to teach me about myself, including some less-than-attractive, unsettling realities. Although the darker truths about myself create discomfort and regret, I have come to trust that I can be instructed by these darker thoughts and feelings. This chapel experience gave me a closer look at the cannibal in me. It was not a coincidence that after I completed my sermon, my thoughts turned to the person in the seminary community who bothered me so. Moreover, I know now what I did not fully comprehend then—that I had in my sermon subconsciously constructed two different messages, text and subtext. The text, for most of my peers and mentors, would be a word of good news, encouragement, and comfort. The subtext would come to rest on the bothersome woman and be received, I hoped, as follows:

- Take a step back, would you? At least when you're talking to me.

- Quit pleading so insistently that the whole seminary subscribe to your vision of the seminary as an affectionate, always-loving, ever-forgiving group of folks. It's not that simple.

- Stop confusing closeness with tightness, and stop being so relentlessly clingy. True closeness respects the choosing of the other. It allows for *chosen* connection and a sense of freedom in relationship; those truly close can choose to come and choose to go. With

overtones of capture, tightness can neither relax into genuine closeness or encourage the capacity for freedom in others.
- Back off. I do not want to be as close to you as you like to be to me (or to anyone else who has fallen into your orbit).
- And change your laugh, please.

As I walked into chapel on the assigned day, I had little awareness of my subconscious longing to use my sermon to create greater distance between myself and the troublesome person. When I saw her in chapel, my fleeting thought was only this: "O Lord, what if she comes up to me after the service, all smiles, telling me what a good job I did, and wants a hug?" I dismissed the thought and focused on the task at hand. One can hide behind the task to be done.

I have long thought that God has a robust sense of humor, one marked by irony, challenge, and healing. In those moments when I have been on the receiving end of that humor, it has seemed to me that God's frequent encouragement to me has been, "Don't take yourself so seriously and don't be so anxious. Lighten up—on others and yourself, too. And I thought that was pretty funny, what I just did. What did you think?"

By now you may have guessed how this chapel episode worked out. After the service, well-wishers and congratulators came to me with kind words. Of course, in their midst, there she stood, all smiles, telling me I did a good job and asking, "Can I get a hug?" And in a moment which I am convinced was one of those that people of faith refer to as a "piece of grace," my impulse to avoid this needy person was superseded by the action of the Spirit who had sought me out. I hugged her. No doubt, I've given warmer hugs in my day, but a jaw-dropping truth about the power of the Spirit is that not only had it led me to hug this unhuggable person, but it had also covered the deficit in my response to her. She walked away, still smiling and apparently content for the moment and perhaps even a bit more whole than before the Spirit moved me on her behalf.

Only one thing further needs saying. The Spirit, that is, my playful, humorous God, was also acting on my behalf that day. In the chapel time, God moved to alert me that I would need to keep working on my well-entrenched tendency to avoid human connection. A false self-sufficiency just would not do. I would need others, need to hold them and be held by them. If I were to translate into words God's comedic and sacred challenge to me during my chapel time, it would go something like this:

You have a long struggle ahead of you, my child. I know you and your inclination to avoid being close, to hide and cut off from others. Yes, at times tightness in relationships can bind and suffocate my people. But on your journey your choices in relationships will be less about escaping smothering tightness than about accepting genuine closeness. Will you choose to let people—and me—in? Will you find a few islands of sustaining closeness and trust that some vulnerability needs to be shared in order for you to be safely known and not alone? You, too, will need safe harbor at times. Just like your fellow pilgrim, your sister, you will need arms to hold you. Remember her, then. Learn from her. After all, I sent you to each other.

And let's keep in touch on your journey. I'll be as close as you'll allow. The choice is yours.

7

The Way of Discipleship

At the heart of his narrative, Mark presents a concentrated vision of the Way (the Road) of Discipleship. This Way is an outgrowth of Jesus's continuing evolution in his understanding of his purpose in the kingdom of God and his ongoing invitation to his disciples to follow him, though the Way be fearsome.[1]

Exploring Mark's Story

CARL WHITAKER WAS AN early pioneer in the practice of family therapy. He believed in treating his patients in the context of their larger family units and that this approach produced more positive and sustainable results than approaches of traditional individual therapies. Dr. Whitaker first came to my attention several years into my professional life as I began training in the specialized ministry of pastoral counseling. As part of my training—and employing technology that today would strike many

---

1. David Rhoads, "Losing Life for Others," 358–69. In chapter 6 I drew on Rhoads's portrayal of the Two Ways as divergent life-orientations out of which persons could live their lives. In this chapter I will consider Mark's use of the concept of "Way" in a similar but perhaps more literal way. That is, "The Way" also carries the literal meaning of "road" (see 8:27, 9:33, 10:17, 10:32, and 10:52). In 8:22—10:52 Jesus and those who follow him are walking the road which will eventually take them all to Jerusalem, and Jesus to the cross. I believe it is beyond safe to say that Mark's use of way/road often includes nuances about both one's life-orientation as well as the path that is leading toward challenging settings and circumstances in which choices will need to be made.

as bordering on the prehistoric—I listened to a number of audio cassette tapes of teachers and proponents of different counseling methods. One afternoon I was listening to a recording of Dr. Whitaker as he engaged in a question-and-answer session following a lecture. A questioner, ignoring the topic of the lecture and speaking in what seemed to me a self-important tone, asked, "Dr. Whitaker, you have become one of the nation's leading authorities on family therapy. Could you tell us, sir, how you found the path that has taken you to such esteemed heights in your profession?" Dr. Whitaker paused briefly and then responded in his best down-to-earth, no-nonsense manner, "Oh, I don't know. I started out headed in one direction and ended up somewhere else."

While I have no idea whether Dr. Whitaker was familiar with the Gospel of Mark, his comment resonates with what I imagine readers of Mark might say after reading through the section of his narrative known as "The Way of Discipleship" (8:22—10:52). Only a few short verses into this material, readers bump headfirst into what Boring calls "a major turning point in the Markan narrative."[2] In the "Way" materials things shift significantly as the narrative builds in intensity. Mark leaves his readers numerous changes to note, understand, and place within his unfolding literary design. What prompts Mark to "head in one direction" in the first half of his Gospel only to begin to pivot in 8:22, a turning that will indeed end the reader up somewhere else?

Mark's Mid-Course Correction

To begin exploration of the Way of Discipleship—a section of Mark's Gospel that has been called "the centerpiece of the Gospel"[3]—let us take note of the changes through which Mark alerts readers to numerous and significant shifts in direction in 8:22—10:52.

Changes in Mark's Narrative Design

No more boats. After the Way section commences, there is no further mention in Mark of a "boat story." Earlier in the Gospel, Mark incorporated a series of boat stories (see especially 4:35–41, 6:45–56, and 8:1–21), but when Mark begins the Way section all mention of the use of a boat as

---

2. Boring, *Mark*, 234.
3. *HarperCollins Bible Commentary*, 911.

The Way of Discipleship 161

a means of undertaking significant missions to advance the kingdom of God abruptly ceases.

On the way. In 8:22—10:52 Mark presents readers with a concentrated use of the phrase "on the way" (or "on the road"). While Mark employs way/road vocabulary at other places in his account seven of his fourteen uses of "on the way" come in 8:22—10:52.[4] Also noteworthy is that the phrase appears both near the beginning of this material (8:27) and at its conclusion (10:52). The way/road vocabulary carries both the literal designation of a highway used for transportation and the more metaphorical designation of a life's orientation or journey.

Mark's literary skeleton. A key feature of Mark's mid-course correction as indicated in his narrative design is a literary skeleton on which he hangs the fuller content of the Way materials.

Mark's Literary Skeleton I: 8:22—10:52
The Way of Discipleship

Book-end I 8:22–26	Theme intro 8:27–30		Focal text 8:31—9:1	Focal text 9:30–37	Focal text 10:32–45	Book-end II 10:46–52
a blind man is sent home	"on the way"		"on the way"	"on the way"	"on the way"	a blind man follows "on the way"
		Each focal text contains three basic elements:				
		1. Passion prediction by Jesus	8:31–32a	9:30–31	10:32–34	

---

4. Boring, *Mark*, 37.

Book-end I 8:22-26	Theme intro 8:27-30		Focal text 8:31—9:1	Focal text 9:30-37	Focal text 10:32-45	Book-end II 10:46-52
		2. Misunderstanding by the disciples	8:32b-33	9:32-34	10:35-41	
		3. Instruction on discipleship (corrects misunderstanding and reissues call)	8:34—9:1	9:35-37	10:42-45	

In Mark's skeleton for 8:22—10:52, the Way material portrays Jesus as shifting the locale of his travels of proclamation from the greater Galilee region, heading instead toward Jerusalem. "On the way" to Jerusalem he engages in three specific moments of encounter with his followers, especially the Twelve. In each of these three pivotal moments, Mark brings to the fore three identical emphases. Namely, as shown in the chart above,

1. Jesus cites the coming fate of the Son of Man;

2. the disciples (again) fail to comprehend what Jesus is clearly stating; and

3. Jesus provides instruction to his disciples in an effort to both correct the disciples' faulty understanding and clarify their ongoing call toward a discipleship grounded not in "human things" but "divine things" (8:33).

It can be said, then, that in 8:22—10:52, Mark has intricately shaped his material into two three-part layers. The first layer is Jesus's three engagements with his disciples. The second layer is the three components of passion prediction, the disciples' misunderstanding, and the corrective instruction; each of these three components appears in each of Jesus's engagements with his disciples. Taken together, these two layers flesh out Mark's literary skeleton for 8:22—10:52.

The bookends. As noted in the chart of Mark's literary skeleton, Mark brackets the Way of Discipleship materials with two bookends, 8:22–26 and 10:46–52. These bookends serve to both introduce the Way section and bring it to its close two and one-half chapters later. The bookends are similar in depicting the restoration of sight in a blind man—the only Markan stories to do so—but there are many and substantial differences between these scenes. The differences offer insight into the nature and scope of Mark's mid-course correction initiated by the Way section. Because of their importance in understanding the major shift Mark begins with 8:22, the bookends receive a more detailed analysis below (see pages 166-70).

Changes in Mark's Content

Even as Mark changes the literary design and structure of his narrative with the Way materials, he also uses the Way section to shift the focus of the thematic *content* of his Gospel. He both adds new themes and refines others; he portrays changes taking place in Jesus, whose maturity increases and self-understanding deepens; and he expands and clarifies what it means to be a disciple and follower of Jesus.

Elaboration upon or refinement of Markan themes. In the Way materials Mark elaborates upon several themes hinted at in the first half of his Gospel.

- As pronounced by Jesus himself, Jesus's ultimate fate includes suffering, being killed and a rising (8:31, 9:32, 10:33–34). Jesus's future involves a funeral.

- Included in Jesus's teachings to the Twelve, the life of discipleship is explicitly coupled with being a servant or slave (9:35, 10:43–44). Discipleship is not an easy path to walk.

- Jesus makes perhaps the clearest statement in the entire narrative of his purpose in God's kingdom (10:45). He is to serve, attending to the needs of others, and engage in a life of self-giving.

- Jesus's self-designation as "Son of Man" is prominent throughout the Way section and is inseparably connected with Jesus's future of passion, being killed, and rising.

- Mark's concept of freedom is clarified through the use of the word "ransom" for the only time in his account (see 10:45). Mark couples ransoming with the liberating effects that result when Jesus gives away, lays aside, his very self.

Jesus's new direction begins to emerge. At this point, readers may find it useful to briefly review Mark's conclusion to the first half of his account.[5] In the several chapters leading up to the beginning of the Way section in 8:22, Mark's main focus is on the two stories of miraculous feedings of large crowds in the wilderness, likely Mark's recapitulation of the account of God's presence and saving action on behalf of the Israelites during their exodus from Egypt. In addition to twice feeding the hungry people of God's kingdom, Jesus is presented as hoping to lead his disciples into a fuller experience of God's arriving kingdom and their place in it. Jesus's efforts with the disciples prove unsuccessful, however, and Mark closes out the first half of his Gospel with Jesus raising a blistering set of nine questions to the Twelve that exposes their hardheartedness and incapacity to understand and live into God's reign. The final question Jesus asks—"Do you not yet understand?"—underscores Mark's portrayal of Jesus's closest followers. The disciples' only answer is silence. Jesus's efforts with the Twelve appear to be of no avail.

However, another possibility opens to Mark's readers with the close of the Gospel's first half. Because of the inability of the Twelve to decipher the significance of Jesus's wilderness feedings, Jesus is confronted with two stubborn, immutable truths: that his core group has not changed and cannot change, at least in the present moment and circumstance, and if they are incapable of changing, he must. Not able to break through the hardheartedness of the disciples to present them with the reality and experience of God's presence and mercy for all peoples, he is called to something new. He verges on the previously unanticipated possibility that something beyond his earlier efforts is required of him. A new course must be set.

With such an evolving self-understanding for Jesus, the need for a change in direction emerges and Mark writes that Jesus sets out on his corrected course. He begins to take a different path. He also continues to invite his followers to come after him, hoping his new Way may become their own.

---

5. See chapter 5 for a more detailed discussion of Mark's conclusion of the first half of his Gospel.

The Way of Discipleship

Jesus's first steps "on the way." Mark's portrayal of Jesus's beginning steps in a new direction comes in 8:27–30. These steps point to a significant shift taking place in Jesus.

> ²⁷Jesus went on with his disciples to the villages of Caesarea Philippi; and on the way he asked his disciples, "Who do people say that I am?" ²⁸And they answered him, "John the Baptist; and others, Elijah; and still others, one of the prophets." ²⁹He asked them, "But who do you say that I am?" Peter answered him, "You are the Messiah." ³⁰And he sternly ordered them not to tell anyone about him.

It is with this scene that Mark begins his heavy emphasis of "on the way," a theme that continues throughout the entire Way section and appropriately concludes it with Bartimaeus following Jesus "on the way" (10:52). What can readers glean from this opening "on the way" scene?

Note that Jesus is still traveling with his disciples. Given the tension between Jesus and the Twelve during their most recent notable meeting (see 8:14–21), readers could have imagined Jesus breaking off association with his core group to continue on his own. But he does not do so. He does not throw up his hands and walk away, declaring himself done with them. Instead, he is gathering them back together; he is still present with them and continuing to teach.

In addition to being "on the way" with the Twelve, Jesus's first words to them center on the question of who Jesus is. This question has been asked previously when Jesus's rebuke of a storm prompts the disciples to ask among themselves, "Who then is this?" (4:41). This identity question has remained unanswered since it was first posed and is to be dealt with yet again "on the way" as Jesus's new direction is initiated. It is also important to note that the dialogue concerning Jesus's identity is not an exercise to pass the time while the group makes its way toward Caesarea Philippi. Chitchat won't do here. Indeed, Jesus intensifies and personalizes the conversation when he asks with great emphasis, "But who do *you* say that I am?"[6] Their answer carries weight; consequences will flow from it. What will they say?

Peter gives an answer, perhaps blurting it out in his best Petrine fashion. While Mark has in 1:1 informed readers of Jesus's identity as Messiah (NRSV translation = Christ), Peter is the first character in Mark's

---

6. Boring, *Mark*, 238. According to Boring, "The 'you' is doubly emphatic in the Greek text."

narrative to bestow this identity on Jesus.[7] Readers know, then, that Peter has given the "right" answer. But something is wrong about it. It falls short by some measure, and Jesus insists that any such talk about his being Messiah must cease. In the past Jesus has rebuked storms and caused winds to cease (4:39 and 6:51). In 8:30 he rebukes (NRSV translation = sternly ordered) all disciples including Peter "not to tell anyone about him." Peter may be "right" in what he says but he and the rest of Jesus's core group are to cease all conversation about Jesus as the Messiah. It is as if they have become a storm to be shushed into a calm quiet.[8]

And so Mark outlines Jesus's beginning steps on his new way, steps that run Mark's readers up against Jesus's seemingly mystifying instructions to his core group. The logic of Mark's Way materials may well convince readers that the imposed prohibition on talk about Messiahship is not meant to be permanent. But the silence it produces in the Twelve seems to give Jesus sufficient time to set straight whatever was awry about Peter's declaration. Jesus begins teaching his followers in the very next scene, and this new instruction presents Jesus's evolving understanding of the kind of Messiah and Son of Man he is being led to be. However, a question remains after Jesus's teachings permeate the Way of Discipleship section: Will his new pronouncements "on the way" be heard more clearly or grasped more fully by the Twelve than they were in the first half of Mark's Good News? Or will the new teachings fail to penetrate the heart and soul of followers, leaving them as blind, deaf, and with hardened hearts as they were before traveling "on the way?"

Mark's Bookends: Similar Narratives, Different Outcomes

As mentioned previously, Mark's bookends allow readers to gain a fuller understanding of the nature and scope of Jesus's mid-course correction. They recount two stories of blind men who regain their sight. As we begin our closer analysis of the bookends, I place them side by side for easy reference and comparison.

---

7. Boring, *Mark*, 238.

8. For more than a century biblical scholars have pondered what is called the "Messianic Secret," that is, the instructions of Jesus that his disciples not speak of his Messiahship. For a summary of the history of this scholarship as well as conclusions about the "secret," see Boring, *Mark*, 264–71.

The Way of Discipleship

Bookend I: Mark 8:22–26
Jesus heals a blind man, and sends him home.

²²They came to Bethsaida. Some people brought a blind man to him and begged him to touch him. ²³He took the blind man by the hand and led him out of the village; and when he had put saliva on his eyes and laid his hands on him, he asked him, "Can you see anything?" ²⁴And the man looked up and said, "I can see people, but they look like trees, walking." ²⁵Then Jesus laid his hands on his eyes again; and he looked intently and his sight was restored, and he saw everything clearly. ²⁶Then he sent him away to his home, saying, "Do not even go into the village."

Bookend II: Mark 10:46–52
Jesus heals a blind man, Bartimaeus, who follows on the way.

⁴⁶They came to Jericho. As he and his disciples and a large crowd were leaving Jericho, Bartimaeus son of Timaeus, a blind beggar, was sitting by the roadside. ⁴⁷When he heard that it was Jesus of Nazareth, he began to shout out and say, "Jesus, Son of David, have mercy on me!" ⁴⁸Many sternly ordered him to be quiet, but he cried out even more loudly, "Son of David, have mercy on me!" ⁴⁹Jesus stood still and said, "Call him here." And they called the blind man, saying to him, "Take heart; get up, he is calling you." ⁵⁰So throwing off his cloak, he sprang up and came to Jesus. ⁵¹Then Jesus said to him, "What do you want me to do for you?" The blind man said to him, "My teacher, let me see again." ⁵²Jesus said to him, "Go; your faith has made you well." Immediately he regained his sight and followed him on the way.

The bookends form the literary boundaries within which Mark presents his lengthy elaboration upon what the future holds for Jesus as the Son of Man, and what a life or path of discipleship will entail for any who choose to follow him. Providing a beginning point and end point for the whole section, the bookends present readers two similar stories that contain distinct differences. Generally speaking, one is of a man whose restoration to sight is insufficient to instill a readiness to take up a life of discipleship; the other is of a man whose restoration of sight is accompanied by a sweeping transformation that moves him toward discipleship. He is ready to follow "on the way," and so he does.

Although the bookends share the common subject matter about the restoration of sight, other aspects of the accounts reveal many important differences.

- **Passive v. active appeals for healing.** In Bookend I the blind man is passive in his dealings with Jesus. His companions bring him to Jesus and beg on his behalf. He is led from the village by Jesus and at the story's end is sent home. In Bookend II Bartimaeus is energized and active. He shouts twice for Jesus, once over the objections of many of those around him; he throws off his cloak, and though blind, makes (stumbles?) his way to Jesus. He knows decisively what he will ask of Jesus, and ask he does with immediate urgency.

- **Role of the people nearby.** In Bookend I the people accompanying the blind man do all the work and on the man's behalf try to secure Jesus's healing for him. In Bookend II members of the crowd initially hinder Bartimaeus, attempting to silence (rebuke) him when he is shouting to get Jesus's attention.
- **Sight v. choice.** In Bookend I Jesus asks a question of the blind man about his ability to see. The man's sight is the focus of the question. In Bookend II Jesus's question to Bartimaeus is about what Bartimaeus wants (chooses) for Jesus to do for him. Bartimaeus's choice is the focus of the question.
- **Direct v. indirect healing.** In Bookend I Jesus's level of involvement and activity is accentuated. He acts twice to secure the restoration of sight. He directs those with the man to take him home, not back to the village. In Bookend II Jesus's efforts are more indirect. Jesus halts before arriving at Bartimaeus's spot along the road and calls Bartimaeus to come to him. After Bartimaeus makes his choice to see again, Jesus points out that Bartimaeus's faith is the agency by which he was healed; Jesus makes no mention of any efforts of his own.
- **The issue of a name.** In Bookend I the blind man does not have a name. In Bookend II the blind man has a name: Bartimaeus.
- **The issue of "called."** In Bookend I there is no mention of the blind man as "called." In Bookend II there are three mentions of Bartimaeus as one being "called."
- **Healer v. teacher.** In Bookend I Jesus acts primarily as a healer. In Bookend II, while a healing happens, Jesus deflects any notion that he healed Bartimaeus, pointing instead to Bartimaeus's faith as the bedrock for his healing. Moreover, Bartimaeus refers to Jesus as "my teacher." In the Way materials teaching is the primary activity through which Jesus relates to the Twelve.
- **A difficult healing v. a faith-filled one.** In Bookend I sight is restored with considerable difficulty, necessitating two healing

touches by Jesus. In Bookend II the restoration of sight happens immediately with Bartimaeus's faith held as the central restorative force at work.

- **Sent home v. following "on the way."** In Bookend I the ultimate outcome of the encounter of Jesus and the blind man is that the healed one is sent home. In Bookend II a sighted Bartimaeus follows Jesus "on the way"—not toward home but toward Jerusalem.

The final difference between the two stories—the difference in outcomes—deserves additional comment. When Jesus sends the man back home this is likely an act of compassion born out of Jesus's recognition that this unnamed healed man is not ready to undergo the rigors of discipleship. Something is not yet in place for him. With Bartimaeus there is no such lack. Given the opportunity, he chooses sightedness; it is a choice of greater purpose than might appear. His choice for sight is of course from a desire to see, but with sight restored, he will be able more sure-footedly, faithfully, and completely to follow. No longer will he be destined to sit by the side of the road, begging. His sightedness frees him to follow, and follow he does. Indeed, our last glimpse of Bartimaeus finds us looking down the road as he fades from view, going after Jesus. In Mark's narrative, we shall not again see another take such a path with such determination and release. Not, that is, until Jesus emerges from the dread but clarity of Gethsemane to walk his resolute and faithful steps toward Judas the betrayer and all that then awaits the Son of Man.

Mark's Bookends: Moving the Gospel Forward

Mark's bookends bracket a body of material that involves his readers in a progression, a defining movement forward in his Gospel. Several instances of this movement are woven into Mark's story. One is present when Mark's story shifts from Jesus's travels taking place throughout Galilee to being "on the way" toward dangerous Jerusalem. Another is present at the beginning of the Way materials when Jesus is still functioning as a healer only later to be called "teacher" at the conclusion of the section by a blind one whose faith has enabled a right seeing. Yet another is present when Mark contrasts the static existence and listlessness of the unnamed blind man sent home with the energy, faith, and active choice exercised by Bartimaeus who follows.

And so Mark's bookends beckon his readers, saying, "Look for the forward movement in the story. Look for the new direction Jesus begins to take. Look for the new teachings with which he will instruct the Twelve. And imagine beyond Bartimaeus's closing scene, for he is the one who follows, showing us that a life of discipleship is possible despite all of its fear-filled hardships. As this faith-filled one follows 'on the way,' new possibilities for discipleship are cracked open for us and for all humankind. Look. Look for these things."

Key Terms in the Way of Discipleship

The following glossary of key concepts may be useful in our more detailed examination of the three focal texts.

Son of Man. In Mark's account this is the term Jesus uses to self-designate. The vast majority of the uses of "Son of Man" are located in the second half of Mark's narrative (12 of 14 occurrences). Thus, in the course of Mark's account this self-designation is ever more frequently associated with the coming passion, death, and rising of Jesus, which he begins to announce and emphasize as the Way section commences. As a result, "Son of Man" becomes increasingly linked to Jesus's approaching fate. The term "Son of Man" appears in all three focal texts.

Rebuke. "To rebuke" in Mark's account means to correct or indicate disapproval with something or someone. When rebuking occurs, it is intended to prevent or interrupt action or speech. To rebuke is to shut a thing down. For example, Jesus rebukes the wind and "the wind ceased" (4:39). In our first focal text, 8:31—9:1, Mark sets the context for a dramatic exchange of rebukes between Peter and Jesus. In 8:30 Mark notes that Jesus rebukes (NRSV translation = sternly orders) all the disciples, preventing them from any mention of him as Messiah. When "Peter finds the combination of Messiahship and suffering incongruous,"[9] Peter attempts to stop Jesus's talk of suffering and being killed. However, Peter's rebuke is countered by Jesus's rebuke, which silences Peter. This series of three rebukes in 8:30–33 lays the groundwork for Jesus's delineation of the Two Ways wherein a person's being and life's direction is oriented toward either "divine things" or "human things" (8:33).

Follow. Mark employs a variety of Greek vocabulary and two levels of meaning to point readers to the process of "following Jesus." The first

---

9. Juel, *Master of Surprise*, 95.

level is the literal one, wherein "following" carries the meaning of taking a position behind Jesus and walking there as the disciples' itinerant Teacher travels. This is the culturally appropriate and respectful location for students as they come after, that is, walk behind, their Teacher. The second level of meaning is the figurative one, wherein "following" refers not merely to the appropriate walking position during travels but also to the reality that "to follow Jesus" is to be or at least seek to be his disciple, one who learns from and practices the path of wisdom offered by his leader. Also, it is fair to say that Mark often invites readers to hold together the literal and the figurative in the same narrative moment. Thus followers on the way/road both walk behind their teacher and are hopeful of becoming disciples. Examples of this dual understanding of following are found twice in 8:34 and 10:32. Also, note that "followers" other than the Twelve appear in Mark's story, most conspicuously the women followers, whom Mark specifically mentions in chapters 15 and 16.

Life. In Mark "life" refers to much more than the biological phenomenon of human existence. It has to do with the very center and core of a person; it is the self, the essence of a person. Life appears repeatedly and centrally in 8:31—9:1, our first focal text, in a series of four references. In 10:32–45, our third focal text, it makes up part of Jesus's climactic statement about the Way of the Son of Man. He, Jesus, comes to serve "and to give his life a ransom for many" (10:45).

Little child. Our second focal text, 9:30–37, includes a reference to a young child, one perhaps small enough for Jesus to hold in his arms. Jesus interacts with his followers about this child, one who in his world lacks influence, standing, or power, and who is not usually attended to or even noticed by others, including the disciples. However, Jesus surprisingly instructs his disciples that through the welcoming or receiving of such a one, they can expect an encounter with the Holy.

Servant and slave. Mark uses the two terms, servant and slave, to point to those who above all else wait on or attend to the needs (or even whims) of others as directed by their masters. Their serving frequently involves much that is menial or unpleasant. Servants and slaves are not held in high regard by those giving them orders. In the society Mark presents as normative, they exist to be "at the beck and call"[10] of more powerful or prominent others.

---

10. *HarperCollins Bible Commentary*, 914.

Ransom. Mark employs the term "ransom" only in our third focal text, 10:32–45, and not at any other point in his narrative. Ransom appears in 10:45 as part of Jesus's final teaching encounter with his disciples in the Way of Discipleship material. In these last words of instruction the Markan Jesus links together his body of teaching delivered to his followers with the chosen Way of the Son of Man—a way of serving and the giving of self. Williamson writes, "'Ransom' comes from a world in which it was possible to buy the freedom of prisoners of war, slaves, or condemned criminals . . . The sum paid was called a 'ransom,' a term used only here (and par. Matt. 20:28) in the New Testament."[11] So, Mark uses this term to point to a process "of setting a person free."[12]

Want/will/choose. This concept (*thelo*) is present in all three of our focal texts of the Way material.[13] Especially noteworthy is Mark's use of it in the third focal text, wherein Mark portrays a contrast between what the disciples James and John want Jesus to do for them and what Bartimaeus wants Jesus to do for him.

The Three Focal Texts: The Heart and Soul of the Way Materials

In approaching the three focal texts for this chapter I take an expanded look at Mark's Way of Discipleship materials. Setting aside the bookends for the moment, along with 8:27–30 (Jesus's first steps on the way), this analysis looks at Mark's literary skeleton (see pages 161-62) from another perspective, focusing on Mark's three essential themes, which stand out vividly: Jesus's passion predictions, misunderstandings by the disciples, and Jesus's corrective instruction on discipleship and reissue of the call.

---

11. Williamson, *Mark*, 190.
12. Williamson, *Mark*, 190.
13. See chapter 6 for a detailed exploration of this theme.

Mark's Literary Skeleton II: 8:31—10:45 Jesus Proclaims his Fate and Teaches about Discipleship

Theme: Passion Prediction / Prophecy

8:31–32a	9:30–31	10:32–34
1. Son of man	1. Son of man	1. Son of man
2. will be killed	2. will be killed	2. will be killed
3. and will rise	3. and will rise	3. and will rise

Theme: Misunderstanding by the Disciples

8:32b–33	9:32–34	10:35–41
Peter misunderstands Jesus's new direction	Disciples misunderstand greatness and firstness	James and John misunderstand privilege and power

Theme: Instruction on Discipleship

8:34—9:1	9:35–37	10:42–45
1. Call (8:34)	1. Call (9:35)	1. Call (10:42)
2. Basic teaching (8:34)	2. Basic teaching (9:35)	2. Basic teaching (10:43)
3. Elaboration (8:35–38)	3. Elaboration (9:36–37)	3. Elaboration (10:45)

Focal Text: Mark 8:31—9:1

8:31–32a: Passion Prediction / Prophecy

[31] Then he began to teach them that the Son of Man must undergo great suffering, and be rejected by the elders, the chief priests, and the scribes, and be killed, and after three days rise again. [32a] He said all this quite openly.

Mark notes that Jesus's initial words about his future constitute a beginning to teach. In adopting the function of teacher Jesus sets himself the task of helping his disciples learn, realize, grasp something they have not known previously. Something new is afoot; he is teaching them so.

The content of that which has been previously unknown by the disciples is revealed in a series of "first mentions" at this point in the narrative. It is here that Mark first mentions (1) that Jesus (as Son of Man) will physically suffer and be killed, (2) that he will be spurned by the members of the religious establishment, and (3) that after three days he will rise. In addition, while Jesus's self-designation as the Son of Man has appeared earlier in Mark's account, it is only with its appearance in this first announcement of his passion that Jesus begins in earnest to reshape the Son of Man designation. Eventually, this reshaping will culminate in the climactic statement regarding the Son of Man as one who chooses to serve and lay aside his core being for the freedom of others (10:45).

Mark invites readers to observe that there is no ambiguity or "fuzziness" about what Jesus is expecting in his future. He speaks openly, clearly, and without qualification.

As we shall see when examining the Passion Predictions in the next two focal texts, the three predictions vary in how they describe the specific events and characters involved in Jesus's suffering and death. However, there is a central and shared message in the three: (1) The Son of Man, (2) will be killed, and (3) will rise.

8:32b–33: Misunderstanding by the Disciples

32b And Peter took him aside and began to rebuke him. 33But turning and looking at his disciples, he rebuked Peter and said, "Get behind me, Satan! For you are setting your mind not on divine things but on human things."

Here in our first focal text the misunderstanding of Jesus by his disciples as they are "on the way" is illuminated in two sides of a conversation between Peter and Jesus (8:32b–33). First, Peter comes forward from his position of following, takes Jesus aside, and tries to correct him by putting a stop to Jesus's words about a Son of Man who suffers, is killed, and rises. Second is Jesus's rebuke of Peter.

To elaborate on Peter's walking forward to Jesus, the context of 32b–33 makes clear that Peter leaves this appropriate position of following Jesus and moves toward him to deal more directly and personally with him. This depiction of disciples who leave off following and walk forward to be beside Jesus is repeated by James and John in our third text. These two accounts are the only instances in Mark when members of the Twelve come forward to interact directly and at such close range with Jesus. In each of these cases Jesus deals with the disciples in a blunt and sharply corrective manner.

From the Markan perspective, disciples are not intended to leave their proper place as followers of the Son of Man and when they do, they find themselves corrected and they face Jesus's expectation that they return to being followers. Furthermore, while on the way, it is only in following that disciples can maintain their vantage point of a clear and steady focus on the One who is out ahead of them, leading them, setting the pace. To be in any other position than following is to lose a right and helpful seeing of Jesus. It is he who is to be out front and they are to follow, all the while keeping their eyes on the One who goes before them.

This Markan perspective is reinforced in our first text after Peter moves forward to walk beside Jesus. He takes Jesus aside and tries to interrupt and silence Jesus. In taking Jesus aside, Peter "takes over as one does with children and the sick."[14] To Peter, Jesus seems to be behaving childishly or in a manner that indicates he is not well. How could Peter view Jesus as fit or maturely grounded when Jesus has just declared that his future will include suffering and being killed? Having heard his leader speak in such an obviously errant fashion, Peter steps in to take charge of a situation that seems to cry out for his guidance and intervention; surely Jesus cannot mean what he has just said. Peter attempts to correct, direct, and set Jesus straight, shushing his foolish talk.[15] Perhaps Peter thought that things could only get better if he could turn Jesus aside for a brief moment, giving him a chance to collect himself. By taking such a Peter-directed break, perhaps the journey could soon resume, back on course again.

As for Mark's second indication of the disciples' misunderstanding of Jesus, readers can hardly miss it: Jesus responds to Peter's rebuke of him with his own two-layered rebuke and correction of Peter. Layer 1:

---

14. Mays, "Mark 8:27—9:1," 176.
15. Mays, "Mark 8:27—9:1," 176.

implicit in Jesus's rebuke of Peter is Jesus's conviction that he, not Peter, holds the more incisive vision of what is to come in his future. It is he who rightly sees what lies ahead. As Mark shapes this scene of dueling rebukes, he pivots the narrative to reflect Jesus's growing recognition that now is the time when a new direction is called for, both for Jesus and his followers. As that new time arrives, the new given for Jesus becomes that his path will involve suffering, being killed, and a rising. Peter, who rebukes his teacher, can envision none of this nor allow himself to hear or trust it. And so, Peter is rebuked.

Layer 2: the Markan Jesus recognizes another matter that is at stake in his conflict with Peter: who will define and direct Jesus's path. The conflict poses a critical question: "Who holds the controlling authority over who Jesus is and how his journey will unfold?" When Peter comes forward to take charge of Jesus and attempts to erase any consideration of a Messiah whose fate is passion and annihilation, Jesus of course (from Mark's perspective) must stop Peter from stopping him. It is only Jesus's prerogative to define who he is and whose he will be as the Son of Man; it is only he—led by the Spirit—who is to be in charge of the direction his steps will take on the Way; it is only he along with the Spirit who will guide his growth into being God's Son (15:39). And so, Peter is rebuked.

Having noted Peter's literal missteps, however, readers are able to adopt a more complete perspective on Jesus's conflict with Peter by reflecting on the corrective aspect of Jesus's rebuke of Peter. As Mays has observed, Jesus's rebuke of Peter is both sharp and corrective, containing stinging confrontation and bracing grace.[16] As for the sharpness, nowhere else in his account does Jesus address any other disciples as "Satan"; even Judas the Betrayer does not warrant this appellation. Moreover, Jesus makes it clear that "satans" like Peter do not have their hearts and minds set on the things of God and God's kingdom; rather, they are anchored elsewhere, in "human things"—that is, in a self-seeking, self-aggrandizing, and self-saving orientation to life. At the same time, and perhaps easier to overlook, grace also permeates the conflict. When Jesus turns to look back toward where Peter has literally just come from—from the group of followers walking behind Jesus—readers might expect Jesus's scathing words to continue. Instead, Jesus leaves the way open to Peter. He will have another chance, for Peter is not prohibited from again following and Jesus does not dismiss him from the Way. Instead, Peter is

---

16. Mays, "Mark 8:27—9:1," 176–77.

told to return to his place among his fellow disciples; it is only there that he can be restored and rightly follow on the way. So, while Peter is subject to firm and even harsh correction, he is also provided a way to resume his journey. "Following" is the precise vantage point from which Peter may yet learn to be saved from human things, or to put it slightly differently, it is the only position on the way from which Peter can be saved from himself.[17]

8:34—9:1: Instruction on Discipleship to Correct the Misunderstanding and Reissue the Call

8:34 He called the crowd with his disciples, and said to them, "If any want to become my followers, let them deny themselves and take up their cross and follow me. **35** For those who want to save their life will lose it, and those who lose their life for my sake, and for the sake of the gospel, will save it. **36** For what will it profit them to gain the whole world and forfeit their life? **37** Indeed, what can they give in return for their life? **38** Those who are ashamed of me and of my words in this adulterous and sinful generation, of them the Son of Man will also be ashamed when he comes in the glory of his Father with the holy angels."

9:1 And he said to them, "Truly I tell you, there are some standing here who will not taste death until they see that the kingdom of God has come with power."

Mark places Jesus's instruction on discipleship in 8:34—9:1 within the context of a summoning of both the crowd and those already drawn to Jesus as disciples. Both Mays and Williamson have indicated that this summons is more than a simple gathering together of the crowd and followers.[18] Rather, the summons carries the meaning that Jesus is issuing a "second" or "redefined" call to his hearers.[19] This reissued call is both similar to and different from the first call of Jesus to Simon and Andrew in 1:16–17. It is similar in that it anticipates following Jesus as a possible response to the call. It differs, however, in that the expected outcome of following declared by Jesus in the initial call was that Simon and Andrew

---

17. Mays, "Mark 8:27—9:1," 176.

18. Mays, "Mark 8:27—9:1," 177; and Williamson, *Mark*, 154.

19. Myers refers to this "second" call (*Binding the Strong Man*, 245); Williamson characterizes the call as "redefined" (*Mark*, 154).

would "fish for people,"[20] while in 8:34, the call is reshaped to include the projected outcome of denial of self and taking up a cross, a more ominous prospect than fishing for people. Moreover, in the second call, the path of following as a disciple is informed by Jesus's recent forecast of his own passion-filled future. If the disciples are to walk behind Jesus on the path he will take, their path, too, will involve suffering—a far cry from what the Twelve have envisioned.

The reissued call, here and in our two remaining texts, contains two constant, defining characteristics: (1) the call issued by Jesus is persistent and recurring, and (2) the decision to respond affirmatively to or decline the call rests solely with those who are recipients of it.

The persistent and prominent nature of the call is indicated by Mark's use of language about "being called" in each of our three focal texts (8:34, 9:35, and 10:42). Jesus's summons is thrice repeated. And each call is issued within the sobering context of Jesus's declaring his own dangerously fraught path toward Jerusalem.

As for the second dominant characteristic of call as Mark portrays it, in each of the focal texts, the choice to pursue or back away from the call is to be made solely by potential followers or those choosing to recommit to following Jesus. That is, Jesus issues no mandated or forced choice for his prospective disciples. To the contrary, he leaves the choosing of discipleship open and hypothetical. His words are: "If any want [choose] to become my followers" (8:34); "Whoever wants [chooses] to be the first" (9:35); and "whoever wishes [chooses] to become great" and "whoever wishes [chooses] to become first" (10:43 and 10:44). It is a hallmark of Mark's understanding of call that discipleship is to be chosen and never compelled or commanded by Jesus; it is ever and always offered by him as that which persons may choose. It is a choice to be faced freely, under no compulsion. A decision for discipleship may be made by those encountering Jesus, but it is equally possible that it may not.

Along with Mark's emphasis on "calling," all of these texts portray Jesus as engaged yet again in his ongoing efforts to teach and instruct his disciples. Williamson outlines a four-part structure for this text: introduction, basic principle, elaboration of the basic principle, and conclusion.[21] Prompted by Williamson's work, I suggest the following questions: (1)

---

20. While the meaning of "fishing for people" is somewhat nebulous, the overall sense of the phrase apparently is to offer a promising prospect to those already engaged in a life of fishing.

21. Williamson, *Mark*, 154.

What is the "basic teaching" in the scene? (I use "basic teaching" here rather than Williamson's "basic principle"); (2) How does Mark go about elaborating on the basic teaching? and (3) What misunderstanding of the disciples is the scene designed to correct? (The same questions are applied in turn to our second and third focal texts.[22])

The basic teaching. In putting forward the basic teaching of our first focal text, Jesus delineates three actions to be taken by those who would become followers; disciples are to "deny themselves and take up their cross and follow me" (8:34). Mays makes the case that these three form a unified whole and "are not acts which are distinct from each other or separable from following."[23] Moreover, self-denial refers neither to abstaining from any specific object, desire, or ambition, nor to pursuing a path born of self-denigration. Rather, it aims potential followers toward a denial of the "grasping" self-promoting and self-serving inclination that forms the center of "human things" mentioned in 8:33.[24] Similarly, taking up one's cross refers not to uncomplaining acceptance of the misfortunes that by chance come our way; it refers rather "to painful, redemptive action voluntarily undertaken for others."[25]

Jesus is growing into his identity as the Son of Man who will suffer, be killed, and rise, and his teaching in 8:34 invites followers to reconsider their relationship to him. Knowing that the road ahead as portrayed by Jesus appears both different from and darker than fishing for people, will they reaffirm their connection to him and follow? Such a course would indicate a striving to keep a suffering Son of Man at their center. But is this One simply too risky to follow?

Mark's elaboration. Mark invites the reader's continuing focus on the basic teaching of 8:34 in two ways that illuminate the fuller meaning of the text. First, he employs a series of four consecutive "for" clauses—one

---

22. Although Williamson does not suggest that his remarks on the structure of 8:34—9:1 could also apply to our second and third texts, his analysis is a helpful lens through which to view 9:30–37 and 10:32–45. As with our first focal text, each of these later texts offer a helpful perspective on (1) a basic corrective teaching of the Markan Jesus and (2) an elaboration Mark employs to refine the basic teaching. Within the three texts Mark's method of elaboration varies; but each basic teaching is broadened by the end of the scene. Consequently, I will use some of Williamson's insights on the structure of 8:34—9:1 in exploring 9:30–37 and 10:32–45.

23. Mays, "Mark 8:27—9:1," 177.

24. Williamson, *Mark*, 154.

25. Williamson, *Mark*, 154.

each in 8:35, 8:36, 8:37, and 8:38.[26] My readers know that a "for" clause signals readers not to miss out on an important moment in the story.[27] By grouping four "for" clauses in a tightly connected series of verses, Mark hopes readers will attend to the content of the clauses and how they expand the meaning of this basic teaching.

Second, Mark's elaboration of the basic teaching relies on multiple uses of the Greek noun *psyche* or "life." The saving of "life" or the losing of it appears in 8:35 (twice), 8:36, and 8:37. The usual translation of *psyche* in the NRSV is "life." However, the Greek noun "means either 'life' or 'soul' and can appropriately be translated as 'self' (NEB)."[28] Through his multiple uses of "life," Mark alludes to the saving or losing of one's essential self—the "whatever it is" that constitutes a human's core being. In this first focal text Mark is letting his readers know that discipleship is the path that leads toward a vibrantly enlivened existence for those who choose to follow Jesus. At the same time, he is indicating that this pulsating aliveness can be forfeited, lost, backed away from by those unwilling to follow. What is involved in "life" is far from the biological process of breathing in and out while one's heart beats. For Mark, the good news holds that (1) life, soul, self are the fundamental realities of existence for followers who choose to pursue Jesus's reissued call, and that (2) if one chooses to walk not merely on this earth, but to enter God's kingdom of radical transformation, aliveness of one's core and soul is what will constitute the future.

The misunderstanding that is corrected. When considering the question of what misunderstanding of the disciples is corrected in 8:34—9:1, caution is the wisest course. To me, Mark is not fully clear about what discipleship misunderstanding is addressed in this first text. Granted, he does offer hints about what is in error when (1) Jesus rebukes the disciples in general and Peter in particular around issues related to Messiahship (8:31–33), (2) Jesus delineates the dichotomy between divine things and human things, and (3) Jesus makes paradoxical statements regarding the saving and losing of life. Even with these three clues, a lack of clarity remains as readers try to ascertain the exact nature and full extent of the disciples' waywardness. This lack may reflect a literary necessity at this point in Mark's story, for his keenest priority in 8:31—9:1 is Jesus's initial

---

26. The NRSV does not reflect the presence of *gar* in 8:37 and 8:38. However, *gar* does appear (and is translated as "for") in the 1953 edition of the RSV.

27. See chapter 1.

28. Williamson, *Mark*, 155.

The Way of Discipleship 181

and full-throated enunciation of the passion-filled fate that awaits him. By having Jesus speak unambiguously about his future Mark postpones for the moment a more specific focus on the disciples' misunderstanding. However, readers can rest assured that Mark addresses the misunderstanding of the disciples more pointedly in the next two focal texts; in these texts Mark will spell out more thoroughly where the Twelve are off track and need correcting.

Focal Text: Mark 9:30–37

9:30–31
Passion Prediction / Prophecy

> ³⁰They went on from there and passed through Galilee. He did not want anyone to know it; ³¹for he was teaching his disciples, saying to them, "The Son of Man is to be betrayed into human hands, and they will kill him, and three days after being killed, he will rise again."

In 9:30–37, Mark again presents the sequence of three crucial narrative themes: passion prediction by Jesus, misunderstanding by the disciples, and corrective instruction on discipleship and a reissued call. By repeating the three themes in the same sequence—in 8:31—9:1, here, and in 10:32–45—Mark creates a structural kinship among the three texts.

Looking specifically at the Passion Prophecy portion of our second focal text, readers find two continuations of features that resonate with the first focal text. First, Mark is again specific about Jesus's teaching function (see 9:31). He flags this instructing activity by placing reference to "teaching" within one of Mark's "for" (*gar*) clauses. Second, the content of this teaching is quite similar, though not identical, to what Jesus has already outlined as his future in 8:31—9:1—that the Son of Man will be killed and rise again. In 9:31, this formula is repeated.

Along with these similarities, Mark adds certain new details, which broaden the reader's understanding of the Way of Discipleship section. Perhaps most notably, Mark has Jesus shift his attention more exclusively and urgently toward his disciples. The crowd that was present in 8:31—9:1 is no longer among those Jesus is teaching. Rather, Jesus is presented as actively avoiding exposure to public throngs. Jesus's choice in 9:30 is to absent himself from the crowd, thereby freeing himself to focus his time and teaching on the disciples. At this juncture on his way to Jerusalem, it is his closest followers Jesus wants to teach.

Another difference between the first two focal texts is that part of Jesus's teaching to his disciples here focuses on Jesus being "betrayed into human hands" (9:31). In comparison, our first focal text speaks of Jesus's suffering and being rejected by various religious factions. While this difference is subtle, it does remind readers that Jesus's passion includes a literal giving Jesus over into the hands of those who will inflict severe physical harm on him before ending his life. For Mark, this betrayal includes the surety of torture, pain, and humiliation. Moreover, according to Mark, those who engage in these practices of pain are not limited to the religious authorities; rather, the category of torturers is expanded to include humankind.

9:32–34
Misunderstanding by the Disciples

³²But they did not understand what he was saying and were afraid to ask him. ³³Then they came to Capernaum; and when he was in the house he asked them, "What were you arguing about on the way?" ³⁴But they were silent, for on the way they had argued with one another who was the greatest.

As in the first and third focal texts (8:27 and 10:32), the setting here is "on the way" (9:34). Also, here again the disciples prove unwilling or unable to absorb Jesus's teachings. Instead, they end up arguing among themselves over which is "the greatest" (9:34). It is not unusual that a debate over greatness would break out among Jesus's followers; as Clifton Black has commented, the issue of a person's or group's greatness is "a point of controversy within social groups of antiquity."[29] Greatness is a familiar and much-argued topic of the disciples as they travel along, and this in itself points to the contrast between Jesus and his followers. Despite Jesus's teaching about what lies ahead, the disciples remain rooted in their usual, everyday, and very human concerns; they are (again) not yet able or willing to see that another Way is being called for, a Way like the one Jesus is walking, and not the way of self-absorption and self-preservation. Mired in their normative and predictable worldview and

29. Black, "The Gospel of Mark," note on Mark 9:34.

manner of moving through life, they demonstrate little to no capacity to envision this other Way—a God-centered, Jesus-walked Way, one able to free them from themselves and compassionately open them to the needs of others. And so they argue.

Mark places in 9:32–34 two very clear indicators of the disciples' failure to understand. The more obvious, of course, is Mark's statement that Jesus's followers "did not understand what he was saying" (9:32). This lack of understanding is apparently compounded because the disciples did not ask Jesus for clarification or further elaboration on what he was attempting to get across. After all, Jesus had specifically set aside this time of instruction in order to talk with his followers. But despite Jesus's efforts, their lack of understanding is unshakeable, leading not to additional explanation or dialogue but only to fear of pursuing the meaning of Jesus's words.

The second clear indicator for the disciples' getting off track comes after Jesus specifically questions them regarding their argument as they were walking on the road. The resounding silence (9:34) is akin to their failure to converse further with their teacher. Also, it is noteworthy that Mark uses a "for" clause to alert his readers to the likely reason behind the silence; they are silent because of their ongoing envelopment by their concern for status, prominence, safety, and power. While these concerns are normative in the social, religious, political, and familial milieu of the day, they are not to be considered so in the time (*kairos*) of God's kingdom and as followers choose to move toward the reign of God. By the time Mark's narrative has reached 9:34, the time is ripe for corrective teaching by Jesus, ably assisted by a small child.

9:35–37
Instruction on Discipleship to Correct the Misunderstanding and Reissue the Call

³⁵He sat down, called the twelve, and said to them, "Whoever wants to be first must be last of all and servant of all." ³⁶Then he took a little child and put it among them; and taking it in his arms, he said to them, ³⁷"Whoever welcomes one such child in my name welcomes me, and whoever welcomes me welcomes not me but the one who sent me."

The basic teaching. When Jesus's question to his disciples is met with mute response, Jesus is alerted that something is amiss and further teaching is needed. As he has in the past, he sits, thereby assuming the position and role of teacher. Equally important in Mark's narrative, as Jesus prepares to teach, he calls his closest followers—the Twelve. In doing so he signals that the teaching of this present moment is directed to his inner circle, those still enthralled with being first and pursuant of normative greatness they had argued over on the road to Capernaum. Over against the disciples' verbal sparring—likely centering on power, wealth, social standing, or familial honor—Jesus in 9:35 promotes a paradoxical perspective by speaking of being great and first as embodied in servants, those who by definition respond to the needs, wants, and even whims of others. Such a call by Jesus—a call to be great and first as a servant—no doubt left the Twelve dumbfounded; it would reverse all that they had come to know and aspire to about becoming honored and admired members of their society.

Mark's elaboration. In our first text Mark made use of two literary techniques to elaborate on the basic teaching: a grouping of four consecutive "for" clauses and a persistent focus on the Greek word for life (*psyche*). Here, in 9:35–37, Jesus is presented as expanding the disciples' grasp of the basic teaching by use of a young child. Jesus presents the child as an object lesson for the Twelve. Within the context of the disciples' discussion of greatness/firstness, Jesus singles out one who is in no way likely to be viewed as prominent or warranting attention.

> Children did not enjoy the central valuation they receive in our culture, often to the child's detriment. On the rabbinic valuation on associating with children, a saying from the *Pirke Aboth*, a collection of rabbinic teachings, is instructive: "Morning sleep and midday wine and children's talk and sitting in the meeting houses of the ignorant people put a man out of the world" (*Aboth* 3:11b, quoted from Danby's edition of the Mishna, p. 451). To use attention to a child, therefore, as an example of greatness in God's kingdom is to fly in the face of rabbinic wisdom that such association is unprofitable for those who would advance religiously.[30]

The prevailing wisdom was that those in pursuit of positive religious and spiritual development could "rightly" expect nothing to be learned or gained from a child; children could profitably be avoided by purposeful,

---

30. Achtemeier, "Mark 9:30–37," 182.

spiritually oriented adults. However, Jesus calls his closest followers to a contrary view of reality in God's reign. For it is precisely a child, in spite of bothersome characteristics and behavior, whom Jesus physically locates at the very center of the disciples gathered around him. Likewise, the child is at the center of Jesus's corrective teaching as seen in both his actions—"taking it in his arms" (9:36)—and his words about welcoming. With both, Jesus indicates that it is the response of his followers toward the child, and toward others who are similarly powerless, difficult, and unrewarding—that will be the true measure of greatness.[31] This is not the greatness sought by the Twelve, but it is greatness nonetheless, instructs Jesus.

The misunderstanding that is corrected. The misunderstanding corrected in our first focal text was somewhat unclear, despite several Markan clues as to its nature. Here in 9:30–37, however, there is little such difficulty for the reader. Jesus sets out to correct the disciples' understanding and practice of greatness/firstness as it intersects with the kingdom of God. In God's arriving reign, Jesus says, greatness is to be coupled with an attentive, servant-like response to those with no societal, familial, political, or religious claim to honor, prominence, regard, or power. Even the likes of chattering children—brimming with distracting behavior and absent any worthwhile contribution to adult learning—are to be welcomed with kindness, treated respectfully, and placed at the center of things. With such corrective instruction at the fore of Jesus's dealing with the Twelve, it is indeed no small thing that Jesus seeks to correct here. It is nothing short of the continuing shift away from the disciples' long-held and practiced worldview. In this second teaching about the Way of Discipleship, no longer does Jesus speak only of self-denial, crosses, and divine things, as if these were not enough. Here, he expands this vision by offering a choice to the Twelve—a choice to pursue greatness by being last, like a servant. The shift in the contours of the Way continues and it is a seismic alteration of what the disciples once believed to be as unshakeable as the earth beneath their feet.

And still Jesus is not finished with his corrective teaching. He advances the Way one step further with his instruction about an additional

---

31. Williamson, *Mark*, 170, indicates that it is unclear whether Mark's portrayal of Jesus as he physically places the child among the disciples implies that he simply stood behind the child, resting his hands around his shoulders, or more dramatically swept up the child in his arms and held him as he addressed the Twelve. Either way, Jesus's attention to the child, touching him respectfully and caringly, would certainly grab the disciples' attention.

reality for those moving deeper into God's kingdom. The additional reality is this: for all who welcome a child, their very welcome places them in the presence of the Holy, the Source of all "divine things," and the Sender of the Son of Man. To welcome a societal "nobody," then, is to position themselves within a sacred relationship. In the welcoming, Jesus's followers meet and encounter as guest and host the great I AM.

And so our second focal text closes. In this scene Mark has implicitly framed a question: "Who could have possibly conceived the outcome of Jesus's dealings with one not notable in society, especially when those with elevated standing or importance are nearby and entitled to receive the lion's share of any such gracious welcome?" And Mark's answer is beyond any human code or wisdom. "Look to the likes of a child," he says. "In God's season and God's realm sacredness breaks forth in such a meeting."

Focal Text: Mark 10:32–45

10:32–34
Passion Prediction / Prophecy

³²They were on the way, going up to Jerusalem, and Jesus was walking ahead of them; they were amazed, and those who followed were afraid. He took the twelve aside again and began to tell them what was to happen to him, ³³saying, "See, we are going up to Jerusalem, and the Son of Man will be handed over to the chief priests and the scribes, and they will condemn him to death; then they will hand him over to the Gentiles; ³⁴they will mock him, and spit upon him, and flog him, and kill him; and after three days he will rise again."

Our third focal text reflects the same Markan literary design mentioned earlier. In the Way materials as a whole, there are three episodes of encounter between Jesus and his followers, and each encounter presents the sequence of three themes: passion prediction, the disciples' misunderstanding, and Jesus's corrective instruction and reissued call.

In 10:32–34, Mark presents readers with a setting that is both similar to and expanded from the settings of our first two focal texts. Again, there is reference to Jesus and his followers being "on the way" (10:32). But there are two additional details that expand the setting. For the first time in the Markan narrative, Jerusalem is identified (10:32–33) as the geographical destination for the journey begun by Jesus and his followers in 8:27. Jerusalem will prove to be the seat of power for the growing opposition to Jesus. This opposition will coalesce until it includes multiple religious authorities, the politically and socially prominent, and those possessing military might throughout the whole of Judea. In addition, Mark speaks of the fear that develops among his disciples: "and those who followed were afraid" (10:32). Certainly, this fear could have been prompted by Jesus's conversation with the disciples in Mark's immediately preceding scene (10:17–31) where Jesus speaks of the persecutions that would accompany their discipleship. It is also possible that the mere prospect of approaching Jerusalem was sufficient to frighten Jesus's followers.[32]

The passion prediction here at 10:32–34 provides an outline of Jesus's passion, death, and rising, which Mark will flesh out, beginning with 14:43 and going through to the end of his narrative.

An additional distinctive feature of this third passion prediction is its focus on the "gentiles" and what they will do to Jesus after his arrest. The gentiles—the Roman political authorities—will mock, spit upon, flog, and kill (10:34). With this passion prediction Mark begins to describe the depth, ruthlessness, and brutality of the power they will exercise toward Jesus. Indeed, they hold life-and-death power over him and all others in their sway.

10:35–41
Misunderstanding by the Disciples

35James and John, the sons of Zebedee, came forward to him and said to him, "Teacher, we want you to do for us whatever we ask of you." **36**And he said to them, "What is it you want me to do for you?" **37**And they said to him, "Grant us to sit, one at your right hand and one at your left, in your glory." **38**But Jesus said to them, "You do not know what you are asking. Are you able to drink the cup that I drink, or be baptized with the baptism that I am baptized with?" **39**They replied, "We are able." Then Jesus said to them, "The cup that I drink you will drink; and with the baptism with which I am baptized, you will be

---

32. The "fear" of Jesus's disciples/followers is mentioned prominently in other Markan scenes. See, for example, 6:50, 9:6, and 16:8. Indeed, Myers writes that "'fear' is a constitutive element of 'following'" (*Binding the Strong Man*, 277). Williamson adds, "Anyone who contemplates following Jesus without fear and trembling has not understood true discipleship, according to Mark" (*Mark*, 195).

baptized; **40**but to sit at my right hand or at my left is not mine to grant, but it is for those for whom it has been prepared."

41When the ten heard this, they began to be angry with James and John.

Mark lays down three markers of the disciples' misunderstanding of Jesus's passion prediction of 10:32–34. These are (1) James and John come forward to Jesus after his third announcement; (2) still anticipating a triumphant future for their leader, James and John ask Jesus for seats of privilege and power in his "glory" (10:37), and (3) the remaining ten closest followers of Jesus react angrily to James and John when they get wind of their request to Jesus. A closer look at each of these markers is in order.

James and John come forward. In yet another example of disciples misunderstanding their role as followers, James and John leave their normative and appropriate positions of walking behind their teacher and come forward to address Jesus face to face. After Mark's description of the outcome of Jesus's encounter with Peter in 8:32b–33, readers might well anticipate that members of Jesus's inner circle would swear off any additional approaches to Jesus; it certainly did not turn out so well for Peter. Not so, says Mark—at least for James and John.

By 10:35 James and John seem to have developed a plan they hope will avoid the flaws of Peter's approach to Jesus.³³ Imagine that prior to their stepping forward to engage Jesus their minds and hushed conversations centered around thoughts and whispered words like these:

---

33. I am obligated to alert readers that I have made ample use of my imagination regarding James and John and thus have entered into the realm of speculation here. I am treading on ground both stimulating and capable in the same moment of leading readers away from the concreteness and spare nature of Mark's account. Indeed, Mark makes no explicit comments about what with certainty goes on in the minds of James and John, or of any conversations they may have had before moving forward to engage Jesus. However, I am hopeful that my speculations will prove evocative for readers and true to the spirit of Mark's narrative. To me, there seem to be clues or hints that James and John's approach to Jesus was more calculating than Peter's earlier outburst. But in the final analysis readers need to decide what they believe regarding James and John, their motivations and possible ploys as they leave off following and move forward to indicate to Jesus what they want (choose) him to do for them.

- Let us approach Jesus with caution and subtlety. Peter failed in part because of his well-known tendency for speaking too quickly and being too blunt.
- Let us approach Jesus with deference and respect for him as our esteemed, wise teacher and leader—one with the authority to grant us a simple wish. Peter failed in part because he acted as though Jesus was not in full possession of his mental faculties.
- Let us approach Jesus as potentially helpful advisors, who could assist him if he would in his glory appoint us. Peter failed in part because he tried to steer Jesus toward his own vision of Jesus's future as the Messiah.
- Let us secure a promise from Jesus before we tell him what we want—approach him as small children might approach their pliable parents.[34] If we play our cards right, we just might end up with those seats of power and privilege we want on his left and right.

With such a plan in mind James and John move forward to try their luck with Jesus.

James and John ask for seats of privilege and power. The request itself is a second marker of the disciples' misunderstanding in 10:32–45. Several aspects of this incident stand out, including the devious way in which James and John frame their request to Jesus. They attempt to secure his promise to give them what they want (choose) before detailing what is involved in their petition; in the parlance of today, they ask Jesus to sign a blank check.

James and John begin by addressing Jesus as "teacher," even as they clearly display their lack of attention to his teaching. Their particular request for seats of power and prominence in Jesus's imagined triumphant future lacks any shred of connection or resonance with what Jesus has been teaching throughout his journeys. Indeed, by the completion of our second focal text (9:30–37), Jesus's teaching has evolved to center on the first being last and disciples hopefully aspiring to be "servant of all" (9:35). But in 10:35 James and John, missing the point altogether, use the title "teacher" to sidle up to Jesus or flatter him so as to get what they want when Jesus's glory time comes.

---

34. Williamson writes of James and John's childlike and manipulative strategy as they attempt to entrap Jesus into giving them what they want (choose) without knowing what their choice entails (*Mark*, 192).

Just as Peter attempted to take charge of Jesus (8:32), in 10:35–37 James and John attempt the same, albeit in a calmer, apparently less boisterous manner. While it is a quieter attempt at control, their goal is identical to Peter's. However, using the vocabulary of wanting (wishing, choosing) in the exchange, Mark presents Jesus as aware of this more subtle attempt to bind his actions and his choices and he deflects James and John, asking, "What is it you want me to do for you?"[35] As the Son of Man, he will not allow James's and John's request to ensnare, bind, or define him; he will not allow himself to be played, even by those closest to him.

The ten react angrily. In 10:41 Mark broadens his account of this incident to show that it is not only James and John who are off track in their errant following of Jesus. His narrative implicates the additional ten close followers as well, hinting that they share James's and John's outlook on privilege and power. Mark clearly states that the ten "began to be angry with James and John" (10:41). Perhaps their wrath is prompted by their wish that they, rather than James and John, had been the ones to approach Jesus. For not only had James and John tried to dupe Jesus into granting their wishes, James and John had also duped their ten fellow disciples by speaking to Jesus on the sly. So Mark closes this section of the discipleship misunderstanding with reference to the simmering and growing anger of the ten. From Mark's perspective, the divisive heat of this conflict springing up among the full complement of disciples reinforces an ongoing Markan storyline—that the disciples persist in their misunderstanding of the Son of Man and the implications of his path for their own.

10:42–45
Instruction on Discipleship to Correct the Misunderstanding and Reissue the Call

> [42]So Jesus called them and said to them, "You know that among the Gentiles those whom they recognize as their rulers lord it over them, and their great ones are tyrants over them. [43]But it is not so among you; but whoever wishes to become great among you must be your

---

35. I remind readers that the question asked of James and John is the identical one asked of Bartimaeus in 10:51. The contrast between the choices being made, however, could hardly differ more dramatically. James and John choose for position, honor, and privilege while Bartimaeus's choice is solely for what he needs in order to more ably follow Jesus. In one sense, James and John give the wrong answer to Jesus's question while Bartimaeus gets it right.

servant, ⁴⁴and whoever wishes to be first among you must be slave of all. ⁴⁵For the Son of Man came not to be served but to serve, and to give his life a ransom for many."

With the conflict escalating among the Twelve, Jesus interrupts, again calling them and preparing to teach. In this call of 10:42 Mark echoes the previous two calls of the Way of Discipleship passages in 8:34 and 9:35. For a third time, then, Jesus is reissuing a call to the Twelve in light of his growing recognition that (1) his path is that of a suffering, dying, and rising Son of Man, and (2) his fate has implications for any who would choose to follow him.

The gentiles. In his first moment of corrective teaching, Jesus reintroduces "the gentiles" into the conflictual atmosphere on the road (10:42). He identifies the Roman political authorities as those who are tyrannical in their role and lord their power over others. Moreover, in his earlier reference to the gentiles in 10:34, Jesus has already established that the logical outcome of the exercise of such tyrannical power is indeed what he anticipates for himself—that the lordly rulers will see to it that the Son of Man is mocked, spit upon, flogged, and killed. Here Mark's readers are invited to consider that Jesus is instructing the Twelve, and all future potential followers, on this singular truth: that the pursuit of power, privilege, and honor bestowed upon the earthly great ones carries with it inevitable, divisive, and destructive results. Those who seek to be great through the use of such unbridled and even life-and-death power over others will never find the Way to a disciple-like way of living. A different Way must be chosen if one wishes to arrive at greatness/firstness in the kingdom of God.

The emphatic, present-tense, and personal "no." Mark's Jesus leaves no doubt about his rejection of all paths that lead to the dominating and brutal use of power. Immediately following his description of the dark center of gentile authority, Jesus issues an adamant pronouncement about who disciples are and how they are able to act if they so choose. His statement is emphatic, delivered in the present tense, and personal. Jesus's adamancy and negation of the gentiles' approach to greatness is shown in two words Mark has Jesus speak to his followers: "not so" (10:43). An essential purpose of this verse, then, is to lay out the confrontive and challenging negation of a particular wayward direction being considered by the Twelve. To seek domineering and potentially crushing power over others is anathema to what Jesus's disciples are to be about. Jesus's words are direct and definitive: "Not so!"

Present tense. A second illuminating feature of Jesus's pronouncement is that he uses the present tense when speaking of his closest followers. By using the present tense, "it is not so among you" (10:43), Jesus anchors the Twelve in the very instant of his teaching. Jesus does this in the midst of their conflict, the raised voices and heat of which are likely still reverberating in the minds and hearts of the Twelve. In God's season and with the arrival of God's reign, the present moment calls for an alternative way of living in the immediate now.

Personal. There is another noteworthy feature of 10:43-44. Jesus uses the phrase "among you" three times—twice in 10:43 and once in 10:44. In doing so Jesus addresses the Twelve in as personal a manner as possible. This message is for them—Jesus's followers—those closest to him, those who have so often failed him, but also those whom he keeps in his heart and projects at the center of whatever is yet to come, even after he is gone.

The basic teaching. In examining 10:43a, we have already taken note of the first portion of Mark's basic teaching contained in the third focal text. In Jesus's first words of corrective instruction, he remains constant in his definition of those who follow him as disciples; namely, that they are not to be like those who seek greatness through securing positions of power and privilege, out of which will inevitably flow ruthless and brutal actions toward others. Said slightly differently, the first half of Jesus's teaching is "You are not gentile-like; you are my disciples, inexorably connected to each other."

The next part of Jesus's instruction spells out the nature of the connection that is to exist between the Twelve. Mark's theme of choice re-emerges through the twice-repeated phrase "whoever wishes" (10:43-44). From Mark's point of view, the positive relationships among the disciples are enabled as they want them to be so, desire them, wish deeply for them, and choose them. It is chosen discipleship that is essential for a successful traveling of the Way of Discipleship. Nothing else will do.

Mark then advances his teaching one step further through his assertion that to be first and great comes through the disciples' choice to be servants, carrying out the duties befitting slaves. Disciples are called to a state of unceasing attention to the needs of (usually) powerless or burdened others. In God's new season and the transforming ethic of the kingdom, the path to being authentically and rightly bound to each other involves the setting aside of one's own self (*psyche*) and human interests, choosing instead to move toward and attend to the needs of others of God's children. It is this stance of other-focused and self-giving servanthood that will in God's season constitute genuine greatness.

Mark's elaboration. As he does in our first and second focal texts, Mark again elaborates on Jesus's basic corrective teaching, this time in Jesus's crystal-clear reference to himself as the Son of Man (10:45). What is most striking about this Son of Man reference is that Jesus—who has already announced that the Son of Man will suffer, be killed, and raised—further develops and expands his identity and stated purpose. New to the Twelve (as well as to Mark's readers) is Jesus's assertion that he, as the Son of Man, comes as servant and gives his very self (core/life/being—*psyche*). And even more than that, Jesus delineates what he expects to be the result of his serving and self-giving. In a metaphor like no other found in Mark, Jesus says that his offered self will be "a ransom for many" (10:45). A ransom in Jesus's day referred to that which secured freedom for those who were in some way unfree—"prisoners of war, slaves, or condemned criminals."[36] In 10:45, then, Jesus is affirming to and for his followers his conviction that service and self-giving culminate in setting others free from the various systems, institutions, and circumstances that hold God's children in their sway. The choices and actions of the Son of Man enable the release and renewed life for the unfree.

In this verse yet again Mark uses one of his "for" clauses (10:45) to invite readers to notice something new. In this instance it is a new dimension of Jesus's identity: Jesus will serve and give himself. At the same time, the clause serves an additional purpose. With this "for," Mark looks both backward and forward in his text; the "for" functions as a connector between the community of disciples on the one hand (10:43–44) and the Son of Man on the other (10:45). The attention of readers in 10:43–44 is drawn first to the Twelve as they are taught about what constitutes greatness and firstness among them and then to the Son of Man and what his service and self-giving will accomplish for the unfree. With this specific "for" Mark assures his readers that the way of authentic discipleship cannot be cut adrift from Jesus and his path of servanthood and offering of self. When taken together, the three verses of 10:43–45 make Mark's point that Jesus is the ultimate paradigm for anyone who chooses to be

---

36. Williamson, *Mark*, 190.

a disciple. So, despite a history of frequent failings and stumbling by the disciples on their Way, the bond between authentic but flawed disciples and Jesus making his way to Jerusalem can never be broken. The two ways are not distinct, separated from one another. In God's time and reign the two are transformed into one. To be sure, Jesus will walk in the lead position and disciples are to follow. But the path is one.

The misunderstanding that is corrected. The nature of the disciples' misunderstanding in the third focal text is revealed by Jesus's words to the Twelve about the holders of tyrannical powers, the gentiles. For the Markan Jesus these political and military authorities stand as the antithesis of his teachings outlined in the Way of Discipleship passages. Jesus cites them because he recognizes what the disciples perhaps do not—that the power of the gentiles is corrosive; it infects its holders and leads them toward acts of brutality, crushing cruelty, and, if necessary, lethal action. Its toxicity is exposed as they engage in their lordly dominance over others, a dominance that will in Jesus's case be used to mock, spit upon, flog, and execute. Moreover, the conflict that arises in this scene springs from the fantasized pursuit of this sort of power by the disciples. Mark's narrative implies that all who would grasp for and hold tightly to such control and dominion will be caught up by deceitfulness, secrecy, anger, tension, conflict, and the breakdown of communal bonds. Given long enough, Jesus implies, this infecting and corrosive force will move all under its spell toward the worst that human beings can do to each other.

From a Markan perspective, then, the Twelve are decidedly off track when they would aspire to occupy such gentile-like seats of power, privilege, and standing on Jesus's right and left. It cries out for confrontation and correction by Jesus. Jesus provides both: "But it is not so among you" (10:43).

Mark's Way of Discipleship: Conclusion

With the delivery of his final and most personal instruction in 10:45, Mark's Jesus has delivered to his disciples a thorough formulation of the Way of Discipleship, providing them a collection of three teachings that both establish and flesh out the meaning of discipleship. Given that discipleship must be chosen and even re-chosen by potential and active followers, to become a disciple means (1) to follow Jesus, the Son of Man whose path leads to passion, being killed, and rising; (2) to be a servant, ever attentive to the needs of those without power, standing, or influence; and (3) to avoid the pursuit and possession of corrosive power over others, and instead serve and give oneself so that the resulting release and freedom proclaim the arrival and ongoing presence of the kingdom of God.

One final point remains to be addressed. Mark's "ransom" metaphor raised the question of what sort of freedom and release Mark implies. In what ways are the inhabitants of his narrative unfree or at least inhibited in their full participation in God's arriving kingdom? Some types of captivity are specifically alluded to in the Way materials, namely, the societal norms of greatness, and the usual methods of seeking prominence and control over others. Other forms of bondage are demonstrated in other episodes. Readers will recall those held captive by the practices of the purity code (see 1:35–45 in chapter 6 and 5:1–20 in chapter 4) or by the expectation of near absolute allegiance woven into the norms of the kinship system (see 3:19b–35 in chapter 4). Similarly, there is a man with a withered hand, made free by Jesus's challenge to and reinterpretation of prevailing religious practices related to the Sabbath (3:1–6).

Broadening even further our understanding of those Mark considers as unfree, we can appeal to Jesus's initial corrective instruction in the Way materials. Here is found Jesus's first mention of the saving and losing of life/self/core (8:35–37). What constitutes Mark's vision of those needing ransom? Mark appears to imply that all persons need to be freed. He understands, through his keen awareness of human nature, that from time to time, knowingly or unknowingly, every person falls under the sway of destructive allegiances and misplaced trust. Even when human beings are attempting to rightly follow, each of us can and does become captive and held in bondage in some manner.

For example, do we not reach for and trust in human systems of safety and security, similar to Markan characters who rely on family membership or prominence of reputation and social standing? Do we not participate in systems of power and control over others, be they systems of religion, politics, wealth, or military force? Do we not seek out other systems or institutions to which we cling in the hope that they will give us life, core, being, or soul—that is, a meaningful and enlivened existence? In my understanding of Mark, such errant allegiances and misplaced trust are ever present and yet in the long run prove bankrupt and idolatrous, for they can in no way save us. To the contrary, any such loyalty and reliance we adopt from the realm of "human things" (8:33) will endanger our very souls and "profit" us nothing (8:36).

Along with his last instruction about discipleship, which contains the ransom metaphor, Mark's Jesus offers another option and choice that humans can make. While it is not an easy choice, persons can follow him after the example of Bartimaeus. It is Bartimaeus whom Mark portrays as sure-footedly following Jesus as he continues on to Jerusalem. The Twelve play no significant role as Mark concludes the Way of Discipleship passages. It is instead the former blind beggar who now sees that any who would follow the Son of Man need only keep him in sight and trust his leading into the future whatever it may hold. It is with this hopeful portrait that Mark closes out the Way of Discipleship section.

But what may Mark's readers take away from the disciples' ongoing and unrelenting failure to understand Jesus despite the extensive and corrective teachings of 8:22—10:52? At least part of what Mark is implying as he completes his Way materials is that even Jesus's wisest and most true instructions about discipleship prove lacking in one important aspect; on their own, they are insufficient. Even after the completion of his three episodes of teaching, Mark's Jesus knows his work is not done and he must continue his journey to Jerusalem. Although with his declaration of 10:45 his teaching function is largely completed, he must still move forward, since he will soon choose not only to teach and speak but also to act. And it is only in Jerusalem in his final hours that Jesus steps beyond his words or, more exactly perhaps, steps into his words, living them out and incarnating his predictions about the Son of Man/Son of God. Only after this final, supreme act of self-giving will it begin to dawn on some in Mark's story that "Truly this man was God's Son!" (Mark 15:39).

And so as we end this chapter we encounter Mark's movement toward the culmination of "the good news of Jesus Christ, Son of God" (1:1). The empty tomb and life-altering promise lie ahead.

Personal Reflection: On Welcoming a Child

I grew up as a child of the church. By that I mean that I hold significant recollections of things like the family's weekly attendance at Sunday School and our local church, favorite Sunday School teachers who knew how to interest young minds and souls, yearly Vacation Bible School complete with songs, crafts, Kool-Aid and cookies, and the Founder's Day Picnic each fall when all former members of the congregation were welcomed back to their religious roots for a day of reunion, food, catching up, and the telling of tales—mostly true I am told. More mundane but nonetheless formative moments occurred in the context of wives cleaning up in the kitchen after Fellowship Hour as the husbands fulfilled their roles outside the church building by smoking, discussing politics or the preacher's sermon, and waiting for their wives. All the while, we children impatiently chafed to get home and free ourselves from our restrictive Sunday clothes. In my later years, there came children's choir practice, weekly youth group meetings, and summer youth camps and conferences.

Looking back, when I narrow my focus to the most prominent impressions drawn from these experiences, one especially stands out. It centers around the eleven o'clock worship time. No doubt, this time is prominent for me because of the particular circumstances in my family's life as of the fall of 1951. In the spring of that year, Dad had died of cancer, leaving behind his thirty-five-year-old wife with two children ages ten and five to care for and raise. After much thought (and ambivalence I learned about later), Mother decided that the best course open to her was to return to Virginia from New York State where Dad had been a Methodist minister and prison chaplain. While Virginia was her childhood home, she had left behind the Commonwealth to accompany Dad to Yale Divinity School in the 1930s and had no intention of returning, primarily because of Virginia's intransigent conservatism and deeply embedded racism. What was available to her in Virginia in 1951, however, was a job and her parents, who stood willing and able to open their home to their northern grandchildren, who needed good people around them and a place to be and heal. So, our family of three headed south, sojourners in an alien land.

The job that awaited Mother in Lynchburg, Virginia—her hometown—sounds anachronistic by today's standards, but in the early 1950s it was deemed a necessity to uphold the mores of that time. She was hired as a "dorm mother" at a local college. In that capacity she was expected both to relate to and be a sympathetic but sensible advisor to the young women in her care as well as to enforce the rules of midnight curfews and monitor "the boys" for mischief or inappropriate behavior. She was, I believe, quite good at her job. However, the down side as far as my brother and I were concerned was that Mother's position called for her to live among her college-age wards. Her days and nights were long and time spent with us was consequently limited to her days off and moments she could slip away from her responsibilities to have dinner with her sons at

Grandma and Granddad's home. Providentially, our grandparents were solidly decent and loving people, and provided us the dependable structure we needed in the midst of our recently shaken world. Looking back, I am amazed at the patience and grounding with which they surrounded my brother and me. But, of course, what they could not do was be our Dad or our Mom. Dad was no longer alive and Mom was not present for us to the same degree as in the past.

Now, back to eleven o'clock Sunday worship. On Sundays—slow work days for Mom—she could often meet the rest of the family at our local church. When we all sat together, always on the left side of the sanctuary on the fourth row of pews, I would often position myself next to her. After the opening hymn and a few other preliminaries, the main event—the sermon—would begin. For any child of six or seven, this is the most boring part of worship and often, after a few minutes—and encouraged by the stillness of the sanctuary, the drone of the preacher's voice, and the warmth that radiated from the closeness of my mother's body—I would find myself leaning over onto her lap, a welcoming space for me, one of comfort, safety, and touch. I rested there and was free to do so. In these moments I took in far more than I was aware of needing, and by the time the closing hymn was announced, I felt surrounded by the presence of spirits for which I had no names. Now I would call these welcomers Touch, Closeness, Warmth, Healing, and Peace. Moreover, I would now venture to say that in those repeated times in that specific place, God approached, joining with a soothing, compassionate, and still-grieving mother to provide what I so achingly needed. For brief but eternal moments, the dominant reality I experienced was a communion long-ago promised and a mystery yet worth pondering: "Whoever welcomes one such child in my name welcomes me, and whoever welcomes me welcomes not me but the one who sent me"(9:37).

So I have come to trust that even though we need not know its name, the Holy surrounds us in any given season of our lives, perhaps especially when we are broken. And receiving its calming and healing presence, we are welcomed home.

8

Resurrections Begin in the Now

With Jesus's dark cry of faith and ultimate act of self-giving in death, God moves to enliven and embolden others to set out on the path of courageous discipleship. Surprising transformations occur; resurrections begin.

Exploring Mark's Story

OF ALL THE SURPRISES Mark's readers may unearth in his Gospel, the concentration of them that appears in the passion and crucifixion accounts of Mark 14 and 15 supersedes any other group of startling or unexpected occurrences in Mark's narrative. In an effort to explore a sufficient but not overwhelming number of these riches, I focus in this chapter on several of the more prominent of these unexpected moments: (1) Mark's account of Jesus's death; (2) the tearing of the temple curtain; and (3) the tapestry of transformation Mark weaves as seen in the centurion, the women followers of Jesus, and Joseph of Arimathea. The scenes involving these Markan personages will make up our three focal texts: Mark 15:39, the centurion; Mark 15:40–41, the women followers; and Mark 15:43–47, Joseph of Arimathea.[1] These focal texts provide a framework

---

1. While the centurion and Joseph of Arimathea are clearly individuals caught up in the events of Jesus's crucifixion, I consider that the several women are best understood as a singular literary character made up of faithful and serving followers of Jesus. That is, the plurality of their numbers is subsumed under the unity of their identity and action as devoted, courageous followers.

to interpret the meaning and significance of Jesus's death from a Markan perspective, the clues about how God responds to Jesus's death, and the transformations that are set in motion through God's presence and activity in the lives of a Roman soldier, a group of women followers, and a respected member of the Sanhedrin.

Jesus Dies and the Temple Curtain is Torn: Mark's Baseline Events in 15:33–38

> ³³When it was noon, darkness came over the whole land until three in the afternoon. ³⁴At three o'clock Jesus cried out with a loud voice, "Eloi, Eloi, lema sabachthani?" which means, "My God, my God, why have you forsaken me?" ³⁵When some of the bystanders heard it, they said, "Listen, he is calling for Elijah." ³⁶And someone ran, filled a sponge with sour wine, put it on a stick, and gave it to him to drink, saying, "Wait, let us see whether Elijah will come to take him down." ³⁷Then Jesus gave a loud cry and breathed his last. ³⁸And the curtain of the temple was torn in two, from top to bottom.

The death of Jesus can certainly be viewed as the most essential and culminating event of Mark's Gospel. In the study note for Mark 15:33–41, Clifton Black writes succinctly, "Jesus' death, Mark's climax."[2] As we have seen, Mark has shaped the last half of his narrative toward this dark reality.[3] Ever since Jesus shifted both his path and pronouncements about the fate of the Son of Man beginning with 8:27, Jesus's being killed has claimed the center of Mark's account. At the same time, however, along with his focus on the killing of the Son of Man, Mark has consistently affirmed through Jesus's words that a "rising" will occur. What will constitute this rising has yet to be delineated in Mark's story even as it nears its end. Consequently, readers remain at a loss to know what it is that Jesus anticipates following his death. With 15:33, Mark begins to suggest his answer to this unknown dimension called rising. By the time Mark completes his three scenes with the centurion, some women followers, and Joseph of Arimathea, readers can draw at least tentative conclusions about the meaning of rising, in the case of Jesus and of those who strive to seek his Way.

2. Black, "The Gospel of Mark," note on Mark 15:33–41.
3. The darkness is both metaphorical and literal for Mark; see 15:33.

A second feature of Mark's baseline found in 15:33–38 is Mark's recounting that Jesus's dying breath is followed hard upon by the tearing of the curtain of the temple. That is, Mark immediately mentions the tearing upon the completion of his portrayal of Jesus's being killed. One could easily—and I suggest, rightly—conclude that Mark sees Jesus's final act of self-giving in death as happening concurrently with the curtain tearing. Mark has, it seems, entwined the two into an inseparable union. Therefore, we should pause our exploration of our three focal texts until we have taken time to consider below how Jesus's death and the curtain tearing inform and relate to each other, thus setting the stage for the three brief scenes that come after Jesus's death and the temple tearing.

Looking Beneath Mark's Dark Tapestry of Crucifixion and Death

The Roman Practice of Crucifixion

To understand the depth of Mark's gripping and horrifying portrayal of Jesus's crucifixion, I now ask readers to delve into the admittedly difficult-to-stomach reality of crucifixion as a practice of imperial Rome in Jesus's day. The nature and specific features of this particular form of torture and humiliation would have been well-known to Mark's first readers. This is less true for those of us who mercifully are centuries removed from this specific form of capital punishment. However, the full impact of Mark's account of Jesus's death is minimized unless we at least glimpse what Jesus endured.

Jouette Bassler vividly describes the cruelty of crucifixion as employed by Rome:

> Condemned persons were nailed or tied to the stake or crossbar, sometimes upside down, sometimes with other sadistic touches added at the executioner's whim. When the object was punishment for individual crimes, several features became fairly standard. The procedure included a flogging, and the victim was usually paraded to the site of execution wearing around the neck a wooden placard proclaiming the crime. The condemned person also carried the crossbar, not the whole cross, to the place of execution, where the upright stake was already in place. Because deterrence was a primary objective, the cross was always erected in a public place. The prisoner was stripped and affixed to the crossbar with nails through the forearms or with ropes. The crossbar was then raised and attached to the upright stake

and the victim's feet were tied or nailed to the stake. The weight of the hanging body made breathing difficult, and death came from gradual asphyxiation, usually after a few hours. To prolong the death and thus increase the agony, a small wooden block was sometimes attached to the stake beneath the buttocks or feet to provide some support for the body. Then death came only after several days, and resulted from the cumulative impact of thirst, hunger, exhaustion, exposure, and the traumatic effects of the scourging. After death the body was usually left hanging on the cross. Because of the protracted suffering and the utter degradation of this manner of execution, it was viewed by the Romans as the supreme penalty, the "most wretched of deaths" (Josephus).[4]

In comments on the practice of crucifixion, Borg emphasizes its political dimension:

> Crucifixion made a statement. There were other forms of Roman capital punishment, such as beheading. Rome reserved crucifixion for two categories of people: chronically defiant slaves and others who challenged Roman rule . . . But he [Jesus] was crucified precisely because it made a public statement; it said this is what we do to people who oppose us. It was state-sponsored terrorism, imperial terrorism, torture and death as deterrent.[5]

When Jesus was crucified, he suffered the full burden of pain, humiliation, and degradation Rome could inflict on a person. Further, according to Mark, Pilate was egged on to order Jesus's execution by shouts of "Crucify him!" resounding from the crowd (15:13–14).

The Prominence of Psalm 22

Mark's account of Jesus's crucifixion and death incorporates several allusions to Psalm 22:

- Mark 15:37, in which Mark quotes the first line of the psalm: "My God, my God, why have you forsaken me?"
- Mark 15:24, an allusion to Ps 22:18: "they divide my clothes among themselves, and for my clothing they cast lots."

---

4. Bassler, "Cross," 212.
5. Borg, *Jesus*, 271.

- Mark 15:29 and 15:31, which remind readers of Ps 22:7: "All who see me mock at me; they make mouths at me, they shake their heads."

Mark's use of these three allusions poses a dilemma for readers, which comes into sharp relief as we examine Psalm 22 on its own terms and not merely as an adjunct to Mark's narrative. In his analysis of Psalm 22, James Mays notes that, "Psalm 22 is a 'prayer for help.'"[6] In it God is addressed by one sorely afflicted, even unto death; the petitioner details his desperate situation and appeals for help and deliverance. At the same time, Mays points out, Psalm 22 contains not only a prayer for help, but also "a song of praise for help."[7] Thus, there are two situations outlined by the psalmist, one of which describes a condition of severe distress or affliction while the other focuses on a condition of deliverance brought about by God. Moreover, Mays asserts that the psalmist intended to unite these two situations and that together they "must be comprehended in one arc of meaning to express what is happening."[8]

But Mark's allusions to Psalm 22 point solely to aspects of distress and affliction that Jesus is undergoing. It is that situation and that situation alone to which Mark directs his readers. On the surface it appears that Mark makes no connection to the more hopeful or rejuvenating features of the psalm, aspects that draw on or reflect praise and thanksgiving to God for God's acts of deliverance. The readers' dilemma is raised by how Mark employs his references to Psalm 22, all of which are in the service of describing Jesus's crushing plight. Given that observation, certain questions are prompted by Mark's account of Jesus's passion and crucifixion. For example, can readers discover why Mark would draw into his narrative only the darker aspects of the psalm? Does Mark intentionally overlook or omit the more hopeful and even celebratory notes sounded in the psalm? In doing so, does he not shatter the unified "arc of meaning"[9] that constitutes the psalm's essential character? Where are the "missing" praising and grateful expressions found in "the song of praise for help"?[10]

---

6. Mays, *Psalms*, 106.
7. Mays, *Psalms*, 107.
8. Mays, *Psalms*, 107.
9. Mays, *Psalms*, 107.
10. Mays, *Psalms*, 107.

Mark Interprets Jesus's Crucifixion and Death: Hope Amidst the Dark

It is clear that Mark's portrayal of Jesus's final hours is more than a mere recounting of the events that happened to Jesus. As gruesomely vivid and memorable as are these events, Mark writes not as an historian or as one whose job is to detail the occurrences of Jesus's waning life. Rather, he writes as a disciple, a theologian, and a revealer of the good news of God's unfolding reign among humankind. For Mark, it is not sufficient to list the harrowing details of Jesus's passion and death; he also shapes an interpretation of the meaning of Jesus's crucifixion and death. Through Mark's Gospel, readers encounter the depth and significance lying beneath the chilling events of the story. For readers to overlook Mark's interpretation is to miss what he has left us. It is not a document for readers to use to pass a couple of hours' time; rather, it is a Gospel—carefully shaped to point to and evoke the possibility of transformation into the life/aliveness that can emerge as readers of this Gospel are enveloped by God's arriving reign.

How does Mark's interpretation of Jesus's story help readers to reach beyond the darkness of Jesus's cry and the breathing of his final breath?

Perhaps the most arresting feature of Mark's interpretive construct is the writer's quotation of Psalm 22: "My God, my God, why have you forsaken me?" (Ps 22:1). For reasons that are not yet clarified for his readers, Mark centers the heart of his good news story in, of all things, Jesus's demise. The death account begins with an affirmation of the severity and terror surrounding the event, and it appears that Mark portrays a Jesus who is completely caught up and destroyed in his last earthly moments. It is as if Mark knows no way out of the darkness of Jesus's dying than by stepping toward it and looking it square in the eye. He uses Psalm 22 to accomplish this.

Mark portrays Jesus as he recites Ps 22:1 as one whose whole and entire being is under assault—physically, socially, emotionally, and spiritually. Jesus suffers at the hands of the powerful; he is deserted by those followers he had gathered around him as his true family. He experiences God only as absent, and his final words recall an ancient plea for help when no help appears in the offing. And with one last, loud, and inarticulate cry, he breathes his last.

However, Mark then begins to move readers beyond the seeming total darkness. With the reference to Ps 22:1 he likely points to more than a cry of desperate desolation. Mays comments that, in Jesus's day, the first line of a psalm carried more significance than it might appear: "Citing the first words of a text was, in the tradition of the time, a way of identifying an entire passage."[11] Given this tradition, Jesus's quotation may stand for the whole, a shorthand expression for the entirety of the psalm. In its fullest form the psalm includes thanksgiving and praise to God for deliverance. With his word-for-word recitation of the psalm's initial line, Mark begins to make room for the possibility that all is not darkness; he leaves the door to good news slightly ajar.

Mark offers a second sign of hope in his depiction of Jesus here. When Jesus cries out in the depths of his abandonment, he cries out to his God: "My God, my God." Jesus's last words suggest that his whole person, his whole self, not only suffers but also still reaches toward God, his God—even while slipping into death. And while God is experienced by Jesus at that moment as absent, the Beloved Son still seeks connection to God—a connection first established when God claimed him as Beloved (Mark 1:9–11), a connection that has guided him ever since, even to this place of crucifixion and death. Schweizer writes perceptively about Jesus's cry, describing it as an act of supreme devotion to God: "a devotion which continues to claim God as 'my' God and will not let him go although he can be experienced only as the absent One who has forsaken [Jesus] . . . This cry clings to the fact that God is real in all times, even in those times when neither experience nor thought can lay hold of him."[12]

In the final analysis, Jesus's cry can be seen as a *dark cry of faith*. In shaping his interpretation of meaning for the crucifixion and death of Jesus, Mark assures his readers that faith is not always calmly spoken, or reasonably presented, or delivered pain-free; rather, it can erupt from costly agony, be interspersed with confusion and despair, and with its ultimate validation only hoped for but not fully assured. Yet such a besieged faith is faith nonetheless; it involves trust in God—a trust that can be beleaguered and has even grown desperate. Through all, however, God is clung to, relied on—a God whose reign is among us and for us.

Mark offers yet one more sign of hope that moves readers ever closer to understanding that the Markan good news is near at hand, even at the very moment of Jesus's last breath. Hope exists ironically in Mark's emphasis that it is the "whole of Jesus" who is present at Golgotha. There he suffers and dies. But it is also there that the entirety of Jesus's being—body, mind, and spirit—is entrusted to God. As he was perishing

---

11. Mays, *Psalms*, 105.
12. Schweizer, *Good News*, 353.

Jesus's full and complete self/core is given over to a seemingly severed connection with God. But with his dark cry of faith, Jesus claims this connection, thereby clinging to it despite God's sensed absence.

Reinforcement for this view can be found in Jesus's summary teaching about discipleship and the personal words Jesus utters in 10:45: "For the Son of Man came not to be served but to serve, and to give his life a ransom for many." These words stand out as Jesus's climactic declaration that serving—attending to the needs of those without standing or power—and the giving of life (self) lie at the center of what he believed to be his purpose; in 15:37 it is this purpose that he lives out. All that remains for readers is to look for whether Jesus's completed path of service and self-giving leads to ransoming, the setting free of captives. Will this indeed happen as Mark's Jesus hoped and expected?

The temple curtain awaits.

The Tearing of the Temple Curtain

We now turn our attention to a brief but crucially significant shift in the Markan narrative. Mark captures this momentous occurrence in a single verse: "And the curtain of the temple was torn in two, from top to bottom" (15:38). In this enigmatic verse, readers find three changes from the immediately preceding verses: (1) the location of the story immediately changes from Golgotha to the temple. (In 15:39, readers are redirected to Golgotha); (2) Mark's focus in 15:38 is not primarily the temple structure in its entirety, but specifically the curtain that sets off the space in the temple that is considered most sacred, the Holy of Holies; and (3) while the person of Jesus is the main focus of the immediately preceding verses, the central actor in 15:38, that is, the one who tears the curtain, is not specifically named. Let us look to see whether Mark leaves clues as to the identity of the mysterious "tearer" and whether the tearer is "up to" more than ripping a piece of cloth.

Mark's Two Tearings: Similarities

Any consideration of the tearing of the curtain of the Temple should include the recognition that an earlier tearing (rending, being ripped apart) has already occurred in Mark's story. From Jesus's baptism scene, Mark 1:9–11, readers may recall this verse: "And just as he [Jesus] was coming up out of the water, he saw the heavens torn apart and the Spirit descending like a dove on him" (Mark 1:10). With the sole exception of a brief teaching moment (2:21), the tearing of the heavens (1:10) and the tearing of the temple curtain (15:38) are the only two uses in Mark of the Greek root *schizō*.[13] Let us briefly explore other similarities in the two tearing stories.

Action occurs outside the arena of ordinary human experience. In the first scene, Jesus's baptism, Jesus is the only named witness to and recipient of the actions that occur. The ripping apart of the heavens, the Spirit's descent, and a voice speaking from heaven center on this man alone and point toward activity performed on a sacred stage and driven by divine purpose. In the second scene, the tearing in the most sacred space in the temple creates a breach in the reputed "residence of God."[14] This space deep in the interior of the temple is considered by Jesus's religious opponents most distinct and removed from normal human interaction. As Borg and Crossan note, "the curtain separated the holiest part of the temple sanctuary—the Holy of Holies—from the rest of the sanctuary. The Holy of Holies was understood to be the particular place of God's presence: God was most present, concentratedly present, in the innermost part of the sanctuary."[15] Access to this space was not granted to humans, except for once a year when the high priest of the temple could enter.[16] Simply put, the Holy of Holies is the place where God is and God's people are not.

A divine force is at work as the primary actor. At Jesus's baptism the action begins with a tearing of the heavens, accompanied by movement of the Spirit and a spoken heavenly message. In the Holy of Holies scene, the action also commences from on high, that is, with the curtain torn "from top to bottom" (15:38).[17] A humanly made tear would necessarily move from bottom to top of a long curtain. The implication is, then, that the veil tearing is accomplished by a non-human force, rending from on high.

Recipients of divine action are persons of no great consequence when tearing occurs. In the lead-up to Jesus's baptism, Mark describes the object of the impending divine action only as coming from Nazareth of Galilee.

---

13. Rich, "Mark 15:25–41," 200–202.
14. Meyers, "Temple, Jerusalem," 1097.
15. Borg and Crossan, *The Last Week*, 150.
16. Borg and Crossan, *The Last Week*, 150.
17. I am indebted to Dr. John T. Carroll of Union Presbyterian Seminary for the insight that the directionality of the tear, from top to bottom, carries suggestive implications concerning the identity of the One who tore the curtain.

Nazareth is not a town where the upper crust of the society of Jesus's day lived. Similarly, those impacted by the effects of the tearing of the curtain, those immediately mentioned by Mark after the tearing of 15:38, are also not persons of particular prominence in their day—a centurion, a group of women followers of Jesus, and Joseph of Arimathea.[18] We will look more closely at these characters when we consider our three focal texts.

Jesus is named as God's Son. As part of Jesus's baptism, a voice from heaven says, "You are my Son," (1:11); in the immediate moment when the centurion sees the manner in which Jesus dies, he surprisingly declares, "Truly this man was God's Son!" (15:39).[19]

Transformation happens. In the first scene, when Jesus approaches the moment of his baptism, he comes as Jesus "from Nazareth of Galilee" (Mark 1:9). But when he emerges from the Jordan River, his identity has been altered; moreover, he will continue to expand that identity throughout Mark's account. As part of his baptism, then, Jesus's new, transformed, and evolving identity has been proclaimed by the voice from heaven: "You are my Son, the Beloved" (1:11). In the second scene, Mark's theme of transformation (rising) is carried by the centurion, the group of women, and Joseph. The actions of these characters function as emphatic examples of the power of transformation unleashed in Mark through Jesus's self-giving and God's response to it.

---

18. Joseph of Arimathea is respected by his colleagues from the Sanhedrin, but that would have been seen as a dubious distinction for Mark and his contemporaries, since those colleagues held Jesus to be "deserving death" (14:64).

19. Some scholars, including Myers (*Binding the Strong Man*, 392–94) view the centurion's words as mocking and sarcastic, employed by Mark as another example of the verbal belittlement Jesus suffers at various points in Mark 15. I am persuaded, though, that the centurion's declaration can be better understood as the first evidence that the curtain tearing has unleashed a divine force which enables positive, life-giving transformation of ordinary folks—empowering them to engage in disciple-like behavior. With this interpretative understanding, the context is established by Mark for additional transformations that will soon occur in his narrative. They will be seen in the lived-out, courageous, and self-giving actions of the women followers near the cross and Joseph of Arimathea. The centurion is not alone in his doing the risky and unexpected, nor in experiencing resurrection.

The Tearing of The Temple Curtain: Prelude to God's Onrushing Presence

There are several additional aspects of the curtain tearing that warrant readers' attention. The first, which can be viewed as a matter of emphasis or nuance, shows readers the dynamism and force with which Mark imbues the curtain tearing scene. Many scholars assert that the curtain scene is a primary symbol, used by Mark to point toward opening "access" to God or God's presence.[20] While I agree that the tearing represents a shift in the relationship between God and humankind, I think "access" is too pale a word to convey the magnitude of the change and the energy unleashed in the rending of the veil. Access is simply inadequate to express the full scope of what happens between God and God's people as a result of the temple tearing.

Some years ago, when composing a prayer to use at the opening of a class I taught on Mark's Gospel, I found that the words for this force, this rending, came to me, almost as a gift—I had very little to do with it except for the quick scribbling I did to get it on paper before it slipped away from me.

> Spirit of God, Who once long ago descended through the torn apart heavens to rest on Jesus, descend yet again into our lives. Open our blinded eyes so that like Bartimaeus, we may yet again see You near at hand, with us, among us, out ahead of us, loosed on us, and preparing us—who are afraid—to follow You on the way, even to Jerusalem. Amen.

Some years later, I ran across the following: "What does the tearing [of the curtain] mean? It may mean, as interpreted in the Letter to the Hebrews (esp. chapters 9–10), that we now have access to God . . . Viewed from another perspective, the image may suggest that . . . God, unwilling to be confined to sacred spaces, is on the loose in our own realm."[21] This observation by Donald Juel solidified my view that the idea of access falls short of the dynamism and energy of God, who, with the curtain tearing accomplished, is moving, flowing, rushing toward humankind with all the force of a flash flood in the desert or a deluge unleashed by a collapsing dam. It is so much more than "access."

---

20. For example, the emphasis on access to God/God's presence is found in Black, "The Gospel of Mark," note on Mark 15:38; Borg and Crossan, *The Last Week*, 150; and Donahue, "Mark," 923.

21. Juel, *Master of Surprise*, 35–36.

Indeed, readers might further imagine the power released in the moment when the curtain is torn by visualizing the following sequence: Just prior to the disruption of the sacred space, the Holy of Holies stands filled to the brim with some liquid, pulsating manifestation of God's presence and deliverance. At the same time, however, this great energy of God's being is isolated and hidden behind the confines of the temple veil. Then, suddenly, this space is unexpectedly, irreversibly altered with the result that the curtain lies completely rent, in shreds on the temple floor. Swirling over its tattered pieces comes the overflowing presence of the One who created Heaven and Earth, loosed on God's people, catching up all in its path, including, as we shall see, a centurion, a group of women, and one Joseph of Arimathea. God on the loose. God loosed on us.

But what is the relationship between the two tearings? The first tearing at Jesus's baptism informs the second at the curtain scene, and the second tearing expands on the first. The baptism scene informs the curtain scene with its tearing apart of the heavens, the accompanying activity of the Spirit's descent, a voice from heaven, and the message poured out on Jesus. The mood at the Jordan is welcoming, celebratory, and expressing the fulfillment of a long-hoped-for movement of God toward God's people. It is a movement expected to fill all creation with God's presence (see Isa 64:1–3). The divine voice exults in the naming and claiming of Jesus as Beloved Son (Mark 1:11), and all that happens at the Jordan and all that begins to happen there is pleasing to God.

Through Mark's baptism scene, readers have a strong hint about what to look for in his second (curtain) tearing. Despite the trauma, pain, and apparent end to Jesus's earthly journey, Mark's curtain tearing—informed by the joyous baptism tearing—surely calls for something beyond despair and defeat. Readers might be prompted by Mark's account of the two tearings to ask questions like the following:

- In Mark 15:38, is Mark inviting his readers to be on the lookout for a second purposeful movement by God, one similar to God's approach toward Jesus at his baptism?
- For consistency's sake, is this second movement also to be filled with joy and amazement, as the divine force approaches other of God's sons and daughters—approaching them with abiding presence, welcome, and the possibility of transformation?
- With all the metaphoric constraints of the curtain demolished and figuratively strewn across the Holy of Holies, is God's Spirit to be

loosed on us as it once was on Jesus, coming our way with the full intensity of a tsunami?

- Does God intend to offer God's people and us even now entry into God's kingdom and rule proclaimed in Jesus's first spoken words (Mark 1:14–15)?
- And finally, is Mark with this temple tearing coaxing us, his readers, ever closer to his understanding and, yes, experience of the Good News?

If the readers' answer to any of the above questions is yes, or even a considered maybe, the tearing of the temple curtain primes Mark's readers to look for how the next three characters mentioned in Mark's story are affected by what is unleashed when God moves into their daily lives. And how does what happens to them portend what is available to us?

The Focal Texts: A Dilemma Resolved

Before we undertake any specific consideration of each of our three focal texts let us revisit the dilemma I posed earlier in the chapter. Remember that Mark alludes to Psalm 22 in his account of Jesus's passion and dying. Mark's allusions draw upon the depiction of acute and desperate distress of the psalmist and include the stark and penetrating opening line, "My God, my God, why have you forsaken me?" (Ps 22:1; Mark 15:34). But Psalm 22 also contains elements of praise and thanksgiving for God's help and deliverance, and Mark makes no specific allusion to the saving emphasis of the psalm. Why does Mark make such obvious and deliberate use of the despairing themes of Psalm 22 but omit any reference to its hopeful elements?

I find resolution to the dilemma in the idea that the more hopeful emphases embedded in the latter portion of Psalm 22 are replaced in Mark's narrative by the curtain tearing scene. That is, even as Mark employs references to the darker and terror-laden aspects of Psalm 22, in the very same scene he introduces the curtain tearing to carry forward the themes of deliverance and divine action. This line of interpretation is supported as we consider that Mark 15:38 looks both backward and forward in the narrative. We look backward to remember the joyous, celebratory mood of the baptism tearing. The exultant mood of that moment—so pleasing to God—informs us as we look forward to the curtain tearing and hints that we need not see Jesus's self-sacrifice through the lens of despair. Mark primes readers to see something very different: with the tearing of the curtain readers again behold a God on the move as God was at the Jordan. With the curtain tearing and the resultant surging Presence rushing toward others caught up in God's reign and rule, readers are invited forward—forward to behold what God's approach brings about for three representative examples of humankind.

Let us turn our attention to our three focal texts to see what happens to these unsuspecting parties as they are enveloped by God's saving and freeing actions.

Focal Text: Mark 15:39
A Centurion Sees and Speaks

³⁹Now when the centurion, who stood facing him, saw that in this way he breathed his last, he said, "Truly this man was God's Son!"

Mark uses the curtain tearing text to point toward the process of transformation for characters in his narrative. In the wake of 15:38 Mark's readers are invited to explore what happens in the lives of the three parties found in the verses immediately following the curtain tearing. Let us note, then, what we can about the centurion, a trio of women, and Joseph of Arimathea. In the case of each we will lay out a basic "before and after" snapshot of the character, drawing on both what clues Mark provides in his account as well as what we can surmise from historical research. First, the centurion.

The Centurion: Before

Prior to the tearing of the curtain, several narrative truths about the centurion's life can be assumed based on what is known about the office of centurion. A centurion was an officer in the army of Rome in charge of approximately one hundred soldiers. The career officers of their day, centurions served a required term of twenty years, with many choosing to stay past their initial commitment.[22] They served as "the actual working officers, the backbone of the army. The discipline and efficiency of

---

22. Gealy, "Centurion," 547–48.

the legion as a fighting unit depended on them."[23] Responsibilities of the office included discipline of troops under their command as well as oversight of punishment and executions of persons condemned of capital crimes. Often a centurion rose through the ranks to his position, one of prestige and importance. The rank of centurion "was the highest to which the ordinary soldier might aspire."[24]

First of all, then, what Mark presents us in 15:39 is a Roman military officer, a man both used to having authority and at the same time obedient to the authority of those of higher rank or standing—in this case, Pilate. Moreover, as Mark has implied earlier, in dealing with Jesus the centurion has been part of a larger gathering of soldiers and officers who have brutalized and mocked Jesus prior to escorting him along with his execution detail to Golgotha (15:16–20). As noted, part of a centurion's duties was to make sure that executions were carried out, and Mark's centurion is initially portrayed as simply going about this task inherent to his job.

A second reality we can ascribe to Mark's centurion is that as a Roman military officer he has sworn his allegiance to the Roman emperor. Moreover, it was the emperor who was considered throughout the empire to be Son of God.[25] The centurion's ultimate loyalty, then, was pledged to the leader of the Roman world. In his narrative, Mark records no hint of wavering in the allegiance or loyalty of this centurion to his Roman Son of God, the emperor. This, of course, is the state of things prior to the curtain tearing scene.

A third noteworthy reality about Mark's centurion as he goes about his responsibilities is that he positions himself opposite the dying Jesus; he faces him. Kelber suggests that Mark's language in 15:39 is reflective of an adversarial or oppositional stance adopted by the centurion as he witnesses Jesus's demise.[26] Indeed, this stance is consistent with the soldier's duty as the one who is to witness that Jesus's sentence is enacted. The centurion sets himself in a position to verify that Jesus does in fact die. Later Pilate draws on the centurion's role as witness when he questions the centurion regarding some of the specifics of Jesus's death (15:44–45).

---

23. Gealy, "Centurion," 548.
24. Gealy, "Centurion," 548.
25. Borg and Crossan, *The Last Week*, 150.
26. Kelber, *The Passion in Mark*, 175.

To sum up our "Before" portrait of Mark's centurion, then, prior to the tearing of the curtain, he is fulfilling his duties as executioner and witness to Jesus's dying.

The Centurion: After

The first and most prominent indication of the transformation of the centurion occurs at Mark 15:39, where the centurion appears as the first human being to directly identify Jesus as God's Son. Granted, others have so identified Jesus in Mark's account, namely the divine voice at both Jesus's baptism and transfiguration, as well as various unclean spirits and demonic forces. Jesus himself has approached using the "Son of God" appellation in telling the parable of the Beloved Son in Mark 12. And perhaps the human who comes closest to referring to Jesus as the Son of God is the high priest when he queries Jesus, "Are you . . . the Son of the Blessed One?" (14:61).[27] However, when the centurion speaks, he does so in a way that indicates a change is beginning to happen in how he experiences a central piece of the reality by which he has lived his adult life. As a centurion, it is he who has just witnessed Jesus's death; and yet, as a fellow human being, it is he who now—after the tearing—sees how Jesus dies, and declares him to be God's Son.

The second indication, crucial to the notion of the centurion's transformation, is what prompted the centurion's declaration. That is, although the centurion's duty was to witness *that Jesus died,* Mark indicates that what the centurion more importantly witnessed was *the way Jesus died.*[28] For the centurion who had likely witnessed many deaths prior to this particular execution, there is something about the manner of Jesus's dying that marks him as different. Mark does not suggest specifically what the soldier observes, but makes it clear that the centurion, in watching Jesus's death process, sees someone who, even as he slips toward the negation of his earthly existence, refuses to break connection with his God. Rather, in crying out to his God, Jesus remains faithful to and trusting of God even unto death. Yes—the centurion has observed—Jesus

---

27. The high priest's use of "Son of the Blessed One" adopts "the traditional indirect reference to Yahweh" (Myers, *Binding the Strong Man,* 376). This traditional manner of indicating the Holy thus maintains the prohibition against speaking God's sacred name.

28. Carroll refers to the centurion's seeing "the mode of Jesus' dying" (*Jesus and the Gospels,* 61).

did suffer; he was anguished; he was profoundly confused by his sense of God's absence. All of this is true. Yet, he breathed his last still reaching toward his *Abba*, Father. This is the manner of his dying. The centurion takes it in and is changed.

The third indication of the centurion's transformation is found in his nearly unimaginable shift in loyalty. Recall that this man is apparently one who has built his life around the principles of loyalty and allegiance. If he is an officer cut from the usual cloth of centurions, his loyalty and ultimate allegiance have been attached to his emperor, one honored as Son of God. For such a man to shift away from one of the foundational components of his life structure and worldview to a different viewpoint that recognizes and speaks publicly that there is in truth another who is God's Son—such a shift would constitute a stunning reversal.

But, Mark says, the inconceivable happens and the transformation occurs. The centurion has journeyed from being executioner, to being witness to a death, to being one who recognizes the strong and unbreakable bond in the kinship between Jesus and his God, to finally, being proclaimer of who in truth is Son of God.

With the example of the centurion, then, the movement God set in motion at the tearing of the temple curtain has reached the very ground on which the centurion stood watching as a dying took place. But, something altogether different from death has happened and a lifelong, loyal officer of the emperor's army speaks: "Truly this man was God's Son" (15:39).

Focal Text: Mark 15:40-41
The Women from Galilee Who
Follow Jesus to Jerusalem

⁴⁰There were also women looking on from a distance; among them were Mary Magdalene, and Mary the mother of James the younger and of Joses, and Salome. ⁴¹These used to follow him and provided for him when he was in Galilee; and there were many other women who had come up with him to Jerusalem.

The Women: Before

At first it seems that Mark provides few indications of the transformation of the trio of women after the tearing of the curtain. This specific group of women—Mary Magdalene, Mary the mother of James and Joses, and Salome—has not been mentioned by name previously in Mark's narrative. Moreover, information about them is scant; Mark notes only that they "used to follow him [Jesus] and provided for [served] him when he was in Galilee" (15:41). However, this brief description contains "loaded" Markan vocabulary. Mark's key words—follow and serve—point to disciple-like actions these three have performed in the past. Even before the tearing of the veil, they have demonstrated compassionate, self-giving behavior and character in response to Jesus, certainly beyond anything done or even contemplated by the twelve male disciples.

The Women: After

When Mark's readers take in the fuller portrayal of the three faithful followers after the curtain tearing, the transformation of the three rises to a more notable level. For example, Mark provides his readers with the names of the three, something he rarely does with women in his account.[29] Moreover, the three have not only followed and served in Galilee; they—along with "many other women" (15:41)—accompanied Jesus to Jerusalem, the very seat of power for those allied against Jesus and determined to kill him. And, most important, these women find the courage to be nearby Jesus at his death. Presumably, the men have fled and sought safety in hiding.

---

29. Jesus's mother (Mary) and Herodias are the only other women identified by name in Mark's narrative (Rhoads et al., *Mark as Story*, 133).

Focal Text: Mark 15:42–47
Bold, Respected Joseph of Arimathea

⁴²When evening had come, and since it was the day of Preparation, that is, the day before the sabbath, ⁴³Joseph of Arimathea, a respected member of the council, who was also himself waiting expectantly for the kingdom of God, went boldly to Pilate and asked for the body of Jesus. ⁴⁴Then Pilate wondered if he were already dead; and summoning the centurion, he asked him whether he had been dead for some time. ⁴⁵When he learned from the centurion that he was dead, he granted the body to Joseph. ⁴⁶Then Joseph bought a linen cloth, and taking down the body, wrapped it in the linen cloth, and laid it in a tomb that had been hewn out of the rock. He then rolled a stone against the door of the tomb.⁴⁷Mary Magdalene and Mary the mother of Joses saw where the body was laid.

Joseph of Arimathea: Before

As described by Mark, Joseph of Arimathea is a man of significant standing, both with the priestly power structure and apparently in the larger Jewish community. His status is confirmed for readers through Mark's mention of his membership in the council, likely the Sanhedrin. But Joseph's membership in the council indicates more than social and religious prominence in Mark's narrative, for it is the "whole council" that has been urgently seeking "testimony" before it that would warrant a death sentence against Jesus (14:55). From a Markan perspective, then, participants in Jesus's trial—members of the council—are complicit in the votes and actions taken against Jesus. As Kelber has observed, there is at least the implication "that Joseph, this respected council member, also cast his vote against Jesus."[30]

Mark further expands this implied possibility through two additional references to the entire council acting in conjunction with the priestly class and other religious leaders: "All of them condemned him [Jesus] as deserving death" (14:64), and "As soon as it was morning, the chief priests held a consultation with the elders and scribes and the whole council. They bound Jesus, led him away, and handed him over to Pilate"

---

30. Kelber, *Mark's Story of Jesus*, 83.

(15:1–2). Thus, while there is no direct mention of Joseph's participation in the vote and additional actions of the council, Mark hints of Joseph's involvement in Jesus's crucifixion and death.

There is yet another feature about Joseph that speaks to his life's orientation prior to the temple tearing. Mark portrays Joseph as a character of complexity and ambiguity; he writes that Joseph "was also himself waiting expectantly for the kingdom of God" (15:43). In this way, Mark puts Joseph forward as one actively on the lookout for God's inbreaking reign and activity, into which Jesus has been inviting his followers since his beginning proclamation. Before the temple tearing, then, Joseph can be viewed as a man in conflict. He has apparently cast a recent vote against Jesus and has gone along with sending him on to Pilate with a recommendation for execution. At the same time, he is one who carries a yearning and openness to the reign of God. He lives not as one with a hardened heart, but as one with a significant longing for God's realm of compassion, justice, release, and equality. Noting that Joseph is never named as a disciple by Mark, Lamar Williamson nonetheless characterizes Joseph in the following generous way: "But Joseph is doing what a follower of Jesus should do; he is looking for (waiting for, looking forward to, living in the hope of seeing) the Kingdom of God."[31] As Mark presents it, Joseph's stance of expectant waiting predates the destruction of the temple curtain, coming prior to the rushing of God toward humankind. However, more than waiting is at hand for Joseph; an even greater transformed life approaches.

Joseph of Arimathea: After

When Joseph learns of Jesus's death—Mark does not specify Joseph's source for this information—he goes to ask for Jesus's body. His attitude in making this request is highlighted by Mark: Joseph "went boldly" to Pilate (15:43). Mark makes sure that his readers realize this bold request requires significant courage. Like the other characters in our sequence of focal texts, Joseph experiences transformation after the tearing of the temple curtain. It is only after God's movement into a world beyond the confines of the temple that Joseph's boldness comes to the fore.

In our focal text Mark provides some additional clues that allow readers to more fully grasp the courage of Joseph. Given that Joseph is

---

31. Williamson, *Mark*, 281.

implicated in the Sanhedrin's machinations, his decision to approach Pilate (15:43) and to provide an "honorable burial"[32] for Jesus both represent a severe breach in his relationship with his former social and religious allies. It is difficult to imagine other council members as anything less than enraged with Joseph.[33] Joseph's courage is seen in the strength and resolve that he will assuredly need in his dealings with his peers—those who had long plotted murder for this troublesome teacher. Anything less than a venomous response to Jesus would not be looked upon favorably by the plotters. Nevertheless, the Markan Joseph boldly goes.

Joseph's courage can be explored from still another angle in Joseph's approach to Pilate. In Mark's account it is Pilate who has exercised the governing authority to send Jesus to the cross, and it is he alone who has the power to grant Joseph's request for Jesus's body. However, when Joseph takes himself into Pilate's presence, he apparently has no reliable information regarding Pilate's mood following the tumultuous events of the day. As far as Joseph knows, his approach and request could prove dangerous; Pilate may be possessed by a still smoldering anger. A few hours earlier, Joseph had acted in concert with the whole council and collaborated with both the high priest and the chief priests to force their will on a reluctant Pilate. Their desire for Jesus's annihilation was so strong that the priestly faction had aroused the crowd to a near fever pitch as Pilate debated with them over Jesus's potential release. In effect, Mark depicts a power struggle between Pilate and Joseph's priestly associates who manipulate the crowd to do their will. In the end Pilate is bested by this coalition in their conflict; he acquiesces to their repeated, shouted demands, "Crucify him, crucify him" (15:13–14). And so a man used to exercising great power is outmaneuvered by the cunning and duplicity of the priestly power structure. Jesus's fate is sealed, and Pilate orders Jesus's execution.

Only a few hours later, Joseph comes into Pilate's presence, seeking favor from this recently outsmarted representative of imperial Rome. He requests Jesus's body.[34] Here Joseph requires the type of courage one

32. Borg and Crossan, *The Last Week*, 153.

33. Myers offers an alternative view of Joseph's actions—that they may suggest "that the Jewish leadership was anxious to hastily dispose of the whole matter before any protest could be made" (*Binding the Strong Man*, 395). In this interpretation, the hurried burial becomes "the final indignity" for Jesus. Other scholars, however, find in Joseph's actions an echo of the proper burial of John the Baptizer provided by his disciples, notably in contrast with the non-actions of Jesus's disciples (Mark 6:29).

34. The body of a crucified individual was usually left on his cross for several days. Such a practice left the body subject to the savagery of wild dogs and birds, and

needs when facing the unknown, the type of courage one needs when engaging an adversary who possesses a recently demonstrated capacity to take life if it suits him. Courage is indeed the currency in which Joseph must deal.

However, despite all we can imagine about this meeting, Mark makes no definitive statement about Pilate's state of mind in his exchange with Joseph, with the single exception that Pilate appears skeptical about the rapidity with which Jesus died. What is clear, however, is Mark's primary focus on Joseph. After all, it is Joseph, not Pilate, who is the main character in our third focal text. And as was true for the centurion and women followers in our previous focal texts, Joseph experiences a personal transformation that leads him to stand alone before Pilate, face to face. No priestly or council colleagues are present to support him; no crowd is nearby to shout and distract Pilate from his singular focus on Joseph. All that Joseph carries into his encounter with Pilate is a divinely bestowed boldness. It is enough.

In our third focal text, then, Joseph changes, or more accurately, is changed. He undergoes a transformation enabled by God on the move. Once again, Mark points his readers toward the reign of God, in which ordinary human beings become truer, more faithful, more compassionate, and more courageous than they have ever been before. It happens "in a moment, in the twinkling of an eye" (1 Cor 15:52), for God is rushing forward to meet God's people.

God Moves Toward God's People

In Mark's story of Jesus's crucifixion and the three focal texts that immediately follow Jesus's death scene, it is necessary, given the descriptions of brutality, fear and suffering in the narrative, to recall that Mark's central purpose for his sixteen-chapter masterpiece is to present his readers with a gospel, a good news. Even with the darkness that pervades 15:33–47, this Markan purpose holds. It is seen most clearly in the movement of God. God's movement has a geography and a timeline—beginning in the now—and it is open to all God's people. The Markan God is powerful, welcoming, enthusiastic, and rushing toward God's people. As such, God

---

completed the humiliation of the offender. Roman officials thus used this practice to intimidate the local populace and deter thoughts/action of significant resistance toward Rome. Mark alludes to the exercise of such power with his comment on gentiles who employ it tyrannically (10:42).

is similar to the pleased God of Jesus's baptism who tore apart the heavens to engage Jesus and claim him as Beloved Son.

The Geography of God's Movement

In considering God's movement toward God's people, I encourage readers to note the geographic sites mentioned after the tearing of the temple veil. Which places does Mark speak of, beginning with 15:39, and, taken as a whole, why are they significant? These Markan locales are as follows:

- Golgotha—where the centurion stands very near to Jesus.
- From a distance—a locale at greater remove from Jesus's execution and the temple. This is the vantage point of the women in general and the trio in particular.
- Arimathea—the home village of Joseph, lying at some indeterminate distance from Jerusalem.[35] Of the three locales mentioned by 15:47, it is the farthest away from where Jesus died and the temple curtain was torn.
- Nazareth and Galilee—these two locales are mentioned beyond the parameters of 15:39–47 at 16:6 and 16:7. They are located at even farther remove than the other sites.

Because the locales lie at ever increasing geographical distances from the place where the temple curtain has been rent, we can deduce that Mark has designed a literary and directional map that delineates God's movement spreading outward from the temple into the larger world. Beginning at the temple—the center of Israel's religious, societal, and spiritual life—God is portrayed as quickly and expansively going forward to greet and engage all humanity wherever they may find themselves, be they near or far. The centurion, the trio of women, and Joseph can be seen as representing all humankind as potential recipients of God's coming. It would appear, then, that Mark envisions a good news even in the shadow of Jesus's death. A tidal wave of God's presence, welcome, and kingdom is loosed yet again, just as it was loosed and engulfed Jesus at his baptism. From the instance of Jesus's last breath, from his faithful cry reaching out to a seemingly absent God, from his ultimate laying aside of self, in the

---

35. The exact location of Arimathea remains unclear; the most likely sites of the village lie outside the bounds of Jerusalem.

hope that freedom, courage, and compassion would begin to stir in others—from all that is part of Jesus's path into his unknown future, Mark envisions this good news:

God is on the move.
God comes to meet humankind.
God rushes toward even the likes of us.

God Enables Resurrections for God's People

A second primary theme of 15:33-47 further elucidates Mark's emphasis on good news even as readers encounter the sobering scene of Jesus's death. This theme is revealed for readers as Mark calls attention to transformations that occur for the centurion, the women, and Joseph. Moreover, these transformative moments can be understood as a foretaste of what constitutes being one of God's resurrected. Let us consider, then, what Mark's story has suggested about resurrection up to this point in his account.

Mark's conception of resurrection is certainly reflected in the centrality of Jesus's three passion predictions. The predictions describe for his followers and others that Jesus, as the Son of Man, will be killed and "will rise again" (8:31, 9:31, and 10:34). This three-fold reference to rising is a key element in the predictions.

However, Mark does not in the predictions describe the nature or characteristics of "rising." With this lack of detail and specificity, Mark leaves his readers to wonder what Jesus may have envisioned about his rising. However, the logic of the predictions of rising serves to aim readers toward the conclusion that the killing of Jesus would not end Jesus's existence. After his killing, something else, something ongoing, something about his being was expected to live on into the present and the future. Thus, while the concrete, specific aspects of rising are not spelled out, Jesus at the point of making his three predictions seems to expect and hope for a good news of some kind, although one of faint delineation.

Mark provides one additional clue about the nature of resurrection (rising) in the final scene of the narrative, 16:1-8. When the three women followers go to Jesus's tomb with the intent of anointing his body after his crucifixion, they encounter a young man who announces among other things that Jesus "has been raised" (16:6). Jesus's hopeful, though vague, forecast of a "rising" has thus been realized and there is no dead Jesus anywhere to be found. In Mark's viewpoint, then, Jesus's resurrection/rising means first of all that his life, soul, self is ongoing.

In addition, Mark implies that Jesus's rising points toward a fuller reality than Jesus's ongoing existence, as centrally important as that is. What is also part of Jesus's rising is that in his aliveness, in his rising, Jesus fully intends to meet his followers again—to be with, advise, challenge, teach, and encourage them. The absent followers are to be told by the women, says the young man, to go to Galilee and see, meet Jesus there. The promise of a future seeing, then, is delivered by the young man, and its fulfillment would appear to rest with the women, who are expected to return to the disciples with this literally promising message.

Jesus's resurrection, then, is intended to initiate a two-part phenomenon: first, Jesus's aliveness continues; second, and equally important, in his full and complete rising Jesus is already going ahead of his followers once more, preparing to engage them in the future just as he has in the past. The good news, then—far from being snuffed out with Jesus's crucifixion—will be ongoing into the future of both Jesus and his disciples. Jesus's resurrection as depicted in Mark is, therefore, in its essential nature a communal event. It is not just about Jesus; disciples also are expected to be part of the transformative experience.

Mark lays out this understanding of resurrection: Jesus's once-prominent deadness is now behind us, and resurrection points toward ongoing life, not only for Jesus but also for the disciples, who are summoned once again and told to go to Galilee and see Jesus there. Resurrection as conceived by Mark, then, is not just an experience of the individual Son of Man/Son of God. Jesus's rising is a foundational event that rests on a promise that will gather up an entire community of disciples in a common, transformed, and shared resurrected life.[36]

---

36. An important detail of Mark's closing scene would seem to invalidate the case I am putting forward for a community of followers who are enabled to participate in resurrection. That is, according to Mark, the women who are told by the young man to give instructions to the Eleven never in fact do so within the parameters of Mark's story. They flee the scene and, caught up in fear, remain silent. An issue then presents itself: did Jesus's core followers even get the word about going to Galilee and seeing Jesus? See chapter 9, where I suggest a solution to this apparent difficulty.

Resurrections Begin in the Now

Returning to our three focal texts for the moment, the question remains whether glimmers of a resurrected life show through in the actions of the three main characters of our focal texts. After the movement of God toward the centurion, the women, and Joseph of Arimathea, how does each of the three commence a life that manifests rising?

We can anchor our answer in the words already familiar, namely those offered by Jesus as his capstone teaching to the Twelve in Mark's Way of Discipleship section: "For the Son of Man came not to be served but to serve, and to give his life [self] a ransom for many" (Mark 10:45). Each protagonist in our focal texts engages in action that resonates with Jesus's words about giving life/self. That is, each sets aside the self-preservation and security that we readers have come to view as deeply ingrained in the followers of Jesus throughout most if not all of Mark's narrative. Mark indeed understands that it is extremely difficult to lay self-promotion and self-concern aside; even at this late point in his narrative Mark is clear that such acts of selflessness have not been adopted as the norm by most of Jesus's followers, including the Twelve. They do not yet understand, and hardness of heart continues for these who have been closest to Jesus.

With our three focal texts, however, Mark again provides good news. As the centurion stands near the dying Jesus and speaks, there is a breach in the focus on self and the maintenance of reputation, standing, and safety. The centurion risks the status and prominence that goes with his office. As one who has once sworn allegiance to the Roman Son of God, he now is empowered to witness to another as God's Son. Similarly, the women risk both their reputations in society and their physical safety by accompanying Jesus into the lair of his Jerusalem enemies, many of whom are bent on murder. Even when Jesus is executed in their sight, they remain nearby. Joseph then risks self in the form of the religious, social, and political connections he has developed over years of apparent community leadership—all to secure a dead body.

All three protagonists find themselves acting in unpredictable, servant-like ways that would not have been possible prior to God's movement. Each of them sets self aside and engages in deeds of immense and God-instilled courage. Preoccupation with self is sacrificed in the immediate moment.[37] These three are meant to represent humankind in

---

37. Rhoads et al. arrive at the following conclusion about the service performed

Mark's design. Whether or not their less courageous or more self-directed concerns reappear at a later time, they remain as good news for us all, standing as reminders that at least in some instances, human transformation is possible. And as those among God's beloved, we too may find that on occasion we are better than we know ourselves to be, more compassionate than is our norm, and braver than we were just yesterday when we failed to speak or act justly. All of this is brought into reality by a curtain-tearing, onrushing God who profoundly loves and reigns. So, the three remind us of good news that infuses our darkest seasons; the age-old message still holds: "The light shines in the darkness, and the darkness did not overcome it" (John 1:5).

He is risen and he calls us to rise and follow him. Again. Always.

Personal Reflection: Good Friday 1996

Today, I wept for Jesus—tears not of my own making, mind you, but wet, honest-to-God tears all the same.

The day began normally enough: alarm, newspaper, toast, juice, shower, and to work. I don't even think it occurred to me that it was Good Friday until I sat down in my office to engage in my ritual of quiet, a time which recently had been anything but quiet with much of the past few months being spent feeling betrayed, angry, and stuck in a relationship with someone who was obviously proving important to me. One's enemies prove important, indeed. Two weeks earlier, I'd had to give up trying to "make progress" or "come to terms" with my feelings toward this person, admit my own failure to love, and say to myself—and whomever might be listening in—that these feelings were so pervasive and persistent that I could do nothing to heal them. Clearly, if anything was going to happen, it would be up to God.

Anyway, when I sat down, I first turned to Luke's Gospel where I had been reading recently. Within a few minutes, though, my old companion Mark was calling out to me. I did recall, then, its being Good Friday and so went straight to Mark 15, the account of the first Good Friday. When I arrived there, I was reminded of the poignant and powerful realities presented: the savagery and ruthlessness of the persons of power who

---

by various "minor characters" in Mark, including specifically Joseph and the trio of women: "The characters who perform these acts of service do so courageously, risking wealth or arrest or reputation to carry them out. These acts mirror the self-giving of Jesus and assure hearers that it is possible to follow him" (*Mark as Story*, 132).

do their human best to break the body and spirit of the one they hail as "the King of the Jews." They accuse, mock, humiliate, spit upon, strike his thorn-crowned head with a reed, whose pliability ensures its bending to the shape of his head while at the same time exerting pressure to drive deeper the tearing spikes. And on his raw, beaten flesh is thrown a royal robe only to be torn away after an interlude of insult, perhaps just long enough for the blood to mingle with the fabric and begin to clot. All this prior to the crucifixion's coming, although come it inevitably does. And even there, in Mark's account, the bandits who are also crucified use what little power and breath they have remaining them to taunt. All human powers do all they can to destroy flesh and soul. Darkness descends, a life ebbs away, and, crying out to his God who seems present only in his absence, Jesus dies.

At that point comes a hauntingly curious verse where God begins to make his peculiar move: "And the curtain of the temple was torn in two, from top to bottom." When I read this again, I immediately flip to the only other place in Mark where a tearing takes place—the tearing of the heavens when Jesus is baptized. I glance again at the footnote, which reminds me of the editor's view that this verse (and its Old Testament predecessor, Isa 64:1) are about the "disclosure of God." I hear myself break the silence in the room by barking out at a scholarship which seems to miss the main point, "IT'S NOT ABOUT DISCLOSURE! IT'S ABOUT PRESENCE!!" Whether at baptism or death God tears away all impediments—be they heavens of his own making or temple veils fashioned at his command—and comes rushing toward an unsuspecting humanity for the purpose of anointing us all to be his beloved children, with whom he is well pleased.

My eyes and heart lead me past the first Good Friday material to Mark's record of the promise: the messenger announces to the women that the dead Jesus, the having-been-crucified Jesus—that Jesus is not here. There is no dead Jesus anywhere to be found. The only Jesus with whom we are left to deal is one who goes out ahead of us in his customary Markan manner and position. And we are promised a seeing: "there you will see him." All we need do is keep our eyes open for a living, going-before-us, preparing-our-way Jesus. Coming Soon, into the lives of the likes of us—the living, out-ahead-of-us, calling-us-to-consider-the-kingdom-of-God Jesus.

And so, with thoughts such as these, I reviewed the story of the first Good Friday, along with a couldn't-wait peek ahead to the Markan Easter promise of 16:7.

About two hours later I was again about my normal plan for the day. It was one of those Fridays when my brother and I get together for lunch and it was my turn to drive to meet him an hour away. I was pursuing my usual ritual reserved for our getting together: I had changed into comfortable clothes, purchased my cup of 7-11 coffee for the road, and turned my attention to the radio to hear what music would accompany me on the journey. Over the speaker came the resonant voice of Martin Goldsmith referencing that some Bach choral music would be coming up. And I thought to myself, "Well, of course. It's Good Friday," and I found myself looking forward to the trip and a chance to hear what Bach might have to say. Somewhere, I think it also crossed my mind to keep my eyes open for the occurrence of the promise. "Maybe something will happen when I'm there," I thought, although I couldn't imagine what vision might break forth over a Pierce's jumbo barbecue sandwich[38] with fries and a Pepsi.

I navigated the road, tossed in my tolls, and—luckily—barely avoided the traffic build-up in the downtown area, due either to an accident or a pre-Easter get out of town rush. I headed on I-64 toward Williamsburg. All the while, the Bach piece was playing. It was lovely and affected me the way much of Bach's music does, where I find myself quietly saying after it's over, "Wow."

When this particular selection was finished, again came the host's voice, announcing, as he always does, the name of the work, as well as where it was performed and by whom. Today, I never heard past the title, however; for as soon as he announced it, "Christ Lay Down in the Bonds of Death," all else was lost to tears. There was no analytic thought process about what he had said, no interlude of recall related to my morning's reading or measured release of feeling, although this is more my accustomed pattern. Rather, it was simply that I heard the words and wept for Jesus.

I was confused by my own response. As best I can remember, I had never done that before. Many's the tear I'd shed for myself, God knows, some out of a maudlin self-pity, others out of a core of sadness that I suppose I shall always carry with me. I'd also wept at the pain of my children, my wife, and others close to me. But never before for him. I found myself

---

38. Pierce's is a well-known locally owned restaurant near Williamsburg, Virginia, that has been serving up delicious BBQ for over fifty years.

doing all I could to defend against the tears. "Wait a minute. It's Good Friday," I thought. "We are called to be joyful because of what Jesus did on our behalf." And so on and so forth. It didn't work, for somehow the truth of this particular Good Friday was different from that. And what was somehow good was that tears were given me and they seemed of God. I do remember thinking fleetingly, "Maybe this means I've ended up being more of a follower of this man than I have realized. If so, when did this happen? And what holy mischief has God been up to, to bring this to pass?" One thing remains clear: I take no credit for any of this; I heard the words and the tears leapt forth.

As I have reflected on that Good Friday of 1996, I have been reminded of a conclusion I reached in my recent engagement with the last eight verses of Mark[39] where it seems to me that part of the message is that, in things that most matter, all human initiative fails. Mark's Gospel ends in the utter failure by the women disciples, with their flight, fright, and silence. But this failure of human initiative serves to throw us back on what we most need—the sure and certain promise of the messenger: "there you will see him, just as he told you." "See" in this verse, can be read in the sense of engage, meet, know, encounter, deal with, perhaps even wrestle with in a Jabbok[40] sort of meeting. In Mark's vision, this "seeing" is the only thing needful. And this only thing we need is presented as a sure thing, a done deal. You can put it in the bank. "There you will see him."

And "you" is "we."

Perhaps that day's moment was one such meeting. I can't say for certain what occurred. I'll never know absolutely. But, today what I best know is that at Martin Goldsmith's words, and without any thought or initiative of my own, I found myself in living resonance with some ancient and ever new words: "But go, tell his disciples and Peter that he is going ahead of you to Galilee; there you will see him, just as he told you."

A movement of grace, these quick and startling tears.

---

39. There remains some lingering dispute that Mark's Gospel concludes with 16:1–8. From very early on in various faith communities, that ending was considered either too unsettling or the result of "losing" Mark's "real" conclusion. Thus, both a "Shorter Ending" and a "Longer Ending" of Mark were added in some later manuscripts. However, the vast majority of scholars now hold that Mark concluded his narrative as he intended—with 16:1–8.

40. Jabbok is the name of the river where, according to Gen 32:22–32, Jacob wrestled with "a man" (often assumed to be God or another divine being). Jacob left that encounter with a limp and a new name—Israel.

9

The Terrifying Good News Promise

In "saving the best for last" Mark underscores both the ongoing aliveness and difficulties of following a still-alive Jesus. And assuredly, whatever may come in the present and at the end, God's kingdom is and ever shall be.

Exploring Mark's Story

FROM TIME TO TIME, in random settings, I have overheard these words: "I'm going to save the best 'til last." It may have happened when an older child, say 10 or 11, who was finally catching on to the advantages of delayed gratification, sized up her stack of Christmas presents under the tree and announced her new strategy. Just last Christmas, she had opened the largest, most interestingly shaped of her gifts straight away, unwilling or perhaps unable to wait and set it aside 'til the end. This year, however, she implements her new approach; she moves her most intriguing and inviting present off to the side, choosing it to be the last she opens.

Or perhaps a friend spoke these words at a fine restaurant, one known for its elegant irresistible desserts. Having made a quick selection of his entrée from the dinner menu, he is unable to curb his anticipation further and asks the waiter to bring him a dessert menu when he serves the water. He simply must have sufficient time to plan for what he intends to be the high point of his dining experience.

And, of course, even Jesus became involved in an incident of saving the best 'til the end when, according to John's Gospel, he changed water into wine, a vintage far superior to what had been consumed earlier during a wedding celebration (John 2:10). In sum, the practice of saving the best until last has a distinguished pedigree.

A case can be made that in the final scene of his Gospel, Mark "saves the best 'til last." This is perhaps most clearly evident in the unexpected ending readers encounter with 16:1–8.[1] In this scene with its curious conclusion, "Mark springs one final surprise on readers."[2] While there are several reasons for readers to be jolted by Mark's closing scene,[3] the overarching surprise is that with this ending, Mark's narrative seems far from complete—all loose ends tied neatly together; instead, his account is left "open-ended"[4] and decidedly unsettled. It attests to both "divine promise and activity, on the one hand, and comprehensive human failure on the other."[5] Therefore, readers are faced with the important task of discerning meaning in these seemingly divergent themes and their implications for Mark's Gospel as a whole. Mark ends his narrative, then, with a peculiarly intriguing scene, leaving much for readers to ponder.

With this chapter, I invite readers to consider three areas of focus: (1) Mark's characters in 16:1–8, (2) Mark's portrayal of discipleship lived in light of the reality of a risen Jesus, and (3) Mark's implications about the nature of God. In his final chapter, Mark completes his Gospel and leaves his readers to carry the good news ever forward—should they so choose.

---

1. See chapter 1 and the conclusion reached there—that Mark's Gospel ends with 16:8.

2. Carroll, *Jesus and the Gospels*, 85.

3. Borg and Crossan, *The Last Week*, 195. Borg and Crossan present several reasons why Mark's Easter scene should "surprise" readers.

4. Carroll, *Jesus and the Gospels*, 86.

5. Carroll, *Jesus and the Gospels*, 86.

Focal Text: Mark 16:1–8
The Terrifying Good News Promise

¹When the sabbath was over, Mary Magdalene, and Mary the mother of James, and Salome bought spices, so that they might go and anoint him. ²And very early on the first day of the week, when the sun had risen, they went to the tomb. ³They had been saying to one another, "Who will roll away the stone for us from the entrance to the tomb?" ⁴When they looked up, they saw that the stone, which was very large, had already been rolled back. ⁵As they entered the tomb, they saw a young man, dressed in a white robe, sitting on the right side; and they were alarmed. ⁶But he said to them, "Do not be alarmed; you are looking for Jesus of Nazareth, who was crucified. He has been raised; he is not here. Look, there is the place they laid him. ⁷But go, tell his disciples and Peter that he is going ahead of you to Galilee; there you will see him, just as he told you." ⁸So they went out and fled from the tomb, for terror and amazement had seized them; and they said nothing to anyone, for they were afraid.

The Characters of 16:1–8

In addition to the risen Jesus, Mark includes three characters of note in his final scene: the women who go to Jesus's tomb, the young man in white seated in the tomb, and in absentia, the missing disciples and Peter.

The Women

In Mark 16:1–8, the women named in chapter 15 continue to play a prominent role. As dutiful followers of Jesus they go to do what they can even though they realize a heavy stone may make access to Jesus's body impossible. As those who had witnessed Jesus's death, they go to anoint the corpse of their dead leader and teacher. Making their way to the place where two of the three saw Jesus's body taken, they act with courage, risking reputation and possible physical confrontation. On being able to enter the tomb to pursue their task of anointing, they are startled to find another already there—a young man dressed in white. When he begins to speak to them, he attempts to calm them. He also delivers unexpected news.

In their encounter with the young messenger, the women are addressed as those who are looking for the having-been-crucified Jesus. Whenever Jesus is "looked for" or "sought" in Mark, he is under threat or in some measure placed at risk (see chapter 6). The threat represented in the tomb scene is that Jesus may be understood by the women to be dead, no longer in existence. They have come expecting contact with a dead Jesus only.

Contrary to their quite understandable human assumption that Jesus is dead—they saw him die, after all—the women are told that (1) there is no such Jesus in the tomb; (2) already raised, he is on the move into Galilee; and (3) Jesus fully intends to have his disciples rejoin him in Galilee, just as he said earlier (see 14:28).

When they hear about the ongoing aliveness and risenness of Jesus, the women flee the tomb, are terrified, and remain silent about all things. With the final words of his narrative, Mark speaks of the utter collapse and failure of even these three—the most loyal, brave, and devoted of Jesus's followers. In the end, their courage and devotion eludes them, they are rendered mute by the news, and they take no action to carry the message of Jesus's aliveness to the other disciples. They in no way "save the day" by publishing the good news in all its miraculous magnitude and as Mark's narrative closes they remain frozen in place. Juel comments on the readers' likely reaction to Mark's final portrayal of the women: "There is surely disappointment as the women flee, dashing hopes that at least one group of followers will prove faithful."[6]

The women in Mark's closing scene raise for his readers what is perhaps the most important and vexing query implicit in his narrative about good news: Are Jesus's disciples ever released from their discipleship path? The answer of the Markan Jesus would appear to be, "No, the path remains before you. Will you yet choose to follow?"

The Young Man

In his closing scene Mark introduces a new character, the young man, who performs a task usually entrusted to God's angels in Scripture—to deliver a message from God to God's people. Mark seems to imply that the angelic youth is enveloped in an aura of holy purpose; the whiteness of his robe is reminiscent of the nearly blinding whiteness of Jesus's

---

6. Juel, *Master of Surprise*, 120.

clothes during a very holy moment—the transfiguration (see 9:3). In addition the young man's first words are the age-old words spoken to frightened souls when God or angels break into their world: "Fear not; don't be alarmed"; or in paraphrase, "I'm not here to hurt you."

Most important, however, is the message he delivers. While part of what he says instills fear in the women, other of his words take readers to the very heart of news that is "good" beyond our deepest imaginings:

> There is no dead Jesus here. Already raised up, Jesus is on his way to Galilee where you and your companions will meet with him again. Again he will walk in front of you, sustain you, and evoke your courage with his vision of the reality of God's realm of compassion, inclusion, and justice for you and all peoples. Go, and meet him there.

And so the young man delivers his message, which profoundly shakes the women. It appears to so unnerve them that they fail to take in the deep good news that he proclaims, namely, that although they and all future disciples are never "done" with Jesus, turn that coin over and we followers will know that *neither is he "done" with us*. He awaits our coming. His promise is sure and welcoming. It overflows with the reality that living as disciples is—with all its stumbles, failures, challenges and moments of fear—possible and a divinely sanctioned path. Now and in the end God will see to God's purposes, and courage, aliveness, and freedom are in our future.

The Missing Disciples and Peter

In one obvious sense, the core group of Jesus's disciples (now the Eleven, not the Twelve) is nowhere to be seen in Mark's closing scene. All except Peter have fled at Jesus's arrest and even Peter a bit later in the story breaks off his following of Jesus, swearing he has no connection to or knowledge of "this man" (14:71). From another perspective, however, Mark presents these absent ones as a major third character in 16:1–8, causing them to stand out even in their absence. They are conspicuous for several reasons. They stand in contrast to the women who risk viewing Jesus's terrifying end. They are conspicuous because they—and especially Peter—are specifically referenced by the young man in the tomb. Also, the missing disciples are invited and even expected to rejoin Jesus in Galilee where he awaits. They are again to follow him, walking behind an out-front

Jesus—disciples once more. They are recalled from their hiding places and re-called by him. The re-call of the absent disciples connotes their restoration to a way of life that will, as in the past, involve their inevitable failures and lack of courage, but these will be more than matched by the constancy of a teacher and leader who refuses to give up on them. Jesus stands ever ready, it appears, to grant them second, third, and fourth chances out to infinity.

Finally, the missing disciples are intended to be the recipients of a stunning promise sent their way by God and delivered by the youth. To those who have consistently failed to understand Jesus's words and deeds about the arrival and availability of God's rule, the promise comes: "There [in Galilee] you will see him" (16:7). At long last a *seeing* by the disciples will happen; understanding will dawn, and hardness of heart will lose its grip on them. It is a promise that can evoke a new life—one characterized, at least on occasion, by courage, freedom, meaning, and like a good servant, by giving oneself away.

What message does Mark send through his curious ending and the interplay of these three characters? It is summed up in three brief statements: We are never done with Jesus. He is never done with us. The promise remains. Stated somewhat differently, would-be followers cannot hope to keep this vibrant, fully alive Son of the Living God dead to their worlds. The cynicism that expects and needs Jesus to be a corpse clashes with the trust that Jesus is risen and already moving into where his disciples abide. There, and alive, he will not be kept from disturbing, challenging, prodding—calling them (and us) to lay self aside as we attend servant-like to the needs of others. At the same moment, he will reject any false conclusion that God is not for us or will give up on us. God's reign is and ever will be. The risen Jesus knows and has experienced that truth that goes beyond all others. Raised, he continues on ahead of all who follow; and calling, he awaits our renewed and ongoing discipleship.

Fear and Promise: Being Disciples of a Risen Jesus

When readers look to Mark's closing scene to assess his final sketch of a life of following one who is raised and on the move, two indelible impressions are conveyed. Embedded in 16:1–8 are both the disciples' fear and an undying promise of persistent hope.

The fear is clearly stated by Mark in his depiction of the women who flee the tomb: "for terror and amazement had seized them and they said nothing to anyone, for they were afraid" (16:8). What thoughts may have led to such paralyzing fears? Perhaps thoughts such as these:

> We cannot just relegate our time and connections to this man to a once-in-a-lifetime, peak experience, now over and done with. We cannot close the book on our life with him and start over on a fresh chapter. We are not released from his presence and call. We will never be able to allow him to diminish toward a fond but ever-fading memory. He is risen. We are afraid.

Mark 16:1–8 culminates with the truth that discipleship goes hand in hand with being afraid. As Williamson writes, "Anyone who contemplates following Jesus without fear and trembling has not understood true discipleship, according to Mark."[7] Mark implies that God well knows that discipleship rightly understood and practiced will engender moments of sheer terror in even the most stalwart of followers. It will be akin to the fear that gripped Jesus as he wrestled in Gethsemane to discern the will of God.

The three women become the first to know the fearful truth that comes to those who would hope to follow the risen Jesus in an ever-committed fashion—that disciples are never finished with him. He has been raised and has promised to be in the future of all followers. Again, Jesus will challenge, invite, nudge, encourage and point followers toward the difficult choices that come with discipleship. He will ever raise the discomforting questions: Can you be servants oriented to address the needs of others? Can you put self aside so that others gain courage and become free?

For Mark, however, fear is not the dominant reality in the lives of those who follow the risen Jesus. Even more vivid and consequential for disciples is the persistent hope and the sustaining promise of good news that becomes ingrafted as disciples follow. In his closing scene Mark reveals the hope and promise through the missing disciples. They are designated to discover in their imminent future that despite all obstacles, despite every failure of nerve, despite all moments of false bravado and human inconstancy, the promise will remain, never to be undone. For all who would seek to follow, "Always he goes before us; always he beckons forward to a new appearance in the Galilee of the nations, in the Galilee

---

7. Williamson, *Mark*, 195.

of our daily lives. We never know where and when we shall see him; we only know we cannot escape him."[8]

An additional hopeful assurance for the recalled disciples is that God's presence and actions will counter their fears several times over. There will be mercy for past failings. There will be restoration to the path of discipleship. There will be ongoing chances to follow even when afraid. Fears that are intertwined with a life of discipleship will be—at least from time to time—held at bay and even overcome. Though doggedly persistent, soberingly real, and thoroughly shaking, in the final reckoning fear will prove no match for the goodness and grace of God.

Another measure of hope for the disciples is found in the words of the young man in the tomb. His message suggests that renewed activity and ministry done in following the risen Jesus may prove more fruitful than the disciples' earlier efforts. Why? Because the promise is founded on the expectation that there will be *a seeing of Jesus*. Finally they will understand him, take to heart his teachings about being servants who attend to the needs of others, and internalize and live into Jesus's example of self-giving. The promise is that discipleship, when it arises from a full seeing of Jesus, will evidence itself in occasions of courage, standing with the powerless, acting on behalf of the isolated and shunned, and tearing down all barriers to inclusion in God's kingdom. God will enable followers of the risen Jesus to be like and act like God's Beloved—ever pursuing God's will for all God's people.

Going after a risen Christ, following him yet again into Galilee, means then that discipleship with its moments of courage, compassion, freedom, and strength beyond our own making is ever and always possible. We can still follow, even now and despite all. There is good and difficult work to be done and we are called to do it. We need not be caught up in deadness and despairing defeat, captured by a self-absorbed cynicism. Meaninglessness, emptiness cannot stand against the promise. No doubt, we will fail, often and at times spectacularly. But when we do we will hear the call of the One out front, saying—not for the first or final time—"You can do this. Try again. Keep your eyes on me. Follow."

---

8. Williamson, *Mark*, 286.

Implications About the Nature of God

Mark 16:1–8 is rich with implications about the nature of God. From its beginning Mark's narrative has bit by bit revealed various aspects of God's character and intentions for humanity, especially as they have manifested themselves in Jesus, God's Beloved. The closing scene—and most especially 16:7 and 16:8—can be viewed as Mark's last and ongoing word about the Holy. And all this is woven together with the author's unanticipated and curious ending. Assuming that Mark's readers across the centuries have engaged his narrative hoping for a greater understanding of the Divine, as well as how God relates to God's children, Mark's closing invites them, and us, to look deeply into what we can discover about God.

Several features of Mark's ending hold theological implications about the nature of God and God's intentions. Intriguingly, Mark leaves us with a unified though complex portrait of how God's kingdom is assured as ongoing and how a discipleship response to God's reign—while flawed and often partial—nonetheless is moved into the future through the power, providence, and constancy of God.

God Alone Brings in God's Reign

The first implication of Mark 16:1–8 is that, theologically speaking, God's reign is and must be advanced solely by God and God's Beloved. It simply cannot be that any human agency can bring such a kingdom into being. Neither can the most merciless acts or savage plans called into play by the dominant earthly or demonic forces defeat God's efforts.

In his ending, Mark lays out a portrait of complete human failure and collapse. This is obvious in the absence of Jesus's male disciples and, somewhat more surprisingly, in the terror and inaction of the women. Given this chaotic and bleak conclusion to a narrative of supposed good news, what positive theological implication about the nature of God can readers draw from such an ending?

One of Mark's most profound implications about the Godhead is that the inbreaking, sustaining, and flourishing of God's kingdom rests ultimately with God. Within Mark's literary and theological framework, it is God who propels the proclamation and furtherance of the gospel. God alone makes certain that the absent disciples (in ways not revealed to Mark's readers) come to learn that God has raised his Beloved. God is the driving force behind the kingdom and God's purposes are neither supplanted nor defeated.

Moreover, the risen Jesus is calling, gathering, and preparing to lead his flawed and oft-failing followers yet again. It is God who brings into being this second inbreaking with its indestructible eternality. Despite all unintentional human failing or the deliberate opposition of Jesus's enemies, God's reign of compassion, justice, inclusion, and service is continuing. As God has done in the past, God will stand with those with little power and status, overcoming all other powers, obstacles, or systems of social, political, familial, or religious bondage that keep God's people unfree. Jesus remains afoot—calling, meeting with, and preparing to lead his disciples. Through him, God is yet "on the loose,"[9] surging forward, carrying all who choose to follow deeper into God's new age.

God Does Not Give Up on Followers, However Flawed

A second Markan implication is that God does not give up on or cut off followers of his Beloved, despite their many ongoing flaws and failures. Even though Jesus's inner circle leaves much to be desired and their vision, courage, and selflessness often desert them at crucial moments, God still wants them, chooses them through God's Son. God will always call disciples to participate in God's arriving kingdom.

God Has the Last Word as Human Language Fails

One final implication is embedded in Mark's concluding verse, "and they said nothing to anyone" (16:8). The women disciples are struck dumb by what they have seen, heard, and been instructed to do. In this instance failure is evidenced in human silence. Mark's emphasis on silence may serve a theological purpose beyond pointing to human limitations. The silence puts forward a contrast between the disintegration of the human capacity for speech and the creative power of divine speech—God's Word.[10] In Gen 1:1—2:4, God speaks into cosmic darkness and chaos. And when God speaks into that primordial epoch, God brings light, life, and beginning to all that is God's creation. Surely, this portrayal of God's

---

9. Juel, *Master of Surprise*, 113. Juel applies this phrase to Jesus. I believe it can equally apply to God here.

10. I assume here that Mark was familiar with the Book of Genesis.

speech stands in contrast to that of Mark's ending where Mark's followers find no capacity or strength to speak words of any consequence or creative power. So, at the end, Mark paints a portrait of a human descent into total silence and wordlessness.

This contrast need not lead readers to ascribe scathing judgment or blame upon Jesus's followers as much as to focus on God and God's word. God's word is desperately needed by flawed human beings and its advancement comes through the creative power of Israel's God—the God who speaks. It is seen especially in God's word and promise in 16:7. There the reality of failed human speech is swallowed up by a God whose word is delivered by the youth at the tomb. And with his ending, Mark hints that God will continue to speak and act through God's newly risen Son. In the end of Mark, then, and in the ongoing movement of God's reign, readers can trust, as Juel writes, "And if this 'good news about Jesus Christ' is God's work within the intimate realm of human speech, there is reason to hope that . . . we will not have the last word."[11]

Providentially for all creation, God has the last word. While human silence can and does come for a season, the greater truth to which Mark invites his readers is that in the risen, Beloved One, God has already spoken and even death cannot silence the ongoing proclamation of and movement toward God's kingdom.

A Never-ending Ending: Mark's Literary Loop

Let us take one final look at Mark's peculiar ending. As noted earlier, Mark's last verses (16:1–8) are unsettling (see chapter 1). They portray the complete collapse of Jesus's most faithful disciples, who are last seen by readers in a frantic, fear-filled retreat into silence. This description of apparent chaos and complete failure raises the question, "Why does Mark end the narrative he puts forward as good news with such a stunningly bleak scene?" Above, we considered one possible theological answer, namely that Mark's portrayal of the women communicates to his readers that it is God alone who ushers in God's kingdom and all human aliveness that results from God's presence and actions.

But there is an additional line of thought regarding Mark's purposes in composing his "unsatisfactory"[12] ending. Mark finishes his story in

---

11. Juel, *Master of Surprise*, 121.
12. Borg and Crossan, *The Last Week*, 196.

such a way that it does not end. With his unsettling and startling conclusion, he may hope that its very starkness will compel his readers back to where God's inbreaking begins: with the river Jordan, a man coming from Nazareth, a baptism, heavens torn apart, a descending Spirit, and a voice from heaven. All of this is followed hard upon by Jesus's initial words, "The time is fulfilled, and the kingdom of God has come near; repent, and believe in the good news" (1:15). These words remind readers not to lose sight of the central motif of Mark's work: that now, in this *kairos* season, the reign of God is arriving and with it comes the possibility of a way, a path, a reoriented manner of living. This motif of God's rule and this way of discipleship is spelled out in the life and self-giving of God's Beloved. Jesus witnesses to an age of justice, compassion, equality, and resistance to all powers opposing the arriving kingdom time. He witnesses with the fullness of his life. He witnesses with the completeness of his laying self aside though it means the death of him. And by the end of Mark 16, God's kingdom is not overthrown, nor do God's daughters and sons remain in bondage. They are freed—freed to be called as often as they need into God's never-ending reign. Freed to face the hair-raising but God-given possibility of laying self aside for the sake of others.

Borg and Crossan speak of this Markan purpose somewhat similarly and in doing so suggest that Mark creates a literary loop: "And perhaps, as some scholars have suggested, the command to 'go to Galilee' means, 'Go back to where the story began, to the beginning of the gospel.' And what does one hear at the beginning of Mark's gospel? It is about the *way* and the *kingdom*."[13]

Mark's ending, then, leads us back to Mark's broader vision of hope, possibility, and good news. Darkness and despair is not all there is in 16:1–8; look again, dear readers, to where Mark writes of Jesus's beginnings. In our return to the commencement of Jesus's path, we are invited to see and to hold fast to our God. God in the beginning, God in the now, and God who will be in our future—Alpha and Omega for all of God's people.

In the end and with its ending Mark's Gospel invites us again and again to take up hope and proclaim good news. God's promise will ever hold.

---

13. Borg and Crossan, *The Last Week*, 198.

Personal Reflection: Continuum— God, Grandma, and Grace

Remember Reader's Digest? That family-friendly publication arrived in the mail monthly, filled with short articles, essays, personal recollections, scientific and health news, plus various repeating features such as "Laughter is the Best Medicine." There were numerous fillers on the magazine's pages—little known facts, tidbits of information or gently humorous stories that invited readers to identify with the foibles of their fellow human beings.

One of the most memorable ongoing features in the Digest was called, "My Most Unforgettable Character." As best I recall, this feature was given over to the writer's recollection of a person who had deeply affected the life or perspective of the article's author. The indelible influence of the "character" might have come in the context of a brief and seemingly inconsequential meeting or over a period of years; it might have involved a stranger or someone so familiar as to be taken for granted; or it might have happened face to face or through means of a letter or a favorite saying or quotation passed on to the next generation. These brief accounts covered the broad spectrum of how human beings find themselves touched and inspired by others.

From my vantage point of some 70-plus years, if I were to single out my most memorable character—at least of my early years—it would be my grandmother, Anna Lewis Morton (known to me as just plain Grandma). My older brother and I went to live with Grandma and Granddaddy, nicknamed H.L., when my brother was ten years old and I was five.

Vocationally speaking, Grandma was a product of her time. In the early 1950s traditional vocations open to women—at least in the South as I remember it—were nursing, teaching, and, of course, being a housewife, although being a housewife was rarely considered "real" work. Coming from a family who valued education, Grandmother gravitated towards teaching, a profession in which she engaged for some forty-plus years until her retirement at age sixty-five. She was apparently quite gifted as a teacher. When former students of hers grew up and had children of their own, they would express great pleasure when their own children were assigned "Mrs. Morton" as their teacher.

Due to her talent and ability, respect grew for Grandma across the years as she was increasingly seen as a knowledgeable and authoritative figure in her school system. She came to bear the title of assistant principal at the school in which she taught, but to my knowledge never aspired to "leave the classroom" and her students to pursue a different or more lucrative position. She loved to teach and she followed her heart on that path throughout her working life.

Grandma lived her life as a person of faith. While it was never of great concern in our family that we loudly and publicly announce ourselves as Christian, this was the faith tradition in which we grew and were nurtured. Looking back, there were numerous church-related activities in which Grandmother participated in those days—again taking on the roles traditionally reserved for women. But what I now most appreciate about her faith journey is that she was in no way what I would call a "sour" Christian. Faith was not seen as a burdensome enterprise, one that must be borne with as much a sense of martyrdom as possible. Rather, all life was laced through with a quality of joy and gratitude. I sensed no bitterness or pettiness in Grandmother around church matters, and in all truth never heard her speak out of meanness about another church member—or family member, for that matter. This has not always been my experience among the Christian faithful in later years, and I hasten to add that I, too, fall short of Grandmother's ability to withhold judgment and quietly accept the peculiarities of others.

I have a favorite black-and-white photograph of Grandmother that captures her authentically accepting and humorous perspective on life. In the photo Grandmother appears with her four sisters, all in their 50s and 60s. From time to time the sisters would get together for some sort of outing, since they truly enjoyed each other's company. On the photo there are no notes to indicate when or where it was taken. In it, all five stand near a dilapidated shed on which a sign had been posted: "For Rent." In the foreground—just in front of the "For Rent" sign—the five sisters, normally quite modest and dignified, had arranged themselves like a chorus line and struck the most seductive poses they could—thereby allowing the sign in the background to stand as silent witness to the certainty of delights that awaited all who could pay the price. But, of course, the true delight reflected by the photo was that of five sisters sharing a moment of poking playfully at extreme and unlaughing moralism and affirming the wisdom of holding a comic worldview.

Grandmother Anna knew the value of living and what was worth living for. In her last years she developed heart trouble and upon medical advice adopted a regimen more restrictive than she liked. One afternoon, I was picked up from school by Mother and Grandma, who were returning from Grandma's latest visit to her doctor. On the way home Mother made a quick stop at her office to collect some work she planned to complete at home. As a 14-year-old, I didn't then have the vocabulary to describe the atmosphere in the car as we waited for Mother's return, but now I would call it "subdued." Grandma seemed not her usual self; she stared trance-like out the front windshield. Finally, speaking to no one in particular and, I believe, not even realizing that she was speaking out loud, she said, "Well, if I have to give up all that, I'd just as soon die." Several days later, Grandma's prayer was granted as she fell to the kitchen floor, set free from an unacceptable and lingering earthly deterioration by her failing heart.

Looking back to that time, what I take away today is that Grandma knew the difference between a person's biological function of breathing in and breathing out when set beside the much more important engagement in a life of meaning, joy, and relationships. In her somber wisdom, she spoke into the hushed stillness of the family car, affirming her lifelong stance of claiming the value of aliveness in its broadest and richest sense. Out of that stance she passed on a great gift—the assurance that at life's end the preservation of biologic function is not the high-water mark of a life well lived. Rather, the supreme pinnacle, at least for some, shows itself in a readiness to let go, declining to settle for an existence shorn of that which makes for gratitude and peace. Such an end need not be born of despair, but is rather grounded in a profound trust in what lies ahead and the sure conviction that whatever comes is gain.

One incident secured Grandmother's place as my most unforgettable character. As mentioned, Grandmother was a teacher. In my elementary school years, I was permitted by the city's school district to attend the school at which she taught. She was wisely resolute, however, that I would never be a student of hers, a situation that would have no doubt proved too pressure-packed for the both of us.

Part of every school day was, of course, set aside for recess—that time when we kids were allowed to run around freely on the school's large playground with a minimum of adult supervision. We could also choose to swing, shoot marbles, or play tag, a game I detested since I was quite slow and therefore "it" more than I thought reasonable. The most popular option at least for the boys was engaging in some loosely organized game involving either a kickball, a football, a softball, or a dodgeball. (Basketball wasn't popular for us fifth graders since we were too short to have much success with reaching the goals set at ten-feet heights.)

One activity forbidden on the playground was belonging to a "gang." In those gentler days a "gang" of fifth graders consisted of a group of approximately five to six boys with a leader who would "ride" around the playground being bossy to other groups or individuals. I say "ride" since in at least some of the gangs, there was evident a strong influence of radio shows popular in those days—shows like the Lone Ranger, or Sergeant Preston of the Royal Mounted Police, or Sky King, the flying rancher who ran the B–B (pronounced "B bar B") ranch. All of these radio heroes rode horses a lot, except for Sky King, who mostly flew, so we gang members would "ride" our imaginary steeds to various locations on the playground, pretending that we had authority to tell the other kids what to do.

In case you haven't guessed by now, I was the self-proclaimed leader of one of these gangs. And at least for a while, my gang was able to evade detection by the playground monitors, since we stayed at some distance from where they patrolled. The trouble started, however, when another gang formed under the leadership of a rival fifth grader. He was far more athletic and coordinated than I—one of those who was always picked first when sports teams were chosen. His emerging gang leadership posed a challenge to the playground dominance I had come to see as my rightful due.

Under my direction my gang and I rode over to where this new gang was active. In trying to reassert my threatened prominence I told him to stop doing whatever he was doing. I don't remember now what he was doing, but I do remember that he refused my "orders." At that point I played what I hoped would be my trump card, saying, "Well you'd better stop because my grandmother is the assistant principal at this school!" This declaration made no impression on my rival but drew enough attention from at least one bystander that my words were repeated to one of the monitors and, apparently, from there to Grandmother.

Later that day, I became better acquainted with one of Grandmother's responsibilities as assistant principal, namely, the disciplining of those who broke the rules of the playground. As I sat in my class a student brought a note to my teacher asking her to send me to Grandmother's classroom. I wasn't quite sure what this was about, but I had a hunch that it wasn't good, especially since such a summons had never happened to me before. As slowly as possible I trudged from my second-floor classroom down the long steps to the first floor, wondering what was going to happen when I entered Grandmother's class. When I entered, Grandma—or, rather at that point, Mrs. Morton—was seated at her desk some thirty to forty feet away. She directed me to move to the front and center of the classroom—closer to her and the entire class of other kids looking on with apparent keen interest, waiting to see what would take place.

My mouth was dry and my knees were shaky. Looking directly at me but speaking in a clear voice audible throughout the classroom, Grandma said, "I hear you have a gang on the playground during recess. Is that true?"

Sensing there was no escape, I replied faintly, "Yes."

"You do know that there is a rule against gangs at this school, right?"

"Yes," I said again and decided I'd better add a "ma'am."

And while I was no doubt caught up by the fear of whatever was still to be said to me, I remember even more keenly the shame and embarrassment as they began to sweep over me. Still very much Mrs. Morton, speaking firmly but calmly, she said, "Well, I want you to break up your gang and stop running around with them on the playground." After a brief, reinforcing pause, she added, "Now, you may return to your classroom."

"Yes, ma'am," I said again. I walked slowly back up the stairs, knees still wobbly, my cheeks burning from Mrs. Morton's discipline.

That afternoon Grandmother and I were to be picked up after school by Granddaddy. After the final bell I got to the car first and climbed into my usual spot in the back seat. I still felt the sting of the day and was filled with dread, sure that Grandma's cool demeanor and scolding would continue when she reached the car. Images of a long ride home filled my head and I expected that additional humbling words would come my way. Granddaddy wasn't much of a talker so we sat in silence for a few seemingly endless minutes as Grandma wrapped up her day, walked to the car, opened the door, and got in. It was deathly quiet as Granddaddy started the engine and we headed home. In the silence I remained braced for an angry blast because I had knowingly, intentionally broken the rule about gangs—a rule I clearly had been told about but had broken anyway.

To my surprise, the silence continued for a few minutes, and then Grandma and Granddaddy began talking about the errands he had run that day and what was planned for supper that evening. No comments were directed towards the back seat where I now sat dazed and confused. This benign lack of focus on me was not at all what I thought would happen and I did not know what to make of it. Soon, however, I began to feel a sense of release, as if I were coming out from under some sort of ominous cloud. Dread began to fade and my fears of additional judgment began to diminish. To top it off, when we arrived home I was free to run into the house, change into my play clothes and tear outside to join my friends just like it was any ordinary afternoon. I was free again. Free, restored, able to get on with being me with no residual recriminations.

I have thought of this incident many times over the years, especially in those moments when I need to remember what is involved in genuine grace, both human and divine. As I look at it now I am both amazed at and grateful for Grandmother's actions that day. She had exercised discipline and corrected my errant expectation that I could regard myself as in any way superior to those with whom I shared the playground. My relationship to her did not entitle me to special standing or privilege in the schoolyard that served as my primary social and relational world.

Grandmother's discipline instilled an ongoing value in me, one I still revisit from time to time. She taught me that my being loved by others is not and should not be predictive of a totally uncritical response to my behavior or expectations about how things should be; being truly loved does not give me permission to manipulate that bond or misuse that affection in a way that eliminates challenge or correction when I choose a path harmful to those around me.

There is yet a second aspect of grace that Grandmother taught me that afternoon. In the extraordinary manner in which she acted following the correction due me—first in her initial silence when she entered the car, and then minutes later when she and Granddaddy began to talk calmly about everyday matters—I received a second gift. It was a treasure of lasting value—namely, coming to know that genuine grace is made complete in the restoration of the one who has at least for a moment, let slip their best self. Even in my time of childhood misbehavior, correction, and vulnerability, I experienced a moment that made all things new again. It was a sacred instant in those early years; it comforts and enlivens me still. Moreover, in a small way perhaps, it was similar for the women disciples who so completely failed, as we learned in the final verse of Mark's gospel. At least I imagine it to be so. For I trust that later, while they were still caught up in the throes of their fear and terror, they began to remember the promise of the young man at the tomb—that Jesus wanted and expected them and the other disciples to follow him, rejoin him, continue on with him, and be engaged once again in their imperfect discipleship, still so needed by a broken world.

Mistakes, errant decisions, and flawed acts are committed by all humans, be they children or adults. But through the living and ongoing grace of God—given once to a child through a most unforgettable grandmother, and given long years ago to some adult followers through a promise delivered by a divine messenger—a child was made free to play and grown men and women were restored to give thanks and take up again the difficult path of discipleship even though afraid. Hope and restoration are possible for us all.

Not to be forgotten, such moments as these.

Appendix 1

Human Lack, Divine Love, and Kingdom Inclusivity in Mark 10:17–31

MARK'S CONSIDERATION OF HUMAN "lack" stands as a key feature in the story of Jesus's loving encounter with the wealthy man who did not follow Jesus's call. Certainly, the lack Jesus mentioned implies a poverty in him that his wealth, possessions, and prominence of social and religious standing failed to ameliorate. Mark's Jesus does not clearly say what is missing, but the logic of this passage suggests what may be absent from this wealthy man's life, and indeed, from the man himself. The wealthy man is unable to follow Jesus into the kingdom (or eternal life); the lack suggested by the flow of Mark's story is this very incapacity or indecisiveness in both following and relating (giving) to others. The wealthy man does not, the narrative suggests, have the freedom to follow or to give, at least during this crucial moment of encounter.

The wealthy man possesses many things but has neither the will to choose a new course or to let go of the very possessions that bind him. He is held by them, captive to them. Their pull is too strong. They have come to occupy such a place in his life that he cannot unseat them for either his own sake or the sake of others. Not free, he walks away grieving. Mark seems to suggest that the wealthy man lacks freedom from that which he places at the center of his life. He holds much wealth, but lacks freedom; he is therefore soul-impoverished despite his riches.

Mark offers three theological implications in this rich scene: (1) an observation about the human condition; (2) a deep truth about the nature of God's love as seen in Jesus; and (3) a key feature of the kingdom of God.

The first theological implication of this text arises because this story resonates with the larger human drama in which we all participate. The passage suggests that we, all of us, are unfree in some significant aspects of our beings or lives. While this story about a man of many possessions points us toward his particular difficulty in becoming free from his wealth and learning to give, his struggle is reflective of our own; he stands in for us. While he cannot free himself from the hold his possessions have on him, each of us wrestle with other gods that hold us captive. Given our human kinship with this wealthy one Jesus loved, Mark's story is about the inability of human beings to become free by their own efforts.

On a personal note, in my thirty years of pastoral counseling work, one of the questions I held in the back of my mind as I attempted to understand those in my care was this: "Where are these persons unfree and what are the forces that hold them back from flourishing and being the kinds of people God is calling them to be?" My counselees taught me much about the numerous ways people can be unfree, captive, or "stuck," to use the vernacular. Some struggled to be free to trust in their hearts that anyone truly cared for them; others could not escape an ongoing sense of profound loneliness and isolation. Some wondered if they would ever be free to love again after experiences of unfathomable betrayal by those they had once loved beyond question; others told of remaining in abusive relationships, struggling to "be faithful" to their wedding vows in the face of a gradually dawning realization of the possibility of danger, physical harm, or even death at the hands of someone who was yet claiming to love them. Perhaps most resonant with the beloved one of Jesus found in Mark 10, some found themselves so tragically consumed and involved with their own wants and needs that they were blinded to the legitimate needs and aspirations of those closest to them.

Indeed, nearly limitless are the ways in which we humans—understandably, but harmfully—can lack freedom and find ourselves bound and unable to move into the flow of life that lies before us, at least during significant periods in our lives. And just as was true for the rich man—one so profoundly loved by Jesus that he was offered a way to free himself from enslavement—we too may find ourselves too debilitated, hurt, stunned, frightened, or (perhaps surprisingly) too blinded by our privileges and our own particular riches that we are—despite being greatly loved—unable to walk a path that would free us and move us away from our poverty of soul to a richness we have not yet known or somehow lost along the way. Something beyond our own efforts and intentions is needed to carry us beyond our lack, our stuckness.

The second theological implication of 10:17–31 aims us towards a profound and sometimes overlooked aspect of divine love. Through Jesus's love for his richly impoverished, unfree questioner, Mark shows readers that in those moments when we are fortunate enough to encounter a sacred sense of being loved, we may hear or sense at least in part a straightforward message about something we lack, something missing in our lives. Mark's text leads us to expect that such moments may involve a love that directs us towards something we yet need for a richer, fuller, and more meaningful life. Love is likely, then, to touch upon the places where we hurt, where we ache, where we remain captive. Fortunately, this passage encourages us to trust that in these potentially revealing, vulnerable, and keenly painful moments, the Divine intent is benevolent. That is, such foretastes of the kingdom are not meant primarily to plummet wayward souls towards any unending morass of shame, guilt, humiliation, or punishment for the past. While hurt and regret may indeed be experienced, underneath lies a call similar to Jesus's call to the wealthy one. It is a call arising out of God's love, beckoning us toward what is needful and benefiting to our lives, our hearts, our sojourns upon this earth—indeed our very cores/souls. Pain may indeed be involved, but it can be the pain of healing. Such moments of being enveloped in God's care may not arrive through "easy," warm, or tepid encounters with the truth. Instead these moments usher us toward love—a love that evermore attempts to reach and enrich us, but in doing so may searingly face us with our lacks.

The third theological implication of Mark's narrative becomes apparent in Jesus's references to the poor (10:21) and again when he mentions those normally considered the first becoming last and the last becoming first (10:31). The two references taken together delineate that those often seen as of least significance or value in society are securely affirmed in Jesus's understanding as included in the reign of God. Indeed, the well-being of the poor and those who are last is elevated above that of the wealthy—so wedded to their riches—and the first—so captured by their pursuit of firstness to the exclusion of all else and all others. Mark, then, points his readers towards this theological truth: the poor and the last are of a certainty included in God's kingdom.

Mark's theological affirmation of the inclusivity of God's kingdom can also be found in Jesus's calls to discipleship in 10:17–31. One call is made to Jesus's wealthy petitioner, a call he declines. But his inability to accept in no way negates Jesus's action to call this prominent, loved man. Another call comes as Peter enumerates the losses that have come to him and other disciples who have answered Jesus's call and "followed" him (10:28). This second call is somewhat different from Jesus's call to the wealthy man. As spoken of by Peter, this call has taken the form of an ongoing struggle to adopt a way of living and acting both urged and modelled by Jesus. In their stumbling efforts to pursue a path of discipleship, Jesus's followers have—as summed up by Peter—become further impoverished. Living under Jesus's call has resulted in no noticeable gain and as Peter expresses it, has led to losing quite a lot.

Jesus issues the call to discipleship to all; in this story, it comes to one with many possessions and also to those who complain of becoming more diminished every day. Mark would have us see that Jesus's call goes out to everyone—rich and poor, high and low, first and last alike. This does not mean that his call results in a movement towards a cushy or more privileged life or even one marked by minimal advancement by the world's standards. But everyone is in some form or another called towards a life in God's kingdom. Just as God's kingdom is inclusive, so is the call that comes to beckon all toward it.

Appendix 2

Resources for Readers

When engaging the Gospel of Mark, readers require three basic tools. First is a "solid," reputable translation of the Holy Scriptures. (A second translation can be useful to broaden or fill out a text's meaning.) Second is a limited number of resources, perhaps three to eight, about the specific passages under study. These resources should draw on the scholarship of those with some standing in the field of biblical studies who write in such a way that their major findings are accessible to non-professionals. Third, curiosity, heart, and passion, as well as an openness to see what it is Mark hopes we will see, are central to the enterprise of biblical exploration. Some of Mark's themes are clear, and others are veiled in a way that invites us to look more deeply and ponder more fully this thing called the Good News of Jesus.

This resource section includes materials I have found useful in providing context, direction, and suggestive interpretation of Mark, both in general and relating to the treasures explored in this book.

HarperCollins Study Bible: New Revised Standard Version. Edited by Wayne A. Meeks et al. New York, NY: HarperCollins, 1993.

For the most part I use this volume, with both Hebrew Scriptures and the New Testament. It contains excellent study notes and is cautious in ensuring that these notes (provided by different scholars in the field) are not presenting any specific theological or ideological ax to grind. When I make an exception to my usual practice, I alert the reader to the alternative translation I am using.

Clifton Black's notes on Mark are helpful both in opening up a deeper understanding of the Markan texts under consideration by readers and in evoking their further imaginative thought.

Black, C. Clifton. *Mark*. Abingdon New Testament Commentaries. Nashville, TN: Abingdon, 2011.

Written by the commentator who provided the study notes for the Gospel of Mark in the 1993 edition of the HarperCollins Study Bible, this commentary provides significant insights that invite readers into the complexities and ambiguities of Mark's narrative. Underlying Black's analysis of Mark is his assertion that God's good news in Mark is of a "peculiar quality" and designed to be experienced by readers. Written with the needs of theological students in mind and containing a wealth of material for the in-depth study of Mark, parts of this work will prove quite a stretch for general readers.

Blount, Brian K., and Gary W. Charles. *Preaching Mark in Two Voices*. Louisville, KY: Westminster John Knox, 2002.

While written specifically for those who preach from Mark, each of this volume's twelve chapters begins with an exploration and analysis of Mark's meaning and message covered in the chapter. Stimulating and evocative interpretation of Mark's story, briefly presented.

Borg, Marcus J. *Jesus: Uncovering the Life, Teachings and Relevance of a Religious Revolutionary*. San Francisco, CA: HarperSanFrancisco, 2006.

Borg provides clear and concise illumination of the various forces brought to bear on Jesus, the central character in Christian faith and practice. His expositions of the religious, social, economic, familial, and political contexts in which Jesus was shaped are extremely helpful. Borg invites the reader to see a flesh-and-blood person existing underneath the overlay of majesty, devotion, and dogma which is often ascribed to him. I believe Borg's approach to be congruent with Mark's emphasis on Jesus as a very human and suffering Son of God.

Borg illuminates the world in which Jesus grew and developed and by which he was shaped. The influences from the cultural, religious, social, and political arenas were no doubt part of Jesus's formation for both good and ill, and I would suggest that Jesus begins to shed some of these learnings after his exchanges with the gentile woman. Borg's work covers this ground, especially 205–17.

Boring, M. Eugene. *Mark: A Commentary.* New Testament Library Series. Louisville, KY: Westminster John Knox, 2006.

Quite thorough commentary, considering in detail the various interpretive understandings of any given passage of Mark. One prominent and distinctive feature of this volume is the numerous excursuses Boring includes in this work. These provide helpful context for placing specific texts within Mark's larger narrative design and theological outlook. This work presents quite a challenge for casual readers.

Carroll, John T. *Jesus and the Gospels: An Introduction.* Louisville, KY: Westminster John Knox, 2016.

This book contains a fine chapter for those seeking an introduction to the Mark's structure, major themes, and characters. Carroll's method of highlighting his findings is especially useful.

Dowd, Sharyn Echols. *Reading Mark: A Literary and Theological Commentary on the Second Gospel.* Macon, GA: Smyth & Helwys, 2000.

Carefully researched and clearly presented, Dowd's commentary emphasizes the centrality of the Markan Jesus as the one who "inaugurated God's reign" in history. To her credit, Dowd asserts that her volume is no substitute for reading Mark's text itself and will make "little sense" unless readers engage Mark's account placed side by side with her work. Another interesting feature of Dowd's work is that, while acknowledging the impossibility of fully understanding Mark's thoughts or the author's intentions for readers, she lays out implications about Mark's mindset as the author shaped the Gospel.

Gaventa, Beverly Roberts and Patrick D. Miller, eds. *The Ending of Mark and the Ends of God: Essays in Memory of Donald Harrisville Juel.* Louisville, KY: Westminster John Knox, 2005.

This collection of essays in memory of Donald H. Juel considers the "disquieting" ending of Mark and the controversies and various interpretations evoked by it. Mark's ending and the Gospel as a whole are explored from varying viewpoints, drawing on both Scriptural studies (Christian and Hebrew) and theological emphases.

Juel, Donald H. *A Master of Surprise: Mark Interpreted.* Minneapolis, MN: Fortress, 1994.

Juel's stated purpose for this refreshing volume is the promotion of modern readers' imaginative engagement with Mark's story. He argues that Mark believed that through this story of Jesus and the arrival of the reign of God, God was at work to change and transform the lives of Mark's readers. Relying on the shocks and surprises Mark includes in the narrative, Juel seeks in our day and time to draw readers ever closer to encountering Mark's God and God's purposes for humankind.

Kelber, Werner H. *Mark's Story of Jesus*. Philadelphia, PA: Fortress, 1979.

Written earlier than other volumes in this appendix, this brief work effectively introduces readers to Mark's narrative as "a single coherent story" organized around a consistent internal logic. Kelber introduces five major themes of the Gospel and well grounds readers in a beginning, insightful understanding of the literary and theological nature of Mark's work.

Myers, Ched. *Binding the Strong Man: A Political Reading of Mark's Story of Jesus*. Maryknoll, NY: Orbis, 1988.

Although this volume presents challenges to the general reader, it provides many gems waiting to be discovered in Mark. It is more thorough than other study aids on Mark and less accessible in places. Its interpretive focus is clearly and deliberately the political themes and implications of Mark's narrative. However, some readers will no doubt find the extra work involved in reading this volume well worth the effort.

The two sections of his work on which I drew related to the Syrophoenician woman's engagement with Jesus and his analysis of the boat stories (187–90) as they contribute to Mark's focus on the tension arising between Jesus and his disciples. The section found in pages 203–4 provided insight regarding the various influences impinging on Jesus as he first meets this gentile mother.

Rhoads, David, et al. *Mark as Story: an Introduction to the Narrative of a Gospel*. Third edition. Minneapolis, MN: Fortress, 2012.

This work focuses on Mark's use of narrative form as a key to appreciating Mark's Gospel. Argues that Mark's first exposure to early congregations of believers was in the form of a play or a dramatic reading prior to the text being written down.

The first edition of this work proved highly significant in the field of Markan studies. The recent edition adds valuable perspectives for Mark's present-day readers. The Two Ways are elaborated in this work as well as additional "nuggets" of sound scholarship, well worth the reader's time.

Williamson, Lamar Jr. Mark. *Interpretation: A Bible Commentary for Teaching and Preaching.* Louisville, KY: John Knox, 1983.

This is a solid and accessible commentary written for both lay and clergy.

Bibliography

Achtemeier, Paul J. "Mark 9:30–37." *Interpretation* 30 (1976) 178–83.
Bassler, Jouette. "Cross." In *HarperCollins Bible Dictionary*, edited by Paul J. Achtemeier, 212. Rev. ed. San Francisco: HarperSanFrancisco, 1996.
Black, C. Clifton. *Mark*. Abingdon New Testament Commentaries. Nashville, TN: Abingdon, 2011.
―――. "The Gospel According to Mark." In *HarperCollins Study Bible*, edited by Wayne A. Meeks et al., 1915–52. New York: HarperCollins, 1993.
Blount, Brian K., and Gary W. Charles. *Preaching Mark in Two Voices*. Louisville, KY: Westminster John Knox, 2002.
Borg, Marcus J. *Jesus: Uncovering the Life, Teachings and Relevance of a Religious Revolutionary*. San Francisco: HarperSanFrancisco, 2006.
Borg, Marcus J., and John Dominic Crossan. *The Last Week: The Day-by-Day Account of Jesus's Final Week in Jerusalem*. San Francisco: HarperSanFrancisco, 2006.
Boring, M. Eugene. *Mark: A Commentary*. New Testament Library Series. Louisville, KY: Westminster John Knox, 2006.
Bowie, Walter Russell. *The Story of the Bible*. New York: Abingdon, 1934.
Carroll, John T. *Jesus and the Gospels: An Introduction*. Louisville, KY: Westminster John Knox, 2016.
Crossan, John Dominic. *Jesus: A Revolutionary Biography*. San Francisco: HarperSanFrancisco, 1994.
Donahue, John R. "Mark." In *HarperCollins Bible Commentary*, edited by James L. Mays et al., 901–24. Rev. ed. New York: HarperOne, 2000.
Dowd, Sharyn Echols. *Reading Mark: A Literary and Theological Commentary on the Second Gospel*. Macon, GA: Smyth & Helwys, 2000.
Gaventa, Beverly Roberts, and Patrick D. Miller, eds. *The Ending of Mark and the Ends of God: Essays in Memory of Donald Harrisville Juel*. Louisville, KY: Westminster John Knox, 2005.
Gealy, F. D. "Centurion." In *The Interpreter's Dictionary of the Bible: An Illustrated Encyclopedia*, edited by George A. Buttrick et al., 1:547–48. Nashville, TN: Abingdon Press, 1962.
HarperCollins Bible Commentary. Rev. ed. Edited by James L. Mays et al. New York: HarperOne, 2000.
HarperCollins Bible Dictionary. Rev. ed. Edited by Paul J. Achtemeier. San Francisco: HarperSanFrancisco, 1996.
HarperCollins Study Bible: New Revised Standard Version. Edited by Wayne A. Meeks et al. New York: HarperCollins, 1993.

Holy Bible. Revised Standard Version, Old and New Testaments. New York: Thomas Nelson & Sons, 1953.

Interpreter's Dictionary of the Bible: An Illustrated Encyclopedia, Vol. 1. Edited by George A. Buttrick et al. Nashville, TN: Abingdon, 1962.

Juel, Donald H. *A Master of Surprise: Mark Interpreted.* Minneapolis, MN: Fortress, 1994.

Kelber, Werner H. "The Hour of the Son of Man and the Temptation of the Disciples." In *The Passion in Mark: Studies on Mark 14–16,* edited by Werner H. Kelber, 41–60. Philadelphia: Fortress, 1976.

———. *Mark's Story of Jesus.* Philadelphia: Fortress, 1979.

Kelber, Werner H., ed. *The Passion in Mark: Studies on Mark 14–16.* Philadelphia: Fortress, 1976.

Levine, Amy-Jill. *Short Stories by Jesus: The Enigmatic Parables of a Controversial Rabbi.* New York: HarperOne, 2014.

———. *The Misunderstood Jew: The Church and the Scandal of the Jewish Jesus.* New York: HarperOne, 2007.

Mays, James L. "Mark 8:27—9:1." *Interpretation* 30 (1976) 174–78.

———. *Psalms: Interpretation: A Bible Commentary for Teaching and Preaching.* Louisville, KY: John Knox, 1994.

Meyers, Carol. "The Temple." In *HarperCollins Bible Dictionary,* edited by Paul J. Achtemeier, 1096–105. Rev. ed. San Francisco: HarperSanFrancisco, 1996.

Myers, Ched. *Binding the Strong Man: A Political Reading of Mark's Story of Jesus.* Maryknoll, NY: Orbis, 1988.

Rhoads, David. "Losing Life for Others in the Face of Death." *Interpretation* 47 (1993) 358–69.

Rhoads, David, et al. *Mark as Story: An Introduction to the Narrative of a Gospel.* Third edition. Minneapolis, MN: Fortress, 2012.

Rich, Matthew A. "Mark 15:25–41." *Interpretation* 70 (2016) 200–202.

Schweizer, Eduard. *The Good News According to Mark.* Translated by Donald H. Madvig. Richmond, VA: John Knox, 1970.

Williamson, Lamar, Jr. *Mark. Interpretation: A Bible Commentary for Teaching and Preaching.* Louisville, KY: John Knox, 1983.

www.ingramcontent.com/pod-product-compliance
Lightning Source LLC
Chambersburg PA
CBHW050842230426
43667CB00012B/2110